M C

# CLASSIC
# FOOTBALL
# DEBATES

# CLASSIC FOOTBALL DEBATES

## SETTLED ONCE AND FOR ALL
### • VOLUME 1 •

# DANNY BAKER
# & DANNY KELLY

EBURY
PRESS

1 3 5 7 9 10 8 6 4 2

Published in 2009 by Ebury Press, an imprint of Ebury Publishing
A Random House Group Company

The Random House Group Limited Reg. No. 954009

Addresses for companies within the Random House Group can be found at
www.randomhouse.co.uk

A CIP catalogue record for this book is available from the British Library

The Random House Group Limited supports The Forest Stewardship Council (FSC),
the leading international forest certification organisation. All our titles that are
printed on Greenpeace approved FSC certified paper carry the FSC logo. Our paper
procurement policy can be found at www.rbooks.co.uk/environment

Pri                                                  )

ISBN 9780091928513

To buy books by your favourite authors and register for offers visit
www.rbooks.co.uk

# Contents

# Why not us?
# An introduction

Hello. Nobody is more aware than Danny and I that the last thing the world needs is another book about football. It is a sombre fact that since the very first publications using movable type were introduced to Britain in 1510 there have been no fewer than 40 different books worrying themselves over this simple peasant pastime.

Even before that there were six separate illuminated soccer manuscripts being painstakingly worked on by monks in monasteries as disparate as York and Tintagel. Incredibly none of these monks was aware of the toils of their brethren and yet frustratingly they were all simultaneously turning out histories of Bolton Wanderers. (Only one of the works was actually authorised and was finally published in 1987 to universally poor reviews.)

So why do we need another one now? Has football changed that much? Can we, a pair of straw-chewing yokels, add anything to that vast 40-book pyramid of prattle about what is, essentially, an old ladies' fascination?

Well we think we can.

The sad truth is that football – once a game that enthralled kings and maharajas, dustmen and charladies alike – is dying. It is an oft-repeated fact that though there were 69,000 souls inside the Olympia-stadion Berlin for the 2006 World Cup final, barely half that number bothered to watch it on TV throughout the world. And yet how many people realise that 'barely half' of 69,000 is 34,498 – a figure that, in the 1980s, Chester City could have comfortably expected to turn up on a wet Monday morning just to watch them train?

This is football in the twenty-first century. Something must be done. Has to be done. And we, a pair of chuckling fat old boys, are here to do it.

Over the next six volumes and 20,000-plus pages Danny and I hope to not only put football into its proper historical perspective but to get among its modern-day guts, wriggle around in its teeming matter, yank out gristle and teeth and say, 'Here. Here, world. Here's your football.'

By putting it in context and reminding both everyday and 'big-pot' people of what it was that folk once found so fascinating about this game of two halves, we believe we can not only cause a surge in world-wide attendances but revive the moribund attitude towards the sport of radio, television and the hundreds of people who use the Internet.

A long time ago it was said that football was bigger than life or death. I think it was death. Danny and I believe that through this book we can get it back to that state of importance, renew our vows with this estranged muddy wife of ours, and collectively make the sequel the whole world really wants to see, yet has forgotten not only that it wants to see it but even where the cinema is situated and what way you face the screen if, and when, you did remember its location. It really is as bad as that.

So welcome home, football. Through oral history, remarkable tales, stunning graphics and big-budget fireworks may this book herald your return. We may not be able to work any magic for the next World Cup but the one after that... Is a global television figure of *one million* reawakened soccer fans merely a dream?

It would be our pleasure.

Danny, 2009

# Can any other sport seriously match up to football?

## Anyone for Kabbadi?

In the introduction to his famous book *The Great American Novel* (it's about baseball and communism) Philip Roth devotes the first seventy-five pages to slagging off rival books that might aspire to the title of *The Great American Novel*. Thus *Moby Dick*, *The Last of the Mohicans*, *The Great Gatsby* and all the rest of those A-level staples get the most terrific kicking. Baker & Kelly are fairer than that, and think that you might like to know, before reading a book of this size and complexity, that other sports are available. What follows, then, is an expert assessment of the other major sports, recreations and pastimes worldwide, and how they compare to soccer. Football first, obviously...

## Association Football

**What's it like?** In its mixture of individual skill and team effort, in its pattern of striving but only very occasional attainment, in its ability to inspire, distress, engage and enthral, football is a grass-bound version of everything that makes life worth living. It lacks only the sexy bits. Even that isn't true if you count the incident in 2001 when José Antonio Reyes (once of Arsenal, but at that time a kid with Sevilla) scored a brilliant goal. In the resultant celebratory pile-up, one of his teammates, Francisco Gallardo, pulled Reyes' shorts to one side and gave him a little kiss on his most private part. Reyes was mildly perplexed. 'I felt a little nip,' he said, 'but I didn't realise what Paco was doing.' The main Spanish sports paper *Marca* took a rather less relaxed view, running a gigantic headline on its front page: INTOLERABLE! Yeah, football is great.

**Who plays it?** Everyone. The United Nations has 192 members. The International Olympic Committee has 205. FIFA has 208.

**Who likes it?** Everybody. Except Americans. And lunatics. In truth, football has captured the globe. In 1998 a group of American scientists infiltrated the murkiest depths of the Amazon jungle to film a remote tribe that had only ever had the most fleeting interaction with the outside world. When they finally made contact, they were greeted by the tribal elder emerging from the dense forest in just a loincloth, and a Barcelona baseball cap.

**Famous fans.** Just a smattering, English clubs only. Prince Harry, Osama bin Laden (Arsenal), Martin Shaw, Prince William (Aston Villa), Michael Parkinson, Dickie Bird (Barnsley), Jasper Carrott, Vernon Kay (Birmingham), Fat Boy Slim (Brighton), Alistair Campbell (Burnley), Melvyn Bragg (Carlisle), Dame Kelly Holmes (Charlton), Richard Attenborough, Michael Caine (Chelsea), Eddie Izzard, Ronnie Corbett (Crystal Palace), Ridley Scott (Hartlepool), the Kaiser Chiefs (Leeds), Englebert Humperdinck (Leicester), Roger Whittaker (Hereford), Daniel Craig, Jimmy Tarbuck (Liverpool), Monty Panesar (Luton), Rick Wakeman, the Gallagher brothers (Manchester City), Jennifer Saunders, Thom Yorke (Manchester

United), Frank Maloney (Millwall), Ant 'n' Dec, Tony Blair, Sting (Newcastle), David Frost, Stephen Fry (Norwich), Michael Foot, Dawn French (Plymouth), Pete Doherty, Michael Nyman, Mick Jones out of The Clash (QPR), the Chuckle Brothers (Rotherham), Kenneth Branagh, Salman Rushdie (Spurs), Glenda Jackson, Patricia Routledge (Tranmere), Frank Bruno, John Cleese, Keira Knightley, Ray Winstone (West Ham).

**Weird.** As this book is busy proving, virtually everything about football is pretty odd. But if we have to pick one thing, try this. There will be a poor-quality prize for the person who can help B&K understand why it is that Londoners are never successful managers outside the capital. Craggy Scots, blunt Yorkshiremen, down-to-earth Lancastrians and a host of other regional stereotypes successfully manage clubs all over the shop – Nicholson, Revie, Clough, Busby, Shankly, Robson, Paisley, Ferguson, Moyes, even George Graham – yet nobody born within the old North/South Circular ring road has ever done the remotest good away from London. What, exactly, is that about?

**Wonderful.** When, in 1950, Uruguay won the World Cup for the second time, half of the nation's population came to the capital, Montevideo, to see the team and the trophy arrive. The nation's president, Tomás Berreta, did not mess about. 'Other countries have their history,' he declaimed, 'we have our football!'

**Suggested improvements.** More games. Cancel the close season. And take up Danny Baker's sister's idea of snazzing up kits with brightly coloured capes.

**Baker & Kelly Rating (points out of 100): 98.** Most wonderful game ever invented. Two points docked because of baleful influence of shark-toothed American tycoons, skulking Russian oligarchs, oil-rich despots and faceless Icelandic financial institutions who've bought the actual clubs. Family silver sold to rag-and-bone men for gin money.

# Test cricket

**What's it like?** Be-flannelled chaps potter about in the sun, waiting for lunch. Or, in the case of the Pakistan team, the chance to start a major diplomatic incident. Or small war.

**Who plays it?** England. And people who used to be beneath the imperial heel of England.

**Who likes it?** The teeming multitudes in India. And TV, cos it's cheap to broadcast.

**Famous fans.** John Major, Sir Mick Jagger, Ben Travers, Siegfried Sassoon, Stephen Fry, Sufi Abdul Jalil (Pakistan's 'Uncle Cricket'), Gravy (West Indies), Jeremy Paxman, John Kettley, Johnny Borrell of Razorlight, Keane, the speccy teenager who plays Harry Potter.

**Weird.** Nearly every cricketer who's ever played for England was born outside the country. Here's just a sample: Tony Greig, Allan Lamb, Kevin Pietersen, Robin Smith, Andrew Strauss (South Africa); Gladstone Small, 'Daffy' DeFreitas, Devon Malcolm (various parts of the West Indies); Adam Hollioake, Tim Ambrose (Australia); Graeme Hick, Phil Edmonds (Zimbabwe); Andy Caddick (New Zealand); Bob Woolmer, Nasser Hussain (India); Owais Shah (Pakistan); Robert Croft, Simon Jones (Wales); Mike Denness (Scotland); Dermot Reeve (Hong Kong); Ed Joyce

(Ireland); Derek Pringle (Kenya); Neal Radford (Zambia); Geraint Jones (Papua New Guinea).

That's Papua New Guinea.

**Wonderful.** It lasts five days. Or longer. In 1939 England and South Africa decided that the final test of the series (in Durban) should be 'timeless' – played beyond the normal five days until a natural conclusion was reached. In the event the game occupied the whole of 3, 4, 6, 7, 8, 9, 10, 11, 13 and 14 March. The England team then had to get the steamship home and so the match still ended in a draw. And they all had tea.

**Suggested improvement.** Softer ball, to give kids a chance.

**Baker & Kelly Rating (points out of 100): 59.** Great game, perhaps lacking just a teensy bit of the MTV wow factor to attract the youngsters. Worth persevering with as every youngster born in the former British empire apparently dreams of playing for England.

# Horse racing

**What's it like?** Huge, specially bred horses are ridden round a big field by tiny, specially bred Irishmen. The tiny Irishmen wear brightly coloured costumes made of silk, even though horse racing often takes place in the iron depths of winter.

**Who does it?** The English-speaking world. And the French. And loads and loads of Arabs.

**Who likes it?** Loads and loads of Arabs. Irish people. Bookmakers.

**Famous fans.** Her Majesty Queen Elizabeth II, Michael Owen, Steven Spielberg, Dennis Hopper, Gene Simmons of Kiss, Ed Norton, Alan Brazil, Andy Capp.

**Weird.** Steeplechasing is so-called because the original races took place between the church of one village and the church of one of its neighbours.

**Wonderful.** Every single racehorse in the world can trace its ancestry to just three Arabian stallions imported into England in the late seventeenth century and used to start the formal breeding of speedy nags. The three lucky creatures were called the Darley Arabian, the Byerly Turk and the Godolphin Arabian.

**Suggested improvement.** Monkey jockeys.

**Baker & Kelly Rating (points out of 100): 67.** Mostly gained by bewildered visits to high-street bookmakers. Indeed, Danny Kelly's family doctor spent almost no time in his surgery and could nearly always be found perched on a rickety stool in William Hill, Essex Road, grumpily filling out prescriptions with one of those stubby pens.

# American Football

**What's it like?** Teams comprising between 80 and 120 formidably muscled African-Americans and square-headed Caucasians from America's farmlands (all armoured like Samurai warriors) charge at each other in the manner of drug-crazed bison. Then they all fall in a big pile. Then they get up and do it again. Occasionally the ball gets thrown.

**Who does it?** Americans. Plus the kind of English blokes who call their kids Chad and Elmer and have Confederate flag stickers on the bumpers of their cars. And who were no good at football at school.

**Who likes it?** Middle-class Americans. Plus the kind of English blokes who call their mates 'the guys' and buy Colt 45 off the Internet.

**Famous fans.** Jon Bon Jovi (New York Giants), Will Smith (Philadelphia Eagles), Ice Cube (Oakland Raiders), Jamie Foxx (Dallas Cowboys), Huey Lewis (San Fransisco 49ers), Snoop Dogg (University of Southern California), Condoleezza Rice (Cleveland Browns).

**Weird.** American football has always reflected the society from which it sprang. The original game, about going up and down the pitch in rushes, reflected the frantic migration of the US population from east to west. After the Second World War, the game started to mirror the shape of the American military, with the mostly black GIs grunting and groaning in the trenches while the ultimate weapon of destruction (the ball) stayed resolutely in the milky-white hands of the quarterback. In recent years more and more of the quarterbacks have been of African-American extraction, until the present moment when, for the first time, they're in the majority. Cue a black president!

**Wonderful.** The players' names have suddenly gone quite mad. Ten years ago 99 per cent of the protagonists were called Joe, Frank, Johnny or Chuck. Now, thanks to the habit of American parents of randomly inventing new monikers, we are blessed with a generation of burly boys with bewildering, quirkily entertaining, handles. Come on down (in alphabetical forename order):

Alge Crumpler (Tennessee)

Arnaz Battle (San Fransisco)

BenJarvus Green-Ellis (New England)

Brodney Pool (Cleveland)

Cadillac Williams (Tampa Bay)

Calais Campbell (Arizona)

Chartric Darby (Detroit)

Craphonso Thorpe (Tennessee)

D'Brickashaw Ferguson (New York Jets)

Devery Henderson (New Orleans)

Frostee Rucker (Cincinnati)

Flozell Adams (Dallas)

Herana-Daze Jones (Denver)

Jermon Bushrod (New Orleans)

Keyunta Dawson (Indianapolis)

Kregg Lumpkin (Green Bay)

Kroy Biermann (Atlanta)

LaDainian Tomlinson (San Diego)

Laveranues Coles (Cincinnati)

Leodis McKelvin (Buffalo)

Lousaka Polite (Miami)

Mackenzy Bernadeau (Carolina)

Mansfield Wrotto (Seattle)

Marshawn Lynch (Buffalo)

Pacino Horne (Detroit)

Ramzee Robinson (Detroit)

Scorpio Babers (Miami)

Shawntae Spencer (San Fransisco)

Sinorice Moss (New York Giants)

Skyler Green (New Orleans)

Syndric Steptoe (Cleveland)

Tashard Choice (Dallas)

Tavares Gooden (Baltimore)

Tearrius George (Miami)

Travonti Johnson (New York Giants)

Wilrey Fontenot (Arizona)

**Suggested improvement.** Even bigger helmets and padding, all heading in the general direction of those huge rubbery giants from *Jeux Sans Frontières*.

**Baker & Kelly Rating (points out of 100): 78.** Massive bruisers knocking seven shades out of each other – what's not to like? Plus Kregg Lumpkin!!!

# Formula 1 Tax Avoiders.

**What's it like?** Skinny, unattractive cars – motorised supermodels – zip round and round and round the track, in exactly the order in which they qualified. A few drops of rain fall. The safety car comes out. The race finishes at 14 mph. Champagne is sprayed. Garb-averse nubiles are entertained in motorhomes. Everyone heads for the courts where the winner is eventually decided.

**Who does it?** Desperate car manufacturers and rich patrons too cowardy-custard to try the real racing and genuine competition of Nascar. The only Americans who take part are those being punished for their mediocrity or some infraction of the rules back home.

**Who likes it?** Jet-setters. Oil-rich sheikhs – why not, it keeps topping up the old current account? Blokes who scour eBay for vintage T-shirts bearing the legend 'Castrol GTX'. Fans of Amazonian girls in hot pants. Carrying flags.

**Famous fans.** Jude Law, Sylvester Stallone, George Lucas, Gordon Ramsey, Pavel Nedved, Vladimir Klitschko.

**Weird.** Between 1976 and 1978 the Tyrrell P34 startled the world with the traditional two big fat wheels at the back plus four small, aerodynamically advantageous, wheels at the front. At its unveiling journalists fainted. But it was fast – it even won a Grand Prix. Other teams also tried the six-wheel trick. As late as the early 80s the Williams team was achieving record testing times with a car that had six full-size wheels (two at the front, four at the back, like a furniture removal van). Then the spoilsports at F1 changed the rules, insisting in future that all cars would have just the traditional four wheels, one at each corner.

Why? Why would they mess with the forces of evolution? Why didn't they follow the example of those in charge of the development of men's razors? Originally one blade was thought sufficient for satisfactory male depilation. Then two became the accepted optimum. Then three. Now five is the minimum requirement for any fellow requiring a smooth shave. In some strip-lit laboratory, no doubt, a boffin is currently working on the seven-bladed razor. Indeed there is a scene in *The Life of Brian* where the firebrand preacher is telling us, in the voice of the Reverend Ian Paisley, about a sword that is 'nine bladed... NINE bladed!' Even that once-impossible-sounding prophecy is now no more than a marketing meeting from reality. If the killjoys that run motor racing had kept their noses out, we could now be watching Grand Prix cars with anything up to two dozen wheels.

**Wonderful.** In a world rife with tabloid hysteria and tut-tut moralising, Formula 1, you might be surprised to learn, has stood as a shining beacon against knee-jerk conservatism. When, in 2008, Max Mosley, president of the Fédération Internationale de l'Automobile (which governs F1), was filmed enjoying a lengthy S&M (not sausage and mash) session with a gaggle of hookers, you might have expected the FIA to show him the door, with extreme prejudice. But no. Despite pressure from less progressive bodies, the FIA allowed Sir Max to keep his job. Only for the old boy to be shown the door a few months later anyway, after he fell out with the top teams over his perfectly sensible plans to cut the ludicrous cost of the sport.

**Suggested improvements.** Races in the proper dark, with headlights on. A figure-of-eight track, no bridge. Cars with a second seat in the back, in which they must carry a celebrity. Less camera-phone footage of Max M's septuagenarian bottom.

**Baker & Kelly Rating (points out of 100): 27.** Mostly for the leggy lovelies that stalk the grid, and a few for James Hunt's legendary pre-commentary relaxation techniques (*see* Recreational Drugs in Sport, page 227).

# Fishing

**What's it like (Britain and Ireland only)?** Early-bird enthusiasts hunch over sultry canals and slow grey rivers. The surface is disturbed only by the small explosions of bulbous raindrops steadily plopping onto the water. Roll-ups are smoked. Flasks of tea and 'special coffee' are drained. Occasionally an inedible fish is hooked, photographed then chucked back into the drink.

**Who does it?** Solitary men in hooded oilskins. And, in more recent times (judging by the canals of Islington and Kings Cross), east European electricians and bricklayers actually hoping to reel in a tasty supper.

**Who likes it?** If the sheer proliferation of angling titles is anything to go by, then great swathes of the UK population. The male population that is. The key phrase here seems to be 'Gets them out of the house.'

Baker & Kelly are equal opportunity authors, as demanded by Section 4, Para 7b of the 2004 Sexual Discrimination in Best-Selling Books Act. We therefore wish to remind all readers that angling is not just for men. To back this up, we can reveal that the heaviest fish ever caught in the UK by a woman is a 66-pound catfish hooked by mother-of-one Bev Street of Skegness, at Bluebell Lakes in Oundell, Cambridgeshire in 2007. Her monster catch broke the record of legendary angler Miss Georgina Ballantine, a member of the famous Scottish whisky family, who caught a 64-pound salmon in the River Tay near Glendelvine, Perthshire, some 85 years earlier.

**Famous fans.** David Seaman (of course!), Chris Tarrant, Gazza, Nick Hancock, Paul Whitehouse, Billy Connolly, Jim Davidson, Jack Charlton, Robbie Williams, Steve Davies, Prince Charles, Norman Schwarzkopf, Jeremy Paxman, Eric Clapton, Emperor Trajan, Sir Ian Botham, Roger Waters, Roger Daltrey, Ronnie Corbett, Bobby Davro, Jim Bowen, Loyd Grossman, Diana Rigg, Marco Pierre White, Nick Faldo, George Bush Snr.

**Weird.** Man has been fishing since the ancients first learned to pull the slippery blighters out of rivers with their bare hands. Fishing magazines have been around for almost as long. You would have thought that by now there would be numerous ways in which successful hunters could display their scaly trophies. But no. In every single photograph, in every single angling journal ever published, fisherman and piscine captive have – as if by some ancient by-law telepathically transmitted down from the Neanderthals and cavemen – to be photographed the same way. Regardless of the size of the fish (or the fisherman); regardless of background scenery; regardless of race, colour or creed... the angler faces the camera and smiles. His arms are extended towards the camera, bent at the elbow, hands palm up, like someone offering you a bundle of invisible towels. The fish is then placed onto the hands, not flat on its side, but on its belly, in profile, for our perusal. It is, in its relentless consistency, a thing of timeless, comforting beauty.

**Wonderful.** Anglers yield to no man in their conviction that their beloved activity is a sport, not a pastime or an excuse to get out of creosoting the fence. In 1991 the *Angling Times* ran a vigorous campaign to get four-time world champion Bob Nudd named BBC Sports Personality of the Year. In the event he garnered over 100,000 votes, enough to make him clearly the winner. The BBC, desperate not to award the prize to someone whose sport was never, ever shown on the telly, concocted some phoney-baloney ruling to deny Nudd his due. Instead they awarded the prize to Scottish distance runner Liz McColgan.

**Suggested improvement.** Only that the people who make the decisions about new record catches should get themselves a rather more imposing address than the one at which they currently reside: British Record (Rod-Caught) Fish Committee, c/o NFSA Head Office, Hamlyn House, Level 5, Mardle Way, Buckfastleigh, Devon, TQ11 0NS.

**Baker & Kelly Rating (points out of 100): 82.** Not least because fishing writers are prone to write meandering, dusty pieces about a long day's search for the perfect zander, only to see their prose headlined RED HOT ROD-BENDING ACTION.

# The Boat Race

**What's it like?** Two high-tech rowing boats. Into each is strapped eight wardrobe-sized toffs – the rowers – and one toff so small he gets pushed around by jockeys, the cox. They row from Putney to Mortlake. Medium-sized toffs cheer them on from the banks. The team that won the toss and chose the Surrey station wins. The victorious microtoff is chucked in the drink. Champagne is quaffed.

**Who does it?** Traditionally, braying hee-haws from the shires. Nowadays, specially imported supermen from the USA and Germany, many with no connection whatsoever to either university, or joined-up writing.

**Who likes it?** Thames-side purveyors of Dom Perignon and quails' eggs. The BBC. Swells, blue bloods, poshoes, toffee-noses, noblemen, peers, the upper crust, members of the aristocracy, the high-born.

Baker & Kelly are equal opportunity authors, as demanded by Section 9, Para 13c, of the 2002 Class Discrimination in Best-Selling Books Act. We therefore wish to remind all readers that the Boat Race is these days no longer the entire preserve of the privileged and moneyed. It is a genuine sporting event between highly tuned teams of top-class intelligent athletes, definitely worthy of your admiration and respect. This apparent volte-face has in no way been motivated by the realisation that the victorious 2009 Oxford crew weighed an average of 17 stone. And may very well live in the London area.

**Famous participants.** Andrew Irvine (mountaineer, Oxford 1922, 1923), Lord Snowdon (photographer, Cambridge 1950), Jeffrey Archer (liar, Oxford 1962), David Rendel (MP, Oxford 1974), Colin Moynihan (sports minister, Oxford 1977) and Hugh Laurie (*Blackadder*, *House*, Cambridge 1980).

**Weird.** It's always the same two teams in the final (copyright every half-baked comedian, circa 1957).

**Wonderful.** The Boat Race played a very important role in the development of British cinema. The 1895 race was filmed by one Birt Acres, an American film pioneer who, among other things, invented the 35 mm camera and the home projector. On 5 May the following year the film (glorying in the snappy title *The Oxford and Cambridge University Boat Race*) was shown at Cardiff Town Hall, thus becoming the first film to be commercially screened outside London.

**Suggested improvement.** Replace the cox with a Ben Hur-style horator, you know, the sweaty ox who beats out the rowing speed on a big drum. 'Row well number 41, and live... Ramming speed!'

**Baker & Kelly Rating (points out of 100): 28.** Most of those points accumulated, let's be honest, by the occasional sight of eight massive marquesses and one diminutive duke sinking into the Thames slime.

# Kabaddi

**What's it like?** Amazing. A mixture of kiss-chase and British bulldog. Two teams line up on a pitch about the size of a tennis court. Then, using various techniques familiar to any British schoolboy (rushing, elbowing, kicking, some gouging), one member of team A attempts to infiltrate the territory of team B. Team B defend themselves by grabbing, elbowing, kicking, some gouging. To the untrained eye it might very easily pass for a particularly violent version of tag.

**Who does it?** People all over India, plus Nepal, Bangladesh, Sri Lanka, Japan and Pakistan. Called *kabaddi*, meaning 'holding of breath' in north India, in southern parts it's known as *chedugudu* or *hu-tu-tu*. Best of all, the good folk of eastern India call it *hadudu* (for the chaps) and *chu-kit-kit* (for the ladies). That's *hu-tu-tu*, *hadudu* and *chu-kit-kit*.

**Who likes it?** Subcontinentals and, for a brief window of time, viewers of Channel 4.

**Famous fans.** Shilpa Shetty, possibly. And the British army, who have adopted the game for fitness reasons and in an attempt, apparently, to attract more recruits from the Asian community.

**Wonderful.** In the early 1990s the game attained brief popularity in the UK when Channel 4, flush with the success of its American Football coverage (or possibly after a long afternoon on the hookah), made it a mainstay of their sports coverage. For the first time the UK viewer was presented with a sport where the attacker had to keep saying '*kabaddi… kabaddi… kabaddi…*' over and over again. When they ran out of breath, they had to retreat to their own half, assuming they hadn't already suffered a good cuffing or a dead leg. Presumably, in other parts of India, the contestants were muttering '*hu-tu-tu… hu-tu-tu…*,' '*hadudu… hadudu… hadudu…*' or '*chu-kit-kit… chu-kit-kit… chu-kit-kit…*'

But the real reason for the early success of *kabaddi* on TV was that C4 chose to show us the women's version of the game, in which tiny pigtailed gals in large shorts grappled with each other in exotic locations. Suffice to say there are stalls in Walthamstow market charging £15 a DVD for far less exciting fare.

**Weird.** Then, out of a clear blue Punjabi sky, some lunatic (possibly under pressure from an EU directive – back off, Brussels!) decided to show the men's game. Exciting though it was to root for West Bengali Police – you know the rule: whenever there's a televised sporting event, even one about which you care less than a whit, you have to pick a team – it soon became evident that watching bear-like Sikh warriors pawing at one another was somehow not the same. And so, with a rapidity that would have impressed Usain Bolt, the golden age of *kabaddi* came to an end. Channel 4 binned it quicker than you could gabble '*chu-kit-kit... chu-kit-kit... chu-kit-kit...*'

**Suggested improvement.** The Indians have had 4,000 years to perfect *kabaddi*, so it seems slightly impertinent to even offer alterations from the other side of the world. But you could have said the same about curry, yet in no time at all Britain has come up with chicken tikka chilli massala, the ultimate dish. Sepp Blatter would no doubt have the females (maybe everyone) playing in 15-denier lace-tops.

**Baker & Kelly Rating (points out of 100): 48.** Possibly brilliant game badly let down by the male variant. Too hairy.

# Swimming

**What's it like?** Shaven-headed, gigantically built hulks propel themselves like sinewy torpedoes through lakes of chlorine. Men do it too. The monotony of watching a line of splashes racing one another is broken only by those tumble turns that look easy as pie and which everyone (admit it) tries in the holiday swimming pool when nobody is looking. They are not, it turns out, easy as pie.

**Who does it?** Triangular-bodied buzz-cut Americans and Australians. Druggy east Europeans. Brits who get up at five in the morning and make 40-mile round trips on sleet-whipped January mornings to dilapidated Victorian communal baths in places like Coventry and Tranmere. Then go on the telly and complain about it. Until they get lottery money.

**Who likes it?** Aussies, obviously. And rednecks, as it's the only major sport not now largely dominated by African-Americans. Oh, and there's ice hockey.

**Famous fans.** Erm...

**Weird.** In the first three Olympic Games swimming was held not in specially built pools but in open water. At the 1896 games in Greece the swimming was held in the Mediterranean; in 1900 in Paris swimming took place in the River Seine; four years later in St Louis all aquatic events took place in a man-made lake.

**Wonderful.** It doesn't matter how many medals Ian Thorpe wins. It's immaterial how many records Michael Phelps breaks. Wonderments though they both are, the greatest swimmer of all time is, and always will be, Australia's Shane Gould. Born on the very first day of competition in the 1956 Melbourne Olympics, she was by her mid-teens a watery phenomenon. She won three gold medals at the 1972 games in Munich, and is the only person ever to hold all the freestyle world records between 100 and 1,500 metres. Unless some GM boffin starts cross-breeding sun-ripened Australians with sailfish (who've been clocked at 65 mph through the water), that latter achievement will never be equalled. And yet she was also blessed with cartloads of common sense and street smarts. When she shocked the world by retiring at the age of 16, the global media could mutter just one question: 'Why, Shane, *why*?' The teenager sat back in her chair, thought – as young women do – about the harmful effects of chlorine, and said, 'Because boys don't date girls with green hair.' That, friends, is a champion.

**Suggested improvement.** 'Exciting? No, it's not. It's dull. Dull. Dull. My God, it's dull, it's so desperately dull and tedious and stuffy and boring and des-per-ate-ly DULL.' So speaks Mr Anchovy in the *Monty Python* sketch about careers advice. He's actually talking about accountancy, but 'Exciting? No, it's not. It's dull. Dull. Dull. My God, it's dull, it's so desperately dull and tedious and stuffy and boring and des-per-ate-ly DULL' just about sums up swimming too. And the main reason it's boring is that we cannot see the faces of swimmers. We have absolutely nothing (bar the occasional glimpse of a postage-stamp Union Jack) to help us identify with them, to make us want to support them, to force us to care.

Baker & Kelly have a plan. We believe that the solution to most of swimming's ills is to mount a large fin on the back (or in the case of backstrokers the belly) of the contestants. The fin would be shaped like shark's or like a sail, about three feet high, and made of an ultra-lightweight material onto which could be projected high-definition images. The benefits are obvious. A lovely portrait of the swimmer could be displayed throughout the race, giving us armchair enthusiasts something to really relate to, to root for, to fall in love with. Obviously this image could alternate during the race with advertising. At low-grade meetings the fin would no doubt carry local endorsements ('Eat at Leo's Snackbox, Braintree'), but at Olympic finals Mothercare, Cleanopine, Vauxhall Nova and Clarks Shoes would all be falling over each other to rent the space.

B&K have contacted the FINA, international swimming's ruling body, with the details of this bold plan plus an estimate of the remuneration we believe we'd be entitled to once the scheme has been universally adopted. We have sent it by post (courier, registered letter and normal second-class post). We have phoned, faxed and emailed. We have contacted the FINA via Facebook, MySpace and Twitter. We got a Native American to send up smoke signals. Despite our best efforts, we have to relay to you the sad, almost unbelievable news that as of yet we have had no response from the aquatic overlords.

Maybe you feel as strongly about all this as us. In which case, why not contact the FINA. Mark your correspondence 'Baker & Kelly's Excellent Fin Plan' and send it pronto to:

FINA

Avenue de l'Avant-Poste 4

CH – 1005 Lausanne

SWITZERLAND

Tel: (+41–21) 310 47 10

Fax: (+41–21) 312 66 10

**Baker & Kelly Rating (points out of 100): 11.** Time for the fin!

# The Final Reckoning

| | |
|---|---|
| Association football | 98 |
| Fishing | 82 |
| American football | 78 |
| Horse racing | 67 |
| Test cricket | 59 |
| *Kabaddi* | 48 |
| The Boat Race | 28 |
| Formula 1 | 27 |
| Swimming | 11 |

# Who got the ball rolling?

One of the most widely held fallacies in football is that the oldest club in the English leagues is Notts County. In fact it is Bristol Rovers. This one simple piece of information not only completely validates the writing of this book but, at a stroke, renders null and void the results of thousands of pub quizzes played up and down Britain over the last 30 years. So write it down and file it away, boys: Bristol Rovers is Britain's Oldest Club.

No hang on, I just looked it up and, as you were, it *is* Notts County. Notts County is, after all, Britain's Oldest Club. Let there be no further argument about that. However, the temptation upon hearing this is to believe that Notts County therefore must have invented football itself.

Well, let Danny and I at least clear that one up. Notts County did NOT invent football. Football has been around a lot longer than Notts County, thank you very much.

That said, quite what was happening before Notts County got together as an actual team neither of us can figure out. Was it simply every man, everywhere for himself? What possible point could a football match have had if it was just 22 separate individuals thrashing away at each other and all claiming eventual victory? Which way would one kick? How was a penalty awarded? Who would ever bother to make a tricky step-over followed by a surprise left-foot cross if they were a team of just one? Lastly, of course, there is that eternal schoolyard conundrum – if Notts County was the original club, who did they play?

To find out the answers to all these questions it is necessary for us to travel back to ancient China. Yes, really. Ancient China. Land of Mandarins, Ming and low, low prices.

Around 1330 the ancient Chinese invented a game called *puya-ni* which was roughly akin to modern tennis, but played with the feet. Also the idea was to get the ball back to an opponent by kicking it *below* a wire strung between two trees rather than above it. The ball was large and made from a light husk prised off a melon-type fruit called an *aagwan*. By decree, the game could only be played after the sun went down, and that meant only on nights when the moon was full enough to grant adequate light. It was customary to smoke long pipes called *tsung-yar*s during the bouts – called *nyar-chii*s – and throughout players would wear heavy floor-length ceremonial gowns embossed with dragons and river scenes. No score was kept. A game of *puya-ni* was only permissible between members of a certain class of society, and it is this revelation that links it to modern tennis.

So where does football come in? Well clearly the aim of having to kick the ball *below* the wire, or bar, is something all football fans would recognise. As they would the only surviving scrap of reporting on a *puya-ni* bout, taken from writing on a wall in 1423: 'Much-tipped prospect San Hoi-gin was presented with a golden opportunity to really settle the fixture in the 88th minute but amazingly he blazed his shot over from barely two yards out.'

However, the key piece of information from this dusty trawl down the millennia is of course the *ball*. The Chinese had begun using a *ball*. Not a very good one and one that I suspect reacted to mild breezes worse than contemporary beach balls but a recognisable bona-fide ball nonetheless.

Actually while we're here, let's think about that. *Why* do men continue to insist, even today, on trying to get a serious game going at the seaside with a hastily purchased super-thin uber-lightweight PVC beach ball? Beach balls are worse than hopeless. The harder you kick a beach ball the more it goes behind you – even when there is no wind. It's like playing with a soap bubble, and you may as well save three quid and stage the kickabout with a seashell or a dead crab. At least when a dead crab goes over the goal line it stays over the goal line. Indeed dead crabs are in many ways nature's own goal-line technology. Beach balls, on the other hand, double back into play with a sort of ghostly waft that then creates more arguments than England's third in the 1966 World Cup final.

As a younger man I used to love going on chaps-only excursions to the coast, but I have lost count of the times I have wasted half the day because I was in the company of cock-eyed optimistic grown men who insisted on blowing up a beach ball till they were weak and giddy, pushed in the valve – and how easy is that to do without losing half the gathered puff? – and then seriously pronounced game on.

Half an hour later the sheer hopelessness of the enterprise has buckled everyone's mood, ruined all sandwiches within half-a-mile's radius and made at least ten babies cry. Let us say it now and say it loud, **Lads, you CANNOT play football with a beach ball.**

In fact you cannot play football on a beach even with a proper ball. Oh, I know they do it in Brazil, but we all really must get over our fascination with Brazil. We have to face up to the fact that Copacabana Bay is not Frinton seafront. It is more than likely that the Brazilians have developed match-friendly, tactic-enriched, samba-filtered super-sand – their economy must run on something. Ours in Britain simply will not allow even the shortest pass to arrive anywhere near its intended destination; sucking the pace from the crispest one-two it defies all known laws of physics. Even the *Wehrmacht* were warned how 'impassable' the UK's coastal beaches were, and from bitter experience I can tell them how infuriatingly true that is.

So, anyway, China gave the world the football and then went on to completely disregard its potential by concentrating on gymnastics instead. Which brings us to one of the richest veins of phone call we've had over the years – people who have also disregarded traditional football and decided, or were forced, to play something else.

# Is the ball necessary?

People, and let's be frank here, *men*, can cause football to happen anywhere, anytime. So long as there is something that even vaguely resembles a ball then nothing else really matters. Tin cans, bottle tops, stopcocks, ball bearings – all these items can apparently do the job every bit as well as the finest that Mitre can make.

We once took a call from a chap who, after a long evening's carousing, had found himself banged up in a cell. He'd done nothing too drastic, simply been picked up for his own good when the police saw him walking down the middle of the road wearing the classic traffic cone as headgear and – and this is a look many of us will have toyed with – a broken umbrella fashioned around his shoulders like armour. When stopped by the constables he responded to their enquiries thus: 'You've got thirty seconds to clear the entire area before I really lose my rag.'

Anyway as the night staggered on, the cell he was in gradually filled up with various other losers, boozers and jacuzzi users, and once there was an agreeable number – six, I believe he said – somebody inevitably lamented, 'If only we had a ball.' It was at this point that the bread roll appeared. A bread roll. Can you picture it? I know I can and it seems entirely play-worthy, doesn't it? Game on. Rather tragically though, the roll was not of the soft and spongy type which might have survived a few skirmishes but, fatally, a crusty one. Within a few minutes of kick-off and with the game still delicately balanced the roll began to break apart. Naturally this led to disputes about which piece was still the official piece (the largest segment surely?), and when one of the lags wafted what was in effect nothing but a large crumb against the opposing cell wall and tried to claim the lead, an almighty fight broke out. Thus what should have been a night that ended with simple police cautions wound up with substantial fines all round accompanied by some strong remarks from the bench.

High spirits aside, what we need to focus on in this tale is the bread-roll-as-ball motif. While in no way an ideal substitute, even casual football followers can see its possibilities. The same can't be said of a six-inch solid metal wing nut – and I mean one of those heavy brutes of the type you see junkyard dogs secured to with rope. And yet, if the British Public is to be believed, these too have been pressed into service so that an impromptu match might go ahead. Surely you would break your foot? 'Well in our game,' the caller insisted, referring to his line of work, 'we all wear steel-toecap boots, and you can shift anything across the floor with those. Besides,' he went on, 'we were only playing till the first goal decided it. We'd always wanted to try out a game with something really heavy.' Again, suddenly I saw the appeal. Not too many crosses and headers, I ventured. He told me not be ridiculous.

Then there was the half-pig's head used during a game staged inside an enormous deep freeze at a meat wholesaler. Or the RAF beret stuffed with newspaper that served for a kickabout in the belly of a massive transport plane at 30,000 feet. Less unlikely but nonetheless notable was the huge roll of gaffer tape that enabled a 4–4 draw to reach its nail-biting conclusion in the bowels of Dungeness Nuclear Power Station. Now I know the Dungeness coast and I challenged the caller that surely they could have visited any of the nearby shops and bought something more suitable. He responded by saying: a) the game was played in the middle of the night, and b) all those nearby shops sell are beach balls and had I ever tried to play with one of those? Thus I was well and truly hoist by my own petard.

The only call about remarkable balls that I outright refused to believe was from a person who claimed to have played in a five-a-side match using a medicine ball. This I simply won't have. They weigh not just a ton but *tons*. You cannot shift a medicine ball. I have no idea what is inside one, but whatever it is, it is on the outer edge of the laws of physics as we currently perceive them. They are round but they won't roll.

Actually, I have no idea whether medicine balls are still manufactured or what they could have possibly been used for, but when I was young every school had one. It was usually locked in a cupboard in the hall and would just plonk onto the floor with a heavy thud when you were trying to fetch out the skittles or skipping ropes or bibs. I remember lifting ours back onto its gloomy shelf and marvelling as to just what it could be that made it so stupendously stodgy. Theories about what was contained within its leathery depths ranged from rags to heavy gasses. And yet I don't know of a single person who hasn't tried to kick one at least once. If you are such a creature then I beg you not to try. They don't budge. Not an inch. Not a centimetre. The flesh of a medicine ball will defy your mightiest strike and simply absorb your instep into its mysterious guts. Then it will send every bit of that energy back up your leg in a lightning bolt of pain that can cause actual matter to issue from the ears.

When I was the writer of the often stunt-based TV show *TFI Friday* I lobbied for us to get a medicine ball into the studio and cut it open live on air. Naturally none of the production staff – average age nine and a half – had ever even heard of this notorious torture instrument of the gym. However, I persisted in my request until one of the special-effects men – a kindly grey-haired guy of about 80 summers – quietly told me to drop the idea. 'Forget it, kid,' he said in a wavering voice. 'Friend of mine did it back in the 50s for the old *Michael Holliday Show*. Leastways they started tests on it in the lab.' Here he stared off wildly into the middle distance and continued in something like awe, 'Flash of light. Huge explosion. Windows shattered for a hundred miles around. Horses fell dead in the street. Nobody got out of there alive. When they found the medicine ball...other than a small puncture hole, not a mark on it. Don't go meddlin' where you don't belong, son.'

So I abandoned my life's dream and in the end we compromised and cut open an Etch-A-Sketch instead, which, let me tell you, is full of a metallic, highly compressed viscous material that forms a giant mush-room cloud when exposed to the air before slowly coming to earth and covering every living thing and structure within a 1,000-metre radius. We're still settling audience lawsuits on that one.

The message from all this is, I suppose, that while both beach balls and medicine balls are called balls they are really nothing of the kind and actually constitute some sort of sick joke. If you want to get a game going and have no proper ball with you, try an acorn. Or a gobstopper. Or a crab shell. Or a wig rolled up and bound with twine. Ah...you're thinking about that last one, aren't you? Be great to volley, eh?

# When did football become Britain's number-one sport?

Football officially became the number-one sport in the British Isles, eclipsing cricket, some time during the winter of 1946. The exact date was lost following a flood in a government warehouse in the 70s. But what caused such a seismic shift and why football?

Well, with troops arriving back on these shores after a violent and extremely filmic world war, the old sporting order with its lbws, polite applause and breaks for tea seemed totally irrelevant and representative of a discredited class system.

Football's time had come, and soccer stadiums sprouted up in the most unlikely places – Wrexham, Mansfield, Ayr, Brechin, Birmingham. At first relatively few of the civilian population were curious enough to go into these grounds to see what the game had to offer – Stamford Bridge with its typically grandiose capacity of 60,000 rarely had more than a few hundred supporters inside – and the music halls looked as though they would continue with their pre-war business as usual. But with demob gathering pace a notable milestone was reached on Christmas Day 1945 at the Sunderland v. Hull City fixture, when the UK's first ever 20,000-plus gate was achieved. Cricket was forced to sit up and take notice but it was too late. When the following day's game between Coventry and Aston Villa notched up an attendance of 25,644, the acrid smell of burning willow and unwashed flannels could be detected wafting across the sacred turf at Lord's.

Why? It must be understood that Britain has traditionally been very fickle when awarding its national sport title. Indeed cricket had only been accepted as number one since May 1921, when it officially replaced the card game bezique. Even during cricket's supposed supremacy it lost the title twice: once in 1928, when the UK craze for miniature golf was at its height, and again in 1940, when the *Daily Mirror* ran an erroneous story that Hitler had once scored 140 runs in just twelve overs. It was subsequently proved that Hitler had done no such thing and actually despised cricket as the 'plutocracy at play'. However, in the brief interim before this became apparent swimming was controversially declared the nation's favourite sport, despite there being only one swimming pool in the whole nation at that time.

Given such an extreme national reaction to the Hitler–cricket story, one can't help but wonder what would have happened to football's reputation had the truth been known – that the Nazis were huge soccer enthusiasts, though because of the international situation (the Second World War) they were forced to play many of their fixtures against the Allied nations under such pseudonyms as Rest of the World XI and Switzerland. It is for this reason that the winners of the notorious 1942 World Cup in Canada, the 'Sudetenland', have since been expunged from the record.

Perhaps the most peculiar and now almost totally forgotten sport ever to dominate the home nations is giant chess. For much of the nineteenth century and for at least two decades of the twentieth, this outsized relative of normal chess completely ruled the sporting roost in the UK. Even the tiniest, filthiest tenement in the Gorbals or most modest hamlet in rural England had, somewhere close by, a massive chequered board and a space in which to house the 32 four-foot-high pieces.

Quite what made giant chess so appealing to generations of Victorians is unclear although one should never underestimate its sheer physicality. One almost has to hug the massive pawns, bishops, rooks and so on in order to get them to where one thinks an attack or defence is best directed, and this would have been hugely erotic in those buttoned-up days. Anyone who has ever read *The Unabridged Letters of Charlotte Brontë* will recall the almost audible sigh of disappointment when on 7 July 1841 she writes, 'Was pleased to play Giant Chess with Sir Robert Peel today but it was all over very quickly.' These days giant chess is looked upon as something of an oddity when one occasionally stumbles across a board in the garden of a country house or roadside inn. However, soon even these bizarre beached survivors may be gone forever following an incident in 1995 when, during some high winds in Oxfordshire, a queen from a giant chess set in the yard of a local pub became airborne and killed a pig in a field several miles away. The *Oxford Telegraph* subsequently instigated a successful campaign to have all giant chess sets in the area demolished 'before we are mourning, instead of a pig, a pensioner', and the hysteria spread to surrounding counties and eventually the whole of the country. Today it is estimated that there are fewer than 900 giant chess boards left in Britain.

It is a statistic our current money-mad soccer mandarins might dwell upon long and hard.

# What was the greatest FA Cup final of all time?

You know the score. Great Cup final blah blah... Liverpool 3 West Ham 3, 2006... blah blah blah... Stanley Matthews, 1953... blah blah... United 3 Palace 3, 1990... blah... Arsenal 3 Man United 2, 1979... Coventry 3 Tottenham 2...Yes, yes. All terrific matches. But to get into this list a final needed something more than just a hatful of goals and spine-snapping drama. You'll see. Now, all together, along with Mr Tommy Steele, 'Abide with me...'

## 10. 1974, Liverpool 3 Newcastle 0 (Wembley)

### Magnificent Magpies claim the Cup! Oh...

Noel Gallagher, speaking on Talksport in 2009, said it best: 'There is no greater sight on *Match of the Day* than fat Geordies crying.' Back in 1974 this was supposed to be Newcastle's day. Yeah, right. The build-up was dominated by the boasts of their players, officials and fans. Foremost among those promising to make linguine of Bill Shankly's boys was England centre forward Malcolm Macdonald. In the event Supermac was reduced to an impotent bystander by Phil Thompson's enormous hooter and bizarrely flowing locks. Kevin Keegan scored two, Steve Heighway the other; even the BBC's normally docile David Coleman was moved to comment that Newcastle's defence had been 'stripped naked'. In 1998 and 1999 Newcastle went on to equally convincing Cup final victories over Arsenal (0–2) and Manchester United (0–2). The 1974 final was an absolute classic for those who understand that football is really about presumption pricked, about dreams trampled mercilessly underfoot, about those TV shots of disbelieving, hollow-eyed losers.

## 9. 1901, Tottenham 3 Sheffield United 1 (Burnden Park, Bolton – replay)

***Tens of thousands ignore pub team winning the Cup.***

How bad was the first game? After a 2–2 draw at Crystal Palace in front of 110,000 fans, this replay set a new world record for evaporating interest. The second match was watched by a crowd 90,000 smaller than the first. Maybe it's something to do with Tottenham: 81 years later they beat Queens Park Rangers in another replayed final in front of 90,000, 2,000 below Wembley's night-time capacity and the only time in history that a Wembley FA Cup final hasn't sold out.

Back in 1901 Sheffield United had started red-hot favourites. And why not? Their London opponents were from the Southern League. But despite the presence of the legendary Fatty Foulkes in the United goal, Tottenham found a way to win and to become the first, and only, non-league club to win the trophy; they didn't join the old Second Division for another six years. It is a record that is unlikely to be beaten. In 2009 William Hill was offering odds of 2,000,000–1 against another non-league side winning the Cup. Compare just 3,000–1 against Elvis Presley and Lord Lucan being discovered, living together in an underground lair. On Neptune.

# 8. 1923, Bolton 2 West Ham 0 (Wembley)

### 'Some people are on the pitch... about a third of a million of them...'

A great final, of course, only because it was the first at Wembley and it had a white horse called Billy – less is heard these days of Billy's rider, the superbly named PC Scorey. What's much more interesting is the story of the site on which the stadium is built, and why all those Cup finals came to be played on top of the blown-up remains of a failed attempt to turn north-west London into a chunk of Paris.

Here's the tale. In 1889 a toff called Sir Edward Watkins, chairman of the Metropolitan Railway, became besotted by the newly erected Eiffel Tower. So much so, in fact, that the old boy hit upon the apparently insane, but tremendously Victorian, idea of building a similar but taller structure on some acres he owned in Wembley Park. Unable to persuade Gustave Eiffel himself to undertake the project, he instead summoned Sir Benjamin Baker, designer of the Forth Bridge, and blueprints were eagerly drawn up. Construction commenced in June 1893. The work though proceeded slowly because the builders were busy (as builders always are) elsewhere, in this case knocking together the Blackpool Tower. Still, by September 1895 four giant legs were finished and the tower itself was begun, eventually rising to some 155 feet. Then the underlying marshiness of the local geology started to make itself felt. The whole thing started to shift and shiver, and work had to be stopped. Forever. Cutting his losses, Watkins built a pleasure garden around the vast iron stump. In 1902 the rusting shambles was declared unsafe. Two years later the monstrosity was dismantled. In 1907 the wobbly foundations themselves were blown up. Much of the resultant rubble became the base on which the sacred turf of the old Wembley pitch was laid.

The Empire Stadium was commissioned for the British Empire Exhibition of 1923. It took exactly 300 days to build over the remains of Watkins' old folly, and it was finished just four days before the Cup final. The terraces were tested by battalions of troops being marched onto the new concrete and ordered to jump up and down; the first piece of turf was laid by King George V. Brilliantly, no one at the FA had thought to sell tickets for the final; instead they expected the crowd – officially the ground held 123,000 – to pitch up and pay at the door.

Which they did, in considerable numbers. A tsunami of humanity poured through the 104 turnstiles. It's now estimated that about 300,000 thrill-seekers actually made it into the ground; another 60,000 milled about outside. It took Billy and his equine chums to clear the pitch (then the biggest in the world; it had later to be reduced in size to comply with new FIFA regulations), and the match started 45 minutes late. Photographs show the hordes of spectators pressed right up to the touchlines; other, hardier, souls made it onto the roof. Oh yeah, Bolton won. And the FA decided, in light of events, that printing tickets for future finals might well be the way forward.

## 7. 1958, Bolton 2 Manchester Utd 0 (Wembley)

### *United's post-Munich fairy tale derailed by inattentive deity.*

Out of the genuine tragedy of the Munich air disaster, this final provided proof, as if proof were needed, that God does not take football seriously. A benign and beneficent deity would take his responsibilities towards the sport seriously, studiously working out from match to match what should happen for the good of the game, its fans and the population of this planet. Instead, our big guy upstairs clearly takes the whole thing for a bit of a giggle, and in matters football rather idly and capriciously rolls his Dice of Godly Power and lets them fall willy-nilly where they may. How else to explain the – roll! – awful events at that snow-duveted Munich airfield, followed by the amazing – roll! – feel-good story of a Manchester United side comprised of reserves and players given to them by rival sides actually getting to the Cup final, only to be beaten in front of a horrified nation – roll! – by Bolton. What kind of God is that? Do you think Gandalf would have let that happen? Do you think a God played by Charlton Heston would have let Nat Lofthouse bundle United goal-keeper – and hero of the Munich rescue effort – Harry Gregg into the net for the Trotters' clinching goal?

And while we're at it, God, can you explain any of the following: Ken Bates? The fact that *Match of the Day* is now so dead that small children poke at its putrefying carcass with sticks? The price of pies at the Emirates? Half-time that seems to last for 25 minutes? Possession statistics that prove absolutely nothing? Sepp Blatter? Referees warming up like they're proper athletes? Joey Barton? The cost of the new Wembley? The colour of Phil Brown? Why, if you wanted him to look like that, didn't you call him Phil Orange? The colour of Wes Brown? Again, Wes Orange! Can you? Explain your lazy-arse self? B&K think not. Amen.

## 6. 1988, Wimbledon 1 Liverpool 0 (Wembley)

### *The Crazy Gang meet a comedy legend. Reds fail to see joke.*

It would be easy to settle on this as one of the greatest finals just because a bunch of dirty dastards beat the best team in England. But to do so would be forgive the so-called Crazy Gang for all their 'zany' antics. The Tottenham-supporting half of B&K feels very little desire to forgive or forget. Not when he remembers martial arts expert John Fashanu almost blinding Gary Mabbutt with his elbow, or a Vinnie Jones tackle that ended Gary Stevens' career, or that same Vinnie Jones playing the human juicer with Paul Gascoigne's procreative bits.

No, the reasons why we must cherish this match are all to do with Wimbledon's goalkeeper Dave Beasant, who that day completed a quadruple of firsts that will never be equalled. He was the first FA Cup winner who lived within actual sight of the stadium. He was the first keeper to save a penalty in an FA Cup final, diving to his left to thwart John Aldridge. When he went up the 39 steps to receive the trophy, he became the first goalkeeper to captain an FA Cup winning team. And, half an hour later, he became the first FA Cup winning captain to be seen jaybird naked by a top comedy actress. June Whitfield – *Terry and June*, *Absolutely Fabulous*, those Birds Eye adverts about telling lies to your loved ones – was a massive Dons fans, and burst into the uproariously celebrating dressing room to be confronted by a soaking wet Beasant wearing nothing but his I've-won-the-Cup-me grin. 'Oh... Joooone...' as Terry Scott would have said.

## 5. 1927, Cardiff City 1 Arsenal 0 (Wembley)

### *Arsenal defeated by New Jersey.*

One of the very best, most lovely and juicy things about these islands is that our complicated, messed-up history means that our national game operates in a complicated, messed-up way. This is a marvellous thing in itself, and is made all the more lip-smacking by the fact that it drives the self-serving pompadours at UEFA loonball crazy. They want order; we bring chaos; they loathe us! They hate it that Cardiff and Swansea are Welsh clubs but play in English leagues. They despise the geopolitical twitch that sees Berwick Rangers located in England but a perennial feature of the lower reaches of Scottish football. They reach for the laven-der handkerchiefs at the realisation that Derry City are in Northern Ireland but display their footballing wares in a neighbouring sovereign country, the Republic. They claw in agony at each other's Christian Dior suits when they remember, despite years of therapy designed to help them forget, that Shrewsbury Town of the English Football League have, on no less than six occasions, won the Welsh FA Cup. And one can only imagine what tortures the gnomes of Nyon endure when they are forced to regard the transnational shenanigans at plucky Chester City. Their set-up straddles the English–Welsh border: the pitch is in the Celtic prin-cipality, the administrative offices in Albion; what's more, the new Dever Stadium was deliberately built this way precisely to prevent interfering Eurocrats from trying to dump City into the League of Wales alongside Airbus UK Broughton, Gap Connah's Quay and Technogroup Welshpool Town. And Abergavenny Thursdays. Back off, Nyon!

But the highlight of this joyful nonsense was when the FA Cup, then the mightiest club trophy on the planet, left England for the first and so far only time. Not just that, but it left in circumstances that these days would have had even the most determined conspiracy theorists saying, 'Nah... that's too far-fetched.'

Arsenal, then under the famous Herbert Chapman, were massive favourites for the match, but this was no ordinary City side. Made up of international players from every corner of Britain and Ireland (goal-keeper Tom Farquharson was rumoured to be a member of the IRA and to carry a gun), they'd lost the final two years previously and were in no mood for a repeat. After 75 minutes the score sheet remained stub-bornly blank. Then Cardiff's Hughie Ferguson picked up the ball from a throw-in and had a routine pot at the Gunners' goal. Arsenal's keeper Dan Lewis flopped onto the ball. In the same movement, so confident was he in his complete control of the orb, he began to make as if to throw it underhand to a colleague. Somehow the ball squirmed out of his grasp, squeezing between his left elbow and his torso like a large bar of soap. Or a small greased pig. As it spun tantalisingly between his prone body and the goal line, Lewis panicked and made a lunge at the ball. He hit it with his elbow; it dawdled into the net. Cardiff won the Cup and carried it triumphantly back across the Severn Bridge – courtesy of Dan Lewis, the only Welshman in the Arsenal side.

Suspicions were aroused. Eyebrows were raised. Skulduggery was scented. But Lewis' explanation for his rick (known in the papers of the day as 'The Howler') was altogether more prosaic. He blamed the new goalkeeping jersey he'd worn for the final, saying the pristine woollen garment was greasy. As a result, Arsenal to this day don't allow their keepers to wear new jerseys in a final.

And UEFA? They took comfort that this was all a terrible aberration, back in the sepia-brown mists of time. It could never happen again, could it? In the age of the Internet, the iPod and the hybrid car, surely a club like Cardiff would never again reach a Cup final (*see* Swiss Town of Nyon Brought to a Halt by Sound of Furballs Being Hawked Up, May 2008, page 498).

## 4. 1911, Bradford City 1 Newcastle United 0 (Old Trafford – replay)

### *The beautiful FA Cup goes home...*

Along with the European Cup and the first World Cup ('Jules Rimet still gleaming') the actual FA Cup is one of the most recognisable trophies on earth. The old pot itself exudes some kind of magic. It always has.

Initially, of course, the Football Association Challenge Cup was a much smaller, less glamorous-looking thing than the current beauty.

That trophy, the 'Little Tin Idol', was won in 1895 by Aston Villa and displayed in the shop window of Birmingham shoemaker William Shillcock, from which it was promptly stolen and, it was learned half a century later, melted down for coins. The theft led to the century-old taunt around the streets of the second city, 'Villa have lost more cups than Birmingham have won.' An exact replica of the original pot was made and served until 1910, when it was presented to the FA's long-serving president Lord Kinnaird. On 19 May 2005 this was sold at Christie's for £478,000. The buyer? David Gold, chairman of Birmingham City, getting some kind of revenge for the 110 years of Villa ragging.

Back in 1911 a new FA Cup was needed, and a nationwide competition was held to design and make one. The winning entry, the wonderment with which we're now so familiar, came from the Bradford firm of Fattorini. They also designed and made the Rugby League Challenge Cup and today still manufacture Lonsdale belts. The new cup was transported down to Crystal Palace just in time for the 1911 final, where a goalless draw meant it remained unclaimed. Four days later, in the first display of its near-mythical romantic powers, the Cup was won, for the first and only time, by Bradford, and made its stately way back whence it came.

That trophy was played for from 1911 until 1991, when it was deemed too fragile to be used any more; it had been simply worn away by generations of loving polishing. It was won for the last time, appropriately enough, by Spurs, who with seven victories in the eighty years of the cup's life, had lifted it more than any other team. Some years later Danny Kelly got to hold this most famous version of the Cup on his *Under the Moon* TV show. Thinking of the hands that had clasped it before him – David Jack, Ted Drake, Stanley Matthews, Jackie Milburn, Danny Blanchflower, Jimmy Greaves, Bobby Moore, Kevin Keegan, Pat Jennings, Bryan Robson, Kenny Dalglish, probably June Whitfield and a pantheon of the game's greats – still makes him slightly sick with excitement today.

The current replica of that trophy was made by the firm of Toye, Kenning and Spencer, makers, according to their website, of 'Masonic regalia, gifts and furnishings since 1685'. While they were at it, they made two. Assuming the current one lasts, like its predecessor, eighty years, and that they then use the spare for a similar period, we're next going to need a new FA Cup in 2151.

## 3. 2001, Liverpool 2 Arsenal 1 (Millennium Stadium, Cardiff)

***Young tearaway totally ruins the old folks' day out in the sunshine.***
A brilliant Cup final because it rammed home once again two critical lessons: 1) it ain't over till the big-boned lady sings; 2) young people are very good at football. Very, very good.

Freddie Ljungberg had given Arsenal the lead with just a quarter of an hour to go. In the ferocious heat Liverpool looked beaten, out on their feet. Michael Owen changed all that. He equalised after 83 minutes and, with just seconds remaining, scored a winner that while rightly celebrated as a finish of the highest quality (up there with his wonder goal against Argentina), was actually more about the relationship between young men and middle-aged men. Its memory is enough to turn the blood of Messrs Baker & Kelly cold...

Owen picked up a long hoof out of defence by Patrick Berger in the middle of the Arsenal half. There appeared no danger. Between the 21-year-old and the goal stood three stalwarts of the English game: Tony Adams (66 England caps), Lee Dixon (22 England caps) and David Seaman (75 England caps). More telling though was the age of this rearguard. Adams was 35, Dixon 37 and Seaman 38. And this was not the hamstrung, shuffling Michael Owen of recent years, but the turbocharged *meep-meep* Roadrunner version of his early career.

A normal player would have received that long punt from Berger and held the ball up, awaiting support. But this is a superboy at the height of his coiled-spring powers. He doesn't actually think about poor old Tony, Lee and David. His brain doesn't calculate that between them they are 110. There is nothing conscious about it at all, just a feeling that comes when the sinew and muscle and will are still young, still untainted by injury and time and failure. He picks up the ball and, with Lee, Tony and Dave in his peripheral vision, just knows – deep in his DNA, right down in his fast twitch fibres – 'You know what? I can piss these...'

## 2. 1981 Tottenham 3 Manchester City 2 (Wembley – replay)

### *Starring 'The Men Who Knew Too Much'.*

People always talk about this as the greatest FA Cup final. It was certainly among the most dramatic, and contained not only the best ever goal in a final (Ricardo Villa's slaloming winner), but also the second best, Steve McKenzie's now lamentably overlooked edge-of-the-box volley after 11 minutes. But 1981 makes this list because on the night of that undulating, heart-stopping replay (Spurs led; City equalised; City went ahead; Spurs clawed their way level; then Villa's gift to the ages) one man watched the whole thing without a care in the world, certain of the result before a ball had even been kicked. That man was Danny Kelly. What follows is, in his own words, his story...

Spurs were strong favourites – for the usual reason: they had the better team – but City, full of courage and tenacity, made the first game a hard-fought affair. Tommy Hutchison put them in front after half an hour, a lead they held until nine tantalising minutes from the end. Then the same player put through his own goal for Tottenham's equaliser. Call me a puff, call me a lily-livered Lily-white, call me Daphne, but dad gum if the whole thing of that equaliser wasn't all too much for me. My head swam, my knees wobbled, I was on the verge of fainting. People, seeing my clay-grey pallor, turned me over to the St John Ambulance, and I was dragged out of the Cup final crowd (with the game still bastard well going on!), taken to a quiet cool room in the bowels of the stadium, given two aspirin and a cup of sweet tea, laid on one of those green examination couches and told to try and calm down. In the event, I drifted somewhere beyond sleep, into a kind of coma-lite.

When I finally came woozily around, the game, extra time and all, was over and the stadium had long since emptied. I muttered thanks to the St John people and tottered through the dank corridors of Wembley's underbelly, then emerged blinking onto the main concourse outside the ground. It was eerily quiet, the vast space completely empty. Except for one thing...

Right next to me, when I finally looked up, loomed a very large vehicle. It was the Manchester City coach, getting ready for the long drive north. In the window directly above my head I recognised one of the City players, their fullback Bobby McDonald. Our eyes met. Then I did something strange. Keeping my gaze fixed on his, I pulled my right index finger across my throat in that universal sign of death. I wasn't threatening him (I was too weak at that stage to threaten a moth), just saying, 'You had your chance today; next time Spurs will win.' And do you know what happened? Bobby nodded at me ever so slightly and mouthed – I swear on all that's holy – 'I know.'

Then I knew too. There was no way City were going to win that replay. And even when they were leading with 20 minutes to go, amid a sea of north London anxiety I was a smiling picture of Zen serenity, knowing – really *knowing* – that Tottenham were going to triumph. It was a wonderful, almost out-of-body feeling, one that I have spent nearly three decades trying in vain to recapture.

# 1. 1970, Chelsea 2 Leeds 1 (Old Trafford – replay)

### *So dirty. So magnificently dirty. Filthy. Disgraceful. Carnage.*

This is not the place to get into an argument about the relative merits of football ancient and modern. But what can definitely be said is that you will never again witness a match like this, which is a shame. Sure, nobody wants to see Marco van Basten kicked out of the game (as the cliché goes). But to watch two teams care so much about the FA Cup (and hate each other so profoundly) that they're prepared to do actual bodily harm, is something you don't readily forget. The PC police will no doubt be knocking at our door for saying it, but this barely contained mayhem was a rare treat.

Of course there were overtones. North–south. Yorkshire grit against the primping dandies of the Kings Road. The decaying industrial heartland taking on the Swinging 6os. Little West Riding Hoods v. Little Lord Fauntleroys. But that is to do Chelsea a disservice. Sure, Leeds' reputation as cloggers was well earned, but the Blues were also heavily armed, not least with 'Chopper' Harris and his apprentices David Webb, Eddie McCreadie and Tommy Baldwin. That's just the way football was. Kick or be kicked.

The first game, a 2–2 draw at Wembley, was bad enough, with only the respective left wingers, Leeds' Eddie Gray and Chelsea's Peter Houseman, floating above a re-enactment of Agincourt on a pitch turned into a quagmire by hosting the Horse of the Year show a few weeks earlier. It was a bloodbath in a mudbath.

But the replay was the real thing. An 18-day gap between the games may have allowed bruises to fade but did nothing to diffuse simmering resentments. The two teams, in scientific terms, attempted to kick the living shinola out of each other, locked together in an unarmed combat in which the ball was rarely the focus of attention. A few years ago respected ex-ref David Ellery – who actually reffed the 1994 final – watched the game for a TV documentary. Applying modern standards, he declared that the 1970 event (it's hard to call it a game) should have seen 20 yellow cards. And six red!

Ron Harris immobilised Eddie Gray. Jack Charlton headbutted Peter Osgood, after first kneeing him. Chelsea's keeper Peter Bonetti was injured after being bullocked into the net by Mick Jones. Then Jones scored. Norman Hunter and Ian Hutchinson swapped punches. Peter Osgood equalised for Chelsea while his marker was busy elsewhere attempting to exact retribution on Ian Hutchison for a dead leg administered a few minutes earlier. David Webb scored the winner. Nobody much cared. In the midst of all this, referee Eric Jennings, officiating in his last match and perhaps fearing for his very life, blundered blithely along, in the end booking just one player. He, erm, let the game flow.

And what a game. Every football fan owes themselves the treat of going down to Blockbuster and viewing this, the greatest ever FA Cup Final, at least once. You'll find it in the kung fu section.

# What is the best squad number to wear?

1. 9
2. 10
3. 7
4. 5
5. 11
6. 4
7. 6
8. 8
9. 2
10. 1
11. 3

This list is final and not negotiable.

# What are the top twelve things that could happen to an opposing team player in any match that a crowd enjoys most?

12. Go round goalkeeper, still miss.

11. Overrun pitch, clatter into advertising hoardings.

10. Get second yellow for kicking ball away or taking off shirt.

9. Air shot with replay on giant screen pinpointing exact moment ball bobbles over fast-arriving boot.

8. Celebrate goal in front of travelling fans while rest of ground knows it won't stand.

7. Any penalty that misses goal completely.

6. Any hopelessly mistimed overhead kick.

5. While still on ground, the helpless and childish look on forward's face as card is produced for 'simulation'

4. Player lets his first touch bobble out for a throw during game after particularly embarrassing newspaper story appears.

3. Player who left for big money being substituted after barely an hour (added derision for kick at inanimate object on way to dugout or last-resort badge kissing in trudge to tunnel).

2. Ball volleyed full into face or balls, resulting in crumpling and obviously genuine agony.

1. Boot that flies off after particularly wild air shot (see 9) plus ridiculous and unnecessary hop affected when going to retrieve same.

# Should footballers be allowed to bring flick knives onto the pitch?

## The junk heap of stuff players have taken onto the field of play

FIFA, normally so fuzzy about things, are actually very straightforward about this. Following the row about the Cameroons' all-in-one kit for the 2004 African Cup of Nations, the game's governing body (in the form, deliciously, of FIFA deputy general secretary Jerome Champagne!!) pointed the Indomitable Lions in the precise direction of the laws of the game: law 4 baldly states, 'The basic equipment of a player is a jersey or shirt, shorts, stockings,* shinguards, footwear.'

So that's it then: shirt, shorts, stockings, shinguards, footwear. Everything else is technically outside the rules. In these days of endless edicts and high-profile crackdowns, you'd think the football authorities would insist that players stick to law 4, wouldn't you? Oh no. Players have

---

* It is kind of weird, is it not, that the laws of the game should refer to 'stockings', rather than the universally accepted 'socks'. Weird, that is, until you remember that Sepp Blatter – head of FIFA and font of a stream of almost unmitigated tosh about the game – was in his student days no less than president of something called the World Society of Friends of Suspenders. The group, from sixteen countries, was formed to express regret at women replacing suspender belts and stockings with pantyhose. So, 'stockings' it is then.

always strolled onto the hallowed turf adorned, augmented and armed with a vast variety of garments, impedimenta and talismans. The most recent addition to the vast array of unlawful junk is a baby's dummy: after scoring for Manchester United against Birmingham at Old Trafford, Carlos Tevez whipped out a soother and stuck it in his gob. Now, if a player can smuggle a pacifier onto the pitch, then why not a Stanley knife? Or a machete? Or a gun?

What follows is a list of the bizarre cornucopia of stuff that players like Tevez have dragged onto the playing surface. It is compiled in the interests of health 'n' safety. One day it's a dummy, the next a Smith & Wesson .44...

**Headbands.** Not such a big thing now, but famously sported in the late 80s/early 90s by the likes of big Steve Foster and Wimbledon's FA Cup hero Eric Young. Headbands are OK but occasionally likely to be confused with one of football's most satisfying sights, the player who had blood gushing from a knock on the noggin and returns to the playing surface encased in enough bandage to suggest they're trying out for a remake of *The Mummy*.

**Alice bands.** So named because they're the chosen hair-control device of her that went through the looking glass. The sporting of this most unmanly of onfield adornments reached extraordinary heights in the 2008 Carling Cup final, when all three goalscorers – Didier Drogba, Dimitar Berbatov and Jonathan Woodgate – were wearing them.

**Scrunchies.** Those little elasticated rings – like brightly coloured calamari – that allow people to scrape their hair into an 'Am I bovvered?' ponytail or a sumo-style topknot, as sometimes favoured by Middlesbrough's well-fed frontman Mido.

**Goggles.** Edgar Davids, a glaucoma sufferer, used to plough about the pitch in what appeared to be a pair of orange welder's goggles. Nobody ever satisfactorily explained the medical benefit.

**Glasses.** In the 1970 World Club Championship match between European Cup holders Feyenoord and South American champs, the murderously violent Argentinians Estudiantes de la Plata, Joop van Daele wore his specs. When Feyenoord scored their winner, van Daele's marker, one Oscar Malbernat, ripped the Dutchman's glasses off his face and trampled them into the mud. The shattered specs now have pride of place in the Feyenoord museum.

**Hat-pins.** The self-same Estudiantes team would sneak hat-pins onto the pitch. At corners they would jab opponents in the thigh and, frankly, arse, before discarding the offending weapons.

**Razor blades.** In a World Cup qualifier between Brazil and Chile in 1989 Chilean goalie Roberto Rojas decided he'd had enough of getting a good stuffing. To get the game replayed, he hurled himself to the ground, stabbed himself in the face with a blade he'd hidden in his glove and claimed he'd been struck by a missile. Cue widespread mayhem and the inevitable abandoning of the match. Video evidence soon revealed Rojas' self-harming. Chile were banned from the next World Cup, and Rojas was slung out of the game for life.

**Wristbands (towelling).** A pioneer, in the fevered imaginations of B & K, of much that is loathsome in the game, Ashley Cole seems to have been the earliest adopter of the tennis-style sweat mops.

**Wristbands (charity).** Lance Armstrong. Anti-racism. Breast cancer.

Anti-bullying. Once ubiquitous, these rubbery rings now seem to have slipped out of fashion.

**Tights.** Clearly a good idea in very cold conditions but now disdained following the hideous gip aimed at poor old Keith Weller when he first took to the sward encased in Pretty Polly 15-denier.

**Roll-neck sweaters.** Once the preserve of old-school goalkeepers like Fatty Foulkes; now largely the preserve of players who've played in Italy, one of the warmest countries in Europe. Yes, I'm talking to you, Francesco Totti.

**Gloves.** Only ridiculous when worn, Chimbonda-style, in mid-August or as part of the short-sleeves-woolly-gloves nonsense combination.

**Diamond earrings.** £2,000 worth of bling covered with 2p worth of Elastoplast.

**Wigs.** Having no hair whatsoever is now the look *du jour* for most footballers; it was not ever thus. How else do you explain the antics of Bulgarian keeper Borislav Mihailov? Early in the 1994 World Cup he was evidently as bald as an 8-ball; next thing he looks like a member of Nirvana. It was an Irish, sir, a syrup! Turned out old Bobby, genuinely hairless, was advertising the wares of a hairpiece company he'd bought. In the quarter-final against Mexico, though, it all went a bit sideways. High temperatures and excessive perspiration meant that the rug came adrift, and the poor man had to take time out – under a towel! – to adjust his tresses.

Mihailov – now top dog in the Bulgarian FA and father of Liverpool reserve keeper Nikolay – is a legend in another way too. In 1995 he joined newly promoted Reading for a club record fee, replacing football's only genuine rocket scientist, Shaka Hislop, in the process. Borislav was a little bit peeved when he turned up at Reading's ground. He'd signed for them because he'd watched the Championship play-offs on TV and assumed that Reading played in front of 80,000 at Wembley every week!

**Hair dye.** We're not talking streaks, highlights and Just For Men here; we're talking dollops of bootblack and barrels of peroxide. Obviously Peter Reid – one minute as silver as a Galway salmon, the next as black as a chaplain's trilby – leads the way, but he's not alone. In his autobiography Tony Cascarino admits he darkened his temples in order to squeeze one last contract out of the fag end of his career. And it was Tony's sometime Republic of Ireland strike partner David Kelly who, for a lower division play-off match, dyed his hair a luminous blonde. When asked why he'd done it, he replied that he hoped that the defenders who'd marked him earlier in the season wouldn't recognise him and remember all his best moves!

**Babies and toddlers.** Our lawyers wish it to be known that Baker & Kelly genuinely do not believe that Dennis Wise is to blame for all the ills that have befallen football, but this one is definitely down to him. When Chelsea won the 2000 FA Cup, skipper Wisey went to collect the trophy. On his way up the famous 39 steps (now since demolished to make way for something much less pleasing) a middle-aged woman passed a very small child to him. Wise Jnr was dressed in a mini Chelsea kit; on the back of the little blue shirt was the legend DADDY. When Wise finally lifted the Cup, he did so with one hand, as he had the child in the other. He had no spare hand with which to receive his winner's medal. The bigwig who was distributing the gongs was, however, very much on the ball. Quick as Theo Walcott, he whipped the lid off the Cup and placed Wise's prize inside the trophy.

Since then no trophy presentation is complete without the players parading around with their offspring. Which makes you wonder: do the losers also have their kids on standby, and how do they explain to the three- and four-year-olds why they didn't come and take them onto the pitch, like all those children whose dads played for the winners?

**Masks (Phantom of the Opera).** For the protection of facial injuries. Paul Gascoigne, Gary Mabbutt, etc.

**Masks (Lone Ranger).** Fulham striker Facundo Sava kept one in his socks, and on the rare occasions he caused the net to ripple used to whip it out and bemuse all and sundry by, erm, wearing it.

**Masks (Hannibal Lecter).** Full, devil-dog-style leather mask as worn by Schalke's Ebbe Sand.

**Masks (Freddie Krueger).** As donned, as he ran out on to the pitch, by Peterborough goalkeeper Fred Barber.

**Brollies.** At the start of the last century, in a famously sleety match between Aston Villa and Sheffield United, several players suffered mild frostbite. Many of the others borrowed greatcoats from the crowd and one, Villa winger Charlie Athersmith, played the second half beneath a black umbrella.

**Seaside-style knotted hankies.** At the other end of the climatic scale, the opening day of the 1906/7 season was absolutely Saharan. In the game between Manchester City and Woolwich Arsenal players were having to be treated for sunstroke. Not so City's Jimmy Conlin, who amazed the assembled throng by protecting his head with a Professor Gumby knotted handkerchief.

**Religious trinkets.** Devout Catholic Damien Duff keeps a Padre Pio medal in his sock.

**Gaffer tape.** A loop of which is worn, for reasons as yet unexplained, over the left knee of Juan Sebastián Verón.

**Electronic tags.** The most modern of all footballers' optional extras. Most recently seen on the ankle of Jermaine Pennant, it was originally modelled in 2000 by Ipswich Town fullback Gary Croft, out of clink following a stretch for perverting the course of justice.

**Bobble hats.** Most famously worn atop the head of Faroe Islands' keeper Jen Martin Knudsen. In fact fourteen-year-old Knudsen had suffered a Petr Cech-style concussion and had been told to wear a helmet. The hat was a compromise; the bobble an optional adornment. Knudsen also kept goal for the islands' handball team and at the height of his powers, when the Faroes famously beat Austria in 1990, was still driving a fork-lift at his local fish factory (of course fish factory!!).

**Skullcaps.** Petr Cech diving. Stephen Hunt running. Hideous collision. Crack! The rest you know.

And so on and so on. We haven't even gone into the murky world of pre-written sloganising vests worn beneath the shirt. The conclusion, however (for those of you attracted to this terribly entertaining list by the sensationalist question posed at its start), is... erm, no, players shouldn't, on balance, be allowed to take flick knives onto the pitch. Sorry.

# Should Jimmy Hill be knighted?

Jimmy Hill is one of the great watersheds of English football, part loved as an affable overhang from a bygone age (and that's just his chin – boom boom!), part despised as a you-didn't-oughta-do-it-like-that duffer of the most tedious type. The truth is of course that he's one of football's great thinkers and innovators. As a players' union rep he opposed the minimum wage, which effectively kept footballers in penury and forced the poor wretches to make their way to matches on omnibuses shared with the evil-smelling hordes who watched the game. Initially the abolition of the minimum wage was thought to be a good thing. Footballers, for the first time, were able to afford Austin Maxis, Matteus Rosé wine and dolly birds. More recently, since Ashley Cole declared that the thought of trying to make ends meet (why do people want to do that?) on a measly 55 grand a week nearly made him crash his car, there's been a bit of a rethink.

As manager of Coventry City he was proper busy. At one stage he threatened to change the club's name to Coventry Talbot, just to cosy up to the club's sponsors (makers, for the teenagers among you, of motor cars that fell apart); he also oversaw the introduction of the first proper football programme and the country's first all-seater stadium. In 1963, like Dennis Waterman in *Little Britain*, he 'wrote the theme tune', penning Coventry's battle cry, which bops along to the tune of the 'Eton Boating Song'. Back then it went like this...

*Let's all sing together*
*Play up, Sky Blues.*
*While we sing together*
*We will never lose.*
*Proud Posh or Cobblers*
*Oysters or anyone,*
*They shan't defeat us*
*We'll fight till the game is won!*
*City! City! City!*

Posh? Peterborough. Cobblers? Northampton Town. Oysters? Your guess is as good as mine. More recently the ditty has been updated to include nose-thumbing at the likes of Spurs, Chelsea and Sir Fergie's gang. Hence...

*Let's all sing together*
*Play up, Sky Blues.*
*While we sing together*
*We will never lose.*
*Tottenham or Chelsea*
*United or anyone,*
*They shan't defeat us*
*We'll fight till the game is won!*
*City! City! City!'*

Hill also went on to invent modern football telly and dozens of other innovations too boring to recount here. But the thing for which he will be longest remembered – long after Ashley Cole's solid-gold house has crumbled to dust – is the idea of three points for a win. Prior to its introduction in 1981 (it took another 13 years for the World Cup to catch up;

America only got on board in 2001), when it was two points for a win, football could often be a dull affair with away teams especially setting their stalls out for a draw. Actually, it is possible to look back on those days with a great deal of affection, since negative tactics were often accompanied by brutal kicking and a collective mentality borrowed from packs of scavenging hyenas. In truth though, three points for a win has been a miraculous success, encouraging more open, attacking, free-flowing football. It has clearly been one of the contributory factors in the game's current global pre-eminence. So, all hail Jim, then, and send him scurrying to the Palace (Buckingham, not Crystal) to bend the knee before the sovereign!

Almost. Like even the most brilliant of innovations, three points for a win does have a downside, one that perhaps means the chinny one's big day out being replaced with a swift size 9 to the pants. Here's the thing: more points for a win means that leagues are more spread out than they used to be: as the season progresses the points gaps between teams become bigger, cavernous even. Now this is not necessarily a great thing. Football fans like their teams relatively evenly matched. Football fans like the contest to be close. That's where the drama lies, in things being on a knife-edge. And it's the reason why I love one of the more amazing league tables in soccer history. It's from the lower reaches of Romanian football in 1983/4 and it reflects the most gut-wrenchingly close league of all time. Ignore the leaders Meresul Deva (of course Meresul Deva!), and check out the rest of 'em. Remember this was in the days of two points for a win. Deep breath...

| Divizia C, Seria A VIII-A, 1983/4 | Pl | Pts |
|---|---|---|
| 1. Meresul Deva | 30 | 38 |
| 2. UTM Timisoara | 30 | 31 |
| 3. Mecanica Orastie | 30 | 31 |
| 4. Minerul Paroseni | 30 | 31 |
| 5. Minerul Moldova-Noua | 30 | 30 |
| 6. Minerul Stiinta Vulcan | 30 | 30 |
| 7. Metalul Bosca | 30 | 29 |
| 8. Dacia Orastie | 30 | 29 |
| 9. Minerul Certej | 30 | 29 |
| 10. Metalul Otelu-Rosu | 30 | 29 |
| 11. Minerul Anina | 30 | 29 |
| 12. Victoria Calan | 30 | 29 |
| 13. Constructorul Timisoara | 30 | 29 |
| 14. Minerul Oravita | 30 | 29 |
| 15. Minerul Ghelar | 30 | 29 |
| 16. Minerul Aninoasa | 30 | 28 |

Check it out, James William Thomas Hill OBE! Nine teams with exactly the same points! Just two points between the runners-up and the second bottom! Just three points between the runners-up and the wooden spoon! And most of the teams have pretty much the same name! Is it not a thing of utter, utter beauty? Not really possible now, with the punitive differential between winning and drawing. And the reason why, in the end, for all his good works, Jimmy Hill must never feel the flat of the sovereign's blade on his bony old shoulder.

# The Godfather recast with football stars

Which football greats would get the star parts if they were recasting *The Godfather* today?

| *Godfather* character (played by) | New footballing actor |
| --- | --- |
| Don Vito Corleone (Marlon Brando) | Luis Phillipe Scolari |
| Michael Corleone, the Don's youngest son (Al Pacino) | Paolo Di Canio |
| Sonny Corleone, the Don's hot-headed bull of a son (James Caan) | Wayne Rooney |
| Fredo Corelone, the Don's lettuce-wet middle son (John Cazale) | Dimitar Berbatov |
| Jack Woltz, film director who ends up with the horse's head in his bed (Jack Marley) | Giovanni Trappatoni |

| | |
|---|---|
| Luca Brasi, Corleone family enforcer (Lenny Montana) | Neil 'Razor' Ruddock |
| Clemenza, ball-shaped Corelone hit man (Richard S. Castellano) | Diego Maradona |
| Sal Tessio, brooding Coreone family lieutenant (Abe Vigoda) | Ricky Sbragia |
| Moe Green, flashy Las Vegas casino boss (Alex Rocco) | Rodney Marsh |
| The young Don Vito Corleone (Robert De Niro) | Paolo Maldini |
| Hyman Roth, goblin-like organised crime guru (Lee Strasbourg) | Paul Scholes |
| Connie Corleone, the Don's wayward daughter (Talia Shire) | Victoria Beckham |
| Carlo, Connie's pretty-boy traitor of a husband (Gianni Russo) | Cesc Fabregas |
| Tom Hagan, the Corleones' trusty *consigliere* (Robert Duvall) | Andy Gray |
| Kay Adams, Michael's long-suffering wife (Diane Keaton) | Fernando Torres |

Don Barzini, head of the Barzini family
(Richard Conte)                          Terry Venables

Virgil 'the Turk' Salozzo, vicious drug
lord (Al Lettieri)                       Juande Ramos

Captain McCluskey, bent cop killed by
Michael (Sterling Hayden)                Ian Dowie

Khartoum, the horse that gets its head
cut off (Khartoum)                       Gareth Southgate

# Are there any mentions of football teams in the film Butch Cassidy and the Sundance Kid?

Unless you count Bolivia, the answer is no.

# Every mother's son

With Mother's Day fast approaching – and whenever you're reading this book, it really is – I have been brooding about footballers' mums.

Have you ever met a footballer's mother? Imagine. Every player – even the snidiest, nigglingest, most divingest greedy Chelsea import – must have had at some point a dear sweet grey-haired old mater wrapped in a threadbare paisley shawl that she would happily sell if it would help put new boots on her little boy's feet or simply a smile on his face. He never calls these days. But that's OK. These noble women are content to remain in shadow, and while their fancy-Dan sons roister and frolic they will eternally weep and wait. Will you excuse me a moment; I have to make a phone call...

I was at school with several boys who went on to be pro players, and I can see their shivering mothers now, waiting to ferry them home as the school bell went at 3.30 or handing across their lunchtime sand-wiches lovingly encased in greaseproof paper each day – though the wrapping from the loaf itself would often make do. Not for nothing was it called Mother's Pride. On match days they would stand at the side of a windswept pitch up on the heath yelling, 'Come on, Gerry! Have a kick!' and nobody had the heart to tell them 'Gerry' had been substituted twenty minutes ago and was actually now the makeshift linesman.

And how about your own mothers? Yes, *you*, who failed, so completely utterly and miserably, to realise Mum's slender dream of having a famous footballing son? What part did she play in your form-ative football-flunking years? Did she steadfastly iron the kit each games day even though you had no chance of getting in the team? Did she buy all the wrong club colours and mangle the basic terms? 'Shoot a score, Bobby!' 'Offtime, ref, offtime!' And worst of all, 'Nil all.' Anybody, other than a mother, who says 'nil all' needs a thorough thrashing. Actually, what about people who say 'flashed' instead of 'thrashed' – ever meet one of those? 'We flashed them 4–0.' Unbelievable.

Was Mum, on the other hand, a feisty old cow who led the singing at home games and was regularly banned from the ground for acts of random violence?

For my own part, I never knew my mother had the slightest interest in football until one day in 1978 when West Ham happened to be on *Match of the Day*. 'Ooh, West Ham,' she said without looking up from her copy of *Titbits*. 'That's my old team.' Aghast I bade her repeat the dreadful phrase. 'No, y' know before y' father. I used to go out with a bloke who used to take me to West Ham. I still like them.' Well I ask you. Should any young man have to cope with such an emotional double blow: 1. your mum went out with someone before dad; 2. she secretly supports West Ham.

Naturally I did the right thing and told her she was now nothing to me, and we haven't spoken since that March day almost 31 years ago. Actually that's not strictly true. When Millwall recently thrashed West Ham 5–1 at the Den I called her up and said coldly, '5–1, Mother. 5–1. There. There's your fancy man for you,' and hung up.

Ernie Haines' mum was a real terror and a champion. Ernie was just about the best schoolboy player in Southwark Park, Bermondsey during the 1970s – a small wiry dribbling wizard with a truly powerful shot who once, and here you can emit a low whistle if you choose, hit a five-a-side goal bar so hard that the entire frame was sent careering head over heels down an embankment and into a duck pond. It was later said that when the goal was eventually retrieved from the pond, the net was full of fish, but I never saw any of that.

Now the Haines were not rich by any stretch of the imagination; in fact nobody ever saw Ernie in anything but the world's most washed-out and mismatched kit. The shirt was a ragged 1960s rugby top of red and black quarters made of a solid material that had no give in it whatsoever – like a particularly coarse denim or what I imagine the sails of a tea clipper might have been fashioned from. If you marked Ernie too closely you suffered abrasions. His shorts were entirely shapeless, possibly once white but now a grey shade of pink after being bunged into too many washes with other things. His socks were woollen and of an embattled black that had long begun the retreat into a paler old age. These exhausted old servants required regular super-human heaves to stretch them just long enough to reach his knee. He played in white plimsolls. Incredibly white. We later found out that he used to paint them between matches with Dulux emulsion from a tin he kept in his shed. But, boy, could Ernie Haines play football. Everyone knows at least one childhood teammate who should have gone on to be a pro, and Ernie was that kid for all of us who gathered to play every night in Southwark Park.. He was brilliant.

Why didn't he go on to conquer the world?

Step forward Mrs Haines. Mother Haines did not take kindly to anyone challenging her boy once he was on the ball. Even fair and legitimate tackles would see her hopping up and down the touchline screaming about 'brutes'. Brutes was far and away her favourite noun. Though a timid and placid soul in every other sphere of life – she looked exactly like Olive Oyl – once one of her Ern's games got under way she turned into a Tasmanian Devil. She would gurn, rotate and gesticulate constantly, issuing tortured shrieks of 'Oh!' if the ball so much as came into the same half as her son. She also had a notorious reputation for accosting other spectators, grabbing them by the shoulders, and shouting, 'Do something!' This could happen if Ernie as much as was beaten to a cross. But it was her pitch invasions that ultimately made Ernie Haines hang up his painted plimsolls.

I think high on the list of any sports fan's favourite memories is that moment back in the 1990s when, during a heavyweight boxing match, one of the bruisers' mothers suddenly enters the ring and starts hitting his opponent with her shoe. This is something we all feel might have happened to any one of us – indeed might still happen to any one of us during a particularly heated business meeting perhaps or an argument with our partners. But it happened to Ernie Haines all the time. Barely a match went by that wasn't broken up by Betty Haines' umbrella. Even on the sunniest of days and with no rain forecast she would have it at the ready.

# Why is Kevin 'Keggy Keegle' Keegan known as Kevin 'Keggy Keegle' Keegan?

Hardly a day goes by without the younger folk asking me this one. Usually I just smile inscrutably and tap the side of my nose but, given that we seem to be settling very few football arguments in this great work, let us at least lay this one bare.

For a long time it looked as though the late, and tremendously great, football commentator Brian Moore would be best remembered as the man who *wasn't* Kenneth 'They think it's all over' Wolstenholme. For it was Brian Moore who did the *other*, rarely heard, commentary on the 1966 World Cup final, working in the shadows for BBC radio. His summation of Geoff Hurst's clinching fourth goal wasn't memorable at all. It ran something like '. . . and England can break here with Hurst, who is charging toward the opposing end. [Long pause with crowd noise swelling to a goal.] And he has scored a fourth. Yes, perfectly good goal...' Happily from such mannered diction Brian went on to join ITV and pretty much invent the fevered, shouty, totally involved man-at-the-mike we expect commentators to be today. Along with Barry Davies and Martin Tyler, Brian Moore heads up the Magnificent Trinity of Greatest Ever TV Soccer Hosts. (I'm sorry, John Motson, but, seriously, face facts.)

However, it was in his later years when he took to a more measured style that Brian delivered some of his most memorable creations. I thought I had found his ultimate epitaph when, during a mid-season First Division clash, as the sides shaped up for a corner, Brian spotted two of the tallest players in the game at that time and duly noted, 'And there they are, international teammates side by side in opposition. Niall Quinn and Tony Cascarino.' There then followed a short thoughtful pause before Brian delivered one of the most wonderful observations in the history of sporting journalism. In a throaty almost rogueish growl he continued, 'Yes, look at them... two peas from the same lofty pod.'

Two peas from the same lofty pod. Lofty pod! What a sentence. In lesser hands we might have had a similar allusion about peas and pods... but with the added 'lofty'? No chance. That was Brian Moore that was.

Ironically though, it was to be in a rare spasm of mangled speech that Brian delivered his legacy. When Kevin Keegan was manager of Newcastle – there's a fair chance he is again whenever you are reading this and, if not, just wait twenty minutes – his team were trailing 1–0 in, I think, a European tie, and as the clock ticked down the camera went in close on Kevin's face. Keegan's eyes betrayed the churning tactical possibilities he now juggled like sticks of lit dynamite.

Cue Brian: 'Yes...what to do. Look at the concentration on the face of Newcastle boss Kevin Keegle, er, Keggy Keegan, er...Keggy Keegle.'

Boom. And he just left it at that.

And that is why all those who truly know football at its raw beating heart will never refer to that explosive little Geordie as anything else.

# How do goalkeepers end up as goalkeepers?

Well the glib answer here is: because they can't play football. However, that also happens to be the right answer, so there you go. However, a more difficult conundrum is: 'Why can't goalkeepers kick a moving ball?'

They can't, and why they can't is one of the great wonders of existence to me. Anyone, *anyone*, can hoof a ball up into the air and across great distances. Children, great big fat blokes, even horses. And yet these professional sportsmen, who live cheek by jowl with some of the greatest players in the world, train with them day in, day out, simply can't do it.

Every time the ball is sent rolling back towards your goalkeeper there is absolutely no guarantee that this grown man will be able to kick it properly. Static balls, yes. They can punt those across three counties. But a rolling one, even a gently rolling one?

Cue torrents of doubt and wild thunderstorms in gangly custodian's brain.

Were it just to happen every now and then, perhaps we might just be indulging in a little topical teasing of football's perennial 'Ringos', but lately I've been keeping a special watch for these phenomena and there is something like a 90 per cent chance of an ugly outcome any time the two protagonists — ball and goalie — are forced to share centre stage. And once a keeper has done it once in a match, he will repeat it ad nauseam.

Now, if an outfield player ballooned a simple pass so grotesquely more than once during a match we would all be nudging our neighbours and saying, 'Old Jenkins is having a right stinker today.' And yet, bizarrely, we almost expect it of goalkeepers. As soon as the ball begins heading towards them, a certain sense of reckless expectation sets in and the crowd sit forward in their seats to see if this experienced professional footballer can actually hit the thing without an element of farce.

Walking my dog on the local heath several years back, I saw an amateur goalkeeper skew a barely moving ball so badly that, two seconds later, it bounced off the roof of a speeding double-decker bus. There is a resounding and unique metallic *groing* sound that accompanies footballs bouncing off the roofs of motor vehicles, almost as if someone far off were playing a drunken kettledrum. This one was so pronounced it caused the birds to fly from the trees for hundreds of miles around. Nobody who saw (and heard) it will ever forget it. The sheer maths involved must be staggering. Imagine the formula required for projecting a ball on to the roof of a double-decker bus when the (overweight) catalyst is at ground level and the double-decker is 90 yards away, behind him, and travelling away from the scene at 30 mph.

However complex, most goalies seem to be able to solve such an equation regularly without breaking sweat. It's not even that unusual to see them miss the ball completely. Think about that. So, as the old adage runs, 'Who'd be a goalkeeper?' Well, chums, I often was. As a youngster, whenever I played impromptu games with the rest of the kids on our part of the estate, I *loved* to go in goal.

Although here the word 'goal' might be stretching it. On the Silwood Estate circa 1970 the agreed goalposts in the square by our flats were marked by the entrance to the stairs and Mrs Gregory's garden wall at one end and some bicycle sheds and a parked car at the other. If no car was parked, we'd use something as flimsy as a pile of leaves or a crisp packet. I promise you that is true. I have played in games where one of the goalposts was a small pile of leaves. Shirts down? Luxury. In the park jumpers might come off or a shirt might get peeled, but on the actual estate, for reasons I suddenly find socially significant, it just wasn't done to strip down in any way. So it was leaves or a kerbside abandoned shoe, or otherwise, 'Someone knock at Sharon Rush's house and ask her dad to pull his Zephyr Zodiac up about five feet.'

Invariably, dads didn't like having their Zodiacs and Hillman Imps used as goalposts, and so, as keeper, I would often make more of an effort to intercept those drives going just wide than I would ones on target. Many's the time an upstairs bathroom window would fly open in our square and an enraged Ronnie Rush, face half-covered in shaving foam, would lean out to bellow, 'Oi, Baker! If there's any f****** dents or marks on that motor when I come down there, I'll kick *you* over the f****** line, all right?'

Baker? Baker? What about Hodges and Millen and King and Micalef and Knight? Hadn't Ron noticed that they were the ones actually propelling the ball towards his Rover? Shouldn't he be putting the attackers off their stroke instead of paralyzing the poor sentry at the gates? No, of course not. I was goalkeeper, see? Just one rung up from being in the crowd,. Yes, I'm kind of playing, but not so involved that I couldn't keep an eye on a few parked cars during all those lulls.

So I was often in goal but I must make it clear that in no way was I our gang's – oh, what would be the proper anachronistic term here? Wally. Yes, wally, that's it. I will concede that, on the whole and by and large, in those days, the wally in the group was usually the one who was shoved in goal. Probably still is.

You would hear such demeaning utterances as: 'Bennett, you've got two choices. Either you can go in goal or I'll kill ya.' Or: 'Lupton, go in and wake your sister up and tell her she's got to go in goal for us.' Or: 'It's OK. We'll have Tank on our side. He can go in goal.' Similarly there was the recognised bargain struck by someone who might already be late for their nan's funeral: 'All right, I'll have a quick game, but I'm not going in goal.'

Three and in was the usual contract. Three and in. Not very hopeful of a defensive stalemate is it? How many goals would be scored in a game where the terms of employment were to change keepers after every three goals and where you might reasonably expect each of the side to serve two or three tours of duty? With such frenzied mathematics involved, it is no wonder disputes arose.

**Tom:** Scotty, you're in goal now.

**Scotty:** No I ain't! Millsy ain't been in yet!

**Millsy:** I was in before Janks. Mulla's the one who ain't been in yet.

**Mulla:** What you talking about? I've just come out! Fennel, go in goal!

**Fennel:** Me? What about Kirky here? He never goes in goal.

**Kirky:** Keep it shut, Fennel – I'm not even on your side!

**Tom:** Oi, Lupton, go in, wake your sister up and tell her she's gotta go in goal.

It's no surprise that virtually every game that kicked off in bright sunlight heard its final whistle by the glow of the moon. And all the time with these reluctant custodians an impossible dilemma raged within embittered minds. Do you play well in goal, thus prolonging the exile, or do you make a few weak waves of the hand as the ball bobbles by and get back in midfield as quickly as possible?

Without question it is this last option that usually won out. This pathetic scuttling of your own side would result in another classic snatch of heated soccer dialogue.

**Tom:** Millsy? Wassamatta with you? You could easily have got that!

**Millsy:** Well, *you* go in goal then!

For many, these are the most chilling words in football: 'You go in goal.' The very phrase is hard-wired into our heads as a threat, an insult, a chore. Thus from childhood it is drummed into us that the goalkeeper is a sulky, wretched and treacherous loser. They can't even kick straight. Indeed it's a small mercy that they can coordinate their own hands, or else they might fall straight into the very last pit of football hell and wind up...a referee.

# What is it like to actually get paid to be at the World Cup?

An extraordinary question and yet one that accounts for so much bad feeling towards Mark Lawrenson.

I mean, what kind of 'job' is this?

You are sent on a plane to the World Cup finals, given tickets to the biggest games, passes to pre- and post-match hospitality, where you are given sumptuous free food and ice-cold beer, superb hotel rooms with merciful daylight-excluding shutters in case you are feeling a little delicate, and all the time there is someone back home saying, 'If you agree to do all of that for about a month then we'll give you this big sack of cash.'

I mean, honestly. In my book it is right up there with being Jennifer Aniston's dresser.

And yet both Danny and I have been hired to perform just such a job. Several times in fact.

Oh don't look so curdled. I mean rather us than someone like, I don't know, Garth Crooks, what? At least when Danny K and I are living high on the FIFA hog we have the good grace to constantly ring friends at home and taunt them about it.

Ex-pros now 'working' for the media at World Cups seem not to have an inkling of how sweet and deep the career gravy in which they paddle actually is. After a lifetime of travelling the world with competing teams they just regard attending more World Cups as tiresome commuting. You see them in hotel foyers and on gantries. They skulk. They scowl. They brood. They plainly have no concept of how Being Paid To Be At The World Cup might be deemed desirable by even a single living soul. 'Bloody World Cups,' you can hear them growling.

Danny and I are different. We somehow seem to immediately grasp the whole concept of Being Paid To Be At The World Cup. We prance, laugh and cavort from the moment we wake up till the time the hotel staff put us to bed. We live each moment in continual pop-eyed wonder. It is all we can do not to walk around the host nation's streets in sandwich boards plastered with the words 'The Wearer Of This Device Is Being Paid To Be At The World Cup'.

And yet some people still refuse to share our joy. There is an undoubted bitter streak in many members of modern society that wishes to sour the good fortune of others. They do not wish to hear that Being Paid To Be At The World Cup is an unbroken ray of sunshine. They demand a reckoning. Instead of giddy good fortune they prefer to hear of the hidden cost in human misery, the wear and tear that Living The Dream will inevitably bring the soul. 'I'm sure this all sounds just fine,' they sneer, 'but show us the worm i' the apple?'

So, to assuage this cynical section, may I present the following shortlist:

## Bad things about being at the World Cup with your best friend and getting paid for it.

I write not in a spirit of prissy, spoilt whining, but merely in the hope it will make our situation more palatable for all who may never go to the World Cup with their best friend and get paid for it. .

To winkle out these recollections took many hours of inner reflection and the sometimes distasteful unearthing of memories best left buried.

I draw these painful experiences from the 2006 tournament but I am sure they are typical of any global sporting event where you are given free food and drink and access to the greatest spectacle humans have ever staged.

**Sundays in Germany.** During any World Cup TV news coverage becomes saturated with non-stop images of colourful supporters draped in flags shouting wild slogans and dancing in foreign fountains. Well, let me assure you, this is a dirty lie. At least on Sundays in Germany it is. Germany doesn't do Sundays.

On the first Sunday of Germany 2006 the other Danny had to write a brief column for the newspaper that, this time around, had put to us the idea of taking cash to attend the World Cup. So I agreed to leave him alone until the first game kicked off at 3 p.m.

Wandering down to reception, I decided to make a few enquiries about local customs. 'Excuse me.' I beamed at the frankly heart-stopping duo of blonde Teutonics on duty. 'Do the shops in Frankfurt open at ten or eleven today?' The two women behind the desk looked at me in stunned disbelief, almost as if I had asked them, 'Excuse me, which of you two wants me the most?'

'It is Sunday,' Gretel said. 'And this is Germany. Nothing is happening today.' There was a silent stand-off for a moment. 'What is it you need?'

I still don't know why, but I said, 'Some shoes.' They almost choked with laughter. 'Shoes! On a Sunday! Shoes! Oh zis is good. *Ja, ja,* go and buy some shoes! Good luck with ze shoes!'

I left them doubled up and went for a walk. In 50 minutes I never saw another living soul, nor did a vehicle pass me. The only noise was the steady *clink, clink, clink* of a flagpole rope vibrating in the wind. I felt like Patrick McGoohan in *The Prisoner*.

Entering the deserted hotel again, I made for the lift. The merry *Mädchen*s were still at it. 'No shoes?' one trilled. 'What a shame! We have a shower cap if you like!' And she waved one at me. I don't know if you have ever had a beautiful girl wave a shower cap at you but it wounds the pride much more than you'd think.

Back in the room I turned on the TV. There was nothing on any channel but endless shots of football fans – somewhere – leaning into camera lenses and screaming with excitement.

I looked out of my window.

*Clink, clink, clink...*

With a sigh I sat down heavily on the edge of my bed and checked my watch. It was four and a half hours to kick-off.

**Getting a drink in Frankfurt Stadium.** The day England played Paraguay it was so hot in Germany that the trees were whistling for the dogs. What with being paid to be at the World Cup and everything, Danny and I were forced to attend the fixture, and it soon became clear that our seats were absolutely dead centre in Frankfurt Stadium's Famous Upper Unshaded Rotisserie Section. Gas Mark 9.

I know it's a cliché to say the sun 'beat down', but it was true. I swear at times I could hear the Roman galley stroke-master from *Ben Hur* hammering out the throbbing tempo on his goat skins. I snapped after about 20 minutes. 'Look, I don't care if I miss a goal,' I said, cascading perspiration like a suburban garden water feature. 'I've got to find a drink from somewhere.'

God, it took me a long time to find the right place. Wandering the dank concrete caverns behind the scenes, I eventually found a very, very long queue of men with sullen faces. 'Are you queueing for drinks?' I asked. 'Wrong end,' the last man said. 'This is for the toilets. You've got no chance with the food and drink.'

Well, he was only half-right. Amazingly, there was no line at all at the giant salty pretzel stall.

For beer and water, though, you'd have thought the cast of *Baywatch* was behind the counter, naked and giving away £50 notes. Eventually, my odyssey brought me to an ice-cream stand that had fewer than 30 people waiting. By the time I got to the front, the pickings were slim indeed.

Thus, half an hour into the opening game, if the camera had picked out our row, you'd have delighted in the unedifying sight of a pair of grown men sucking on sickly cola-flavoured Calippo ice lollies as if their very lives depended on them. As, indeed, they did.

**German TV.** Never, ever complain about football coverage on British television again. And I'm even talking about ITV here. While Germans seem to have mastered the visuals during the games themselves, everything else around them is a calamity. Most bewildering of all is the commentary. In Germany the concept of a co-commentator – an Andy Gray, if you will – is alien. Now you may say this is a good thing, and flying solo never hurt Brian Moore or Barry Davies. But that's because they were Brian Moore and Barry Davies.

German commentators tend to lean towards the spare, the minimal, the terse even. Again, this may strike you as a bonus – no unnecessary yabbering – but I promise you it is eerie. Huge stretches go by with just the audio of a strangely muted crowd accompanying the pictures. Then up pops matey-boy. 'Peter Crouch,' he will say in a creepy, flat monotone, before bowing out for another two minutes to consider his next utterance.

It is commentary on a strict need-to-know basis. Even at their most garrulous, the German Mottys tend to inflect as though they are watching the match in replay. Then there are the pundits' studios. The thinking here seems to be that those introducing and picking over the action must appear in a setting as far divorced from the event as possible. Thus, within seconds of the half-time or full-time whistle, we are whisked away to an enormous garish studio that looks for all the world as if Cilla Black will come galloping from the wings.

Here, some ruddy-faced fellows in suits sit in front of a quiet studio audience and presumably dissect what we've seen. I say presumably, because nowhere near them is a window onto the emptying stadium or a giant plasma screen pouring out highlights, or indeed anything to link them to the sport we've just seen.

The first time I saw this I swear I thought somebody in the bar had sat on the remote control and turned us over to *Question Time Mit Hans Und Franz.*

Even this alien landscape is not a constant. On another occasion Rudi Völler was plonked on a huge circular dais in the centre of a market square with a series of different anchormen. Surrounded by what appeared to be thousands of football fans sent straight from central casting, Völler must have put in a 12-hour shift. As night fell, with the crowd surging about him and the arc lights blazing, the exhausted Völler looked for all the world as if he had just been evicted from the *Big Brother* house.

**Milk at breakfast.** I remember that at some hotels during that World Cup Danny and I just couldn't get semi-skimmed milk at breakfast. Every morning we had to make a special request. On one occasion I got fed up of waiting and put cream into my tea out of sheer frustration, and of course it was simply undrinkable.

I seem to have run out of legitimate Bad Things About Being At The World Cup With Your Best Friend And Getting Paid For It. Sorry about that. But still, how was that for a glimpse at the grim underbelly of show-biz, eh? The heat, the solitude, the bad local TV coverage. Make no mistake, privilege comes at a price, my friends. So if you do happen see the pair of us sitting by a pool in South Africa, holding ice-colds and fanning ourselves with tickets to the next England match, look closely into our haunted eyes. We earning it, sister...

# What was the greatest ever World Cup in the opinion of Baker & Kelly?

## Baker & Kelly at the World Cup 1990

*Kelly splits up a band. George Graham gets held up at gunpoint.*

**DK remembers.** As Italia 90 came around, I was editor of the *NME*. As such I had constantly to sign bits of paper that sent my colleagues jetting off to all points of the globe, where they hung out with bands, got drunk and trashed, and informed local lovelies that yes, they were a member of the group. For myself, I was so devoted to the job that I remained resolutely chained to my desk on the 19th floor of Kings Reach Tower in Blackfriars, the highest building in Britain south of the River Thames. No foreign trips, no freebies, no backstage passes and no geisha girls. In retrospect, I was an enormous schmuck.

Back in those days, you see, when the pre-downloading music industry was awash with money, the whole thing was oiled by a weird kind of bribery. Nothing so obvious or sleazy as actual coinage changing hands; but if you wanted your useless band to grace the pages of Britain's premier music mag, then taking a hack to some luxurious and exotic location to see or talk to the band usually did the trick. That's why you'd always see groups from Ashton under Lyne being interviewed by a London journo halfway up Mount Kilimanjaro or while playing a private gig for the Sultan of Ubercash in his air-conditioned, gold-plated yurt in the Maldives.

But I gave off an air of utter incorruptibility. So much so that despite being in control of the most important music magazine in the world, I was never once offered money, women or drugs to favour an act. This despite the fact that any one of those – and certainly any combination of two – might, I suppose, have done the trick.

The one exception to this life of hair-shirt asceticism came as the World Cup in Italy approached. My desire to get out there and see at least one game overcame my innate contempt for the sleazy machinations of the Biz. My head spinning with desire to witness World Cup football, I embarked on a scheme of such self-interested cunning that even a modern British politician might have rejected it as overly cynical.

In this endeavour I was aided and encouraged by photographer Kevin Cummins, with whom I tended to do most of my work and who was, if anything, an even bigger fan than me. Let's tell the truth here: Kevin was nuts about football. More accurately, he was nuts about Manchester City. And hideously opposed to anything to do with Manchester United. He refused to wear, or touch, anything red. In deference to the great City goalkeeper who was on the plane, he referred to the Munich Air Disaster as the Frank Swift Tragedy. Once we went to New York to look for the then still fairly obscure rap group Public Enemy. After several days of fruitless search, Kevin started to panic. He rang the record company and said that it was their fault that they hadn't produced the band, and that he now needed to get back to Manchester in order to see City's next home game. They, he insisted in the way that only rock photographers can, must fly him from New York to Manchester, then back again to rejoin me. The label, bless them, agreed to this frankly ludicrous plan, but soon found their generosity foundering on another snag. The only suitable New York–Manchester flight was with United Airways, and Kevin refused to fly United. Flatly and absolutely. Hence it was that he made a 48-hour round trip New York–London– Manchester–Maine Road–Manchester–London–New York.

My office, three weeks before the World Cup: me and Kevin sweat-beaded with concentration; on the table a roll of wallpaper laid out, blank face up. On the wallpaper has been written a grid of fiendish complexity. The horizontal axis shows every record company in Britain. The vertical axis lists every band on those labels that has a record coming out around the time of the World Cup. Thick red pencil lines have crossed out those companies who don't have the cash to send us to the tournament. More crimson slashes disqualify those labels with whom we have either very good, or very bad, relations. Yet further scarlet scribbles winnow out labels without suitably scheduled releases, and bands with a suitable timetable but not the remotest interest in the world's most popular game.

Through this spaghetti junction of selective ink one label and one record release starts to emerge. EMI (nice people, plenty of dough) are putting out the new one from noisy electronic funkateers Tackhead (who I happen to adore) smack dab in the middle of the World Cup. Tackhead comprised three Americans (bassist Doug Wimbish, percussionist Keith LeBlanc and guitarist Skip McDonald, who eight years earlier had revolutionised music when, as the house band at Sugarhill Records, they'd played on the very first rap record to make a global impact, Grandmaster Flash's 'The Message') plus one east Londoner, their genius producer and mixer Adrian Sherwood. And Adrian – God be praised! Pass me the phone! – was football crazy. A couple of calls later, including one conscience-clearer to a delighted Sherwood, and we were on our way –

11 June, Cagliari in Sardinia, England versus the Republic of Ireland. Cue the sound of a 24-trumpet fanfare going off in my head.

We flew out to Sardinia from Heathrow, the Americans polite but clearly bewildered with the travel arrangements. They obviously felt we could manage a conversation and photo shoot in, say, Ladbroke Grove. Poor, deluded fools.

Once safely arrived, our despicable ignorance of the island's geography soon became painfully evident. Cagliari (where we landed and hired our cars) is on the southern tip of the island; Baia Sardinia, where our nine-star hotel was situated, is at the extreme north. No problem, we thought, this is a tiny island, a belief entirely based on a vague map, without scale, printed on the matchbooks we were given on the flight. OK, we'll drive to the hotel this evening. It was only after a couple of hours of pitifully slow progress up windy tracks, with the Mediterranean sun beginning to slide away, that somebody bothered to pull a proper map from the glove compartment. Rustle, unfold, peer, frown. Oh. Sardinia, so very small when viewed between the thumb and forefinger on a matchbook, is, it turns out, the size of Wales, and we are embarked on a drive of over 200 kilometres. Still, no matter, press on...

Pretty soon, with a full moon rising ever higher in the Sardinian sky, we realised that our despicable ignorance of the island's geography was matched only by our despicable ignorance of the island's topography. OK, so we know that the blinking thing is 200 k long; now we're discovering that the whole middle of the isle, so flat when viewed on a car-hire road map, is actually made up of a series of vertiginous mountain ranges, through which slither some of Europe's most half-baked roads. It is going to take the whole night to get anywhere near our resort basecamp. Oh well, press on...

A while later, in the deep heart of the Sardinian night, high in bandit-infested sierras, we realised that our despicable ignorance of the island's geography and topography was matched only by our despicable igno-rance of the island's rail network. After several hours of hairpin driving, our way was suddenly blocked by a rail track, guarded by a huge red-and-white-striped pole barrier. Cue one crisis meeting, complete with much ill-tempered stabbing of forefingers into the map spread out on the flinty ground, illuminated by the yellow headlights of two Fiat Puntos. We can't go forward; there's a barrier and a train may come. We can't retreat; it's a million kilometres back to Cagliari and there's nowhere to stay.

It was one of those moments that the ladies never understand, one of those moments when the extra 5 per cent of testosterone that courses through the male body insists that action – regardless of how stupid, inappropriate or likely to end in premature death – just has to be taken. With the bickering and finger-stabbing still in full swing, I marched over to the barrier. Starting at the end that swung free, unattached to the box containing the electric lifting gear, I stooped down and put my right shoulder under the four-inch diameter shaft. Standing shakily up, I cut the dash of one preparing to perform the pole vault, except there had been a clerical error in the equipment room, and I was attempting the feat using the foremast of the *Cutty Sark.* By taking groaning, wobbly, pigeon steps forward, I began to force the vast pole upward. When I was halfway along its length – now I looked like a misguided amateur at the Highland Games, about to finish last at caber-tossing – there was just enough room for a car to pass beneath. The musicians, finally taking the hint, gingerly edged the Fiats past my panting carcass and across the tracks. Three bumpy hours later, with the yellow fingers of dawn flam-ing up out of the sea, we arrived at our destination, bone-tired and utterly determined to take an adult education course in Mediterranean geography, topography and rail networks.

Baia Sardinia is magnificent. A crescent of porcelain sand tilts gently into a lapis lazuli sea; the sun beams its approval on the scene. With the match still 24 hours away, we spent the day floating blissfully about on pedalos, the reverie broken only by the need for refreshments. Even this didn't require a return to dry land, just an occasional desultory pedal to the palm-roofed boat-bar that bobbed about in the sea some 30 yards from the tide line.

But there was trouble in paradise. The Europeans were aboard one pedalo; the equally relaxed Americans grooved about on another. After several hours of calm, the Yanks made glacial progress into our general area. Incredibly, given an afternoon of blissful laziness, they seemed agitated. They'd been thinking. They'd been talking. They'd come to a conclusion. Staring at me, Kevin and Adrian they declared, 'You f***ers don't give a damn about the band. You're only here for the mother****ing football. We're going to the airport. We're out of here.' With that they started to pedal – their evident anger somewhat diluted by the cartoon slow motion of their exit – toward the beach. I shot their band-mate a 'What shall we do?' look. He gave me a 'Sod 'em' shrug. Three quarters of Tackhead disappeared – with as much dignity as men powering a yellow pedalo can muster – from view and a major rock group splintered; they didn't play live together for another 14 years.

Next day's drive back to Cagliari was rendered more bearable by the simple, if unBritish, expedient of asking the advice of the locals. Turns out there's a coastal motorway that avoids craggy bluffs, hairy brigands and unmarked railroads. 'Take you two hours, tops.'

In the capital city the authorities were dealing with a swarm of England supporters whose reputation for beery mayhem was then at its zenith. As you saw the ancient town turned into an armed camp, you genuinely wondered whether any football match could be worth all this. *Polizia* and *carabinieri* brooded on every street corner; helicopters fluttered overhead; armed troops, many of them looking like they were yet to do their O levels, scowled from the depths of helmets. On the way into the match we were searched three times; at the last checkpoint, beside the Stadio Sant'Elia itself, the soldiers patted down every single spectator – man, woman and child – at gunpoint.

Once inside, we watched a match whose plodding tediosity was in direct contrast to the drama of its setting. As the sun deserted the sky, the rain pummelled down, and an electrical storm saw the open bowl of the stadium licked and flicked by snaky tongues of lightning. Gary Lineker scored early; Kevin Sheedy, inadvertently aided by the hapless Steve McMahon, equalised near the end.

The real highlight, though, happened on the terracing just below me. Sat on his own, with his sculpted hair and immaculate suit, was Arsenal manager George Graham. At half-time, with the rain threatening serious bedragglement of the Graham groomage, he rose purposefully and made for one of the exits. His path was blocked by a soldier who could not have been old enough to vote. There was an exchange of views. The uniformed boy seemed to suggest that the hooligan pig-dog return to his designated seat. The suave Scot may well have been trying a variant of the old 'do-you-know-who-I-am-I-organise-the-Arsenal-offside-trap-me' gambit. Most of this was conducted in the international language of exasperated arm-waving and curt head-nodding. To this vocabulary, the private now introduced a new phrase. Without warning he swivelled his sub-machine gun, previous dangling off his shoulder, to waist height and aimed it at George's glistening belt buckle. I think he may even have given him a couple of back-up-buster pokes.

The message got through. George sullenly rejoined the saturated masses to ignore the football and enjoy the lightning. High above the Atlantic, the American remnant of what until so recently had been Tackhead were in an equally dark mood, continuing no doubt to curse the mother****ing soccer.

# Baker & Kelly at the World Cup 1994

*An amazing match. An amazing radio show. And O.J. Simpson in a lap-dancing club.*

**DK remembers.** In the summer of 1994, at the height of the wonderful madness of Matthew Bannister's reign at Radio 1, Danny B had a Satur-day- and Sunday-afternoon gig on the nation's favourite; I was his side-kick. The show itself was both pretty brilliant and, as a seriously relaxed Matthew used to point out to us in the Crown & Sceptre, enthusiasti-cally contributing to the tailspin decline in the station's listening figures. Pearls, swine, etc.

As the World Cup in America approached someone in the BBC's Bril-liant Ideas Dept decided it would be a top wheeze to send the pair of us to the States do a couple of shows from the tournament. Now, say what you like about B&K, but we are not the kind of guys to defy an edict from BBC management and so, with some reluctance, we accepted the oner-ous task of, as the Baker would describe it, 'going to the World Cup free of charge with your best friend'.

Nowadays both Dannys are roaring drunk after two amontillado sher-ries, but back then we fancied ourselves a little more robust. Hence the plan was simple: a 72–hour no-sleep chapfest that would include the bawdier bars of 42nd Street, as brill a radio show as we could manage and the juiciest-looking match of the entire World Cup, reigning cham-pions Italy versus my beloved Republic of Ireland in the most Italian city and most Irish city outside Europe. In prospect, the itinerary looked a corker; in reality it exceeded even our most schoolboyish expectations.

We arrived amid a typical New York summer heatwave, hot as hell, sultry as Ava Gardner. It was late evening as we dumped our stuff in the posh Midtown hotel into which the Beeb had been kind enough to place us. Then it was off into the night. Given that my first destination of choice – the Guggenheim Museum – was closed, we instead took a cab to the other end of the cultural waterfront, a bar called Private Eyes. I say bar, and sure enough you could definitely buy a libation there, but the main feature of this establishment was a full-sized fashion-show-style runway on which young people of the feminine persuasion seemed intent on defying the establishment's excellent air conditioning by removing a high percentage of their already inadequate clothing. Bewildered then, I now know that we were in a lap-dancing club!

Now, if these dancers relied for their livings on the undivided attention of the audience, then that night may well have been the least remunerative of their careers. Because, just as Dan and I were ordering the second stein of foaming ice-cold, something quite extraordinary started to happen. The club, like all good American bars, was liberally sprinkled with TV sets – the locals seem to like to combine their evident love of dancing with sports, news and, I'm guessing, the latest from the Dow Jones index. On the multiple screens there started to appear live helicopter shots of what at first appeared to be a reduced-energy auto pursuit on one of those *America's Thickest Crooks* shows. But instead of being a ten-second clip, this thing went on and on and on. Gradually more and more of the punters found their gaze drawn from the obvious attractions of the runway to the sunlit pictures being beamed from distant California.

Oh. My. Giddy. God. It's O.J. Simpson, legendary gridiron footballer and resolutely tree-like actor in, among much other rubbish, *Roots*, *The Towering Inferno* and the *The Cassandra Crossing*, in which he, Richard Harris, Martin Sheen, Burt Lancaster, sultry Ava Gardner, Sophia Loren and Lee Strasberg did their best to capture the award for the Worst Many-Stars-No-Script Film Ever Made. Yes, ricocheting Chinese whispers confirm, it's O.J. Simpson in a white Bronco, probably armed, most likely nuts, doing his best to escape from the Feds, who are now convinced that he's done in his missus with malice aforethought. All eyes – punters, bouncers, barmen, scantily-clads – now stare in cartoon disbelief at that most contradictory of entertainments, a low-speed car chase. Above me, I finally notice, a transfixed lady in just frilly knickers is beginning to shiver. I give her my jumper. By the time Simpson finally gives himself up, we are firm friends.

The rest of the night is spent trawling from bar to bar, laughing about O.J. and chuntering about the next day's match. As the beer and jet lag significantly reduce the horsepower of my brain, I briefly hallucinate that we are joined by then-huge Irish folk rockers the Saw Doctors. It seems unlikely, but no more so than watching a sporting god going on the slow-mo lam in a strip joint...

Next day, we're off to the game in the Giants Stadium. A nation that can bring the world both the hula hoop and atom bomb is unlikely to worry overmuch about getting 75,000 people from the centre of Manhattan to the suburbs of New Jersey. And sure enough, America once again proves its genius for organisation, seamlessly bussing the lot of us from place to place with the minimum of fuss.

The only moment of slight conflict I witnessed was outside the Port Authority bus station. Like on any other Saturday, some Nation of Islam adherents – sombrely scowling young black men in formal suits and dickie bows – were using booming hip hop and loudhailers to aggressively broadcast their message of racial segregation. They create a forbidding, slightly scary climate, and they do it deliberately. How bewildered they seemed, then, when slightly drunken fellows in green shirts and felt leprechaun hats kept weaving up to them and enquiring, in broad brogues, what exactly was making them so mad. And why they were dressed for a tea dance.

The grand old Giants Stadium is situated on the road made

legendary by Simon & Garfunkel, Bruce Springsteen, Chuck Berry and the opening sequence of *The Sopranos*, the New Jersey Turnpike. On that Saturday afternoon it was the most exciting place on earth, and certainly one of the hottest. Again the Yanks excelled themselves. All along the route to the ground, and every 20 yards inside it, smiling students proffered plastic skiffs of twinkling, icy lager. 'Buck a beer!' they hollered, like some modern-day good Samaritans, 'Buck a beer!' Have to admit, we took them up on their offer. Seemed impolite not to.

The match itself was a bona fide classic. In the 100-degree heat Paul McGrath, dodgy knees and all, gave the grittiest defensive performance I've ever witnessed (at the other end of the pitch, legendary backs Franco Baresi and Paolo Maldini must have looked on in awe), and Ray Houghton scored the winner. After just eleven minutes the Aston Villa midfielder took advantage of a weak header, scurried to the edge of the Italian box, then slightly shinned a shot. The ball made a sickly, leisurely loop over the bewildered goalkeeper Pagliuca before flopping into the net.

What followed was beyond pandemonium: 37,000 Irish fans bellowed their delight while 37,000 Italian voices screamed in anguish and anger. I've never heard such a noise. I don't think such a noise has ever been made. Go to YouTube and play the clip; hear the American commentators straining to howl over the cacophony; hear the feedback as the TV microphones struggle to cope with the sheets of noise. This mayhem went on for what seemed an eternity. When we finally began retaking our seats I noticed that the boy Baker had never risen to his feet. He smiled when I finally collapsed next to him: 'I get it. I'm the only Protestant in this whole stadium.'

In the end it proved perhaps the most famous win in Ireland's history, a zenith that the country's team may never again replicate. It was a wonderful day, full of feelings one wants to keep fresh but which, in the normal rough and tumble of passing time, might be expected to fade and flake. But I have been very lucky. These days I talk rubbish on Talksport radio, and once or twice a week I get to work with Ray Houghton. He is a good analyst and a top bloke, but it wouldn't matter if he was tongue-tied and the devil in high heels; his very presence repeatedly reactivates those gorgeous memories from the Giants Stadium all those years ago. And though in real life he's only the same height as Jeanette Krankie, because of everything that happened to him and me on that incredible day he will always be, in my eyes, a giant.

After the match we once again eschewed the hotel's serene facilities in favour of buzzing bars, where we drank (carefully) and chatted and laughed into the small hours before making our way to the BBC's tiny studio on Broadway. In order to be live in the UK, we were broadcasting – from Broadway! – at five o'clock in the morning. For the second time in twelve hours we found ourselves in the most perfect place on the planet. By now we looked like the Grateful Dead and smelled like the actual dead, but Danny was in the most brilliant form. He started the show with Gershwin's 'Rhapsody in Blue' and segued it into Dylan's 'Subterranean Homesick Blues'. Breathtaking. I was close to tears, thinking that this could hardly get much better. At which exact moment the studio door swung open; in trooped the Saw Doctors, armed with their instruments and a cheery determination to, yes, make it much better. By now I was genuinely struggling to differentiate reality from a lovely dream.

When the show ended, and we staggered blinking into the early-Sunday-morning sunshine, there was one more chunk of unplanned delight yet to unfold. Tired but delighted, our firm (the Dannys, Stewart the studio engineer and a couple of Saw Doctors) made its way to one of the most famous entertainment-business diners in New York. Its walls are covered – side to side, floor to ceiling – with framed photos of the showbiz personalities who have eaten there. Groucho Marx jostles for space with

Bob Hope, John Lennon, Judy Garland, Phil Silvers and myriad others from the very top shelf. Inevitably, given the sheer number of these portraits, there are also, shall we say, some folk of the less-celebrated variety.

I mention all this because as we chomped down the ham, eggs and hash browns, the waiters asked us what we were doing on Broadway so early in the morning. Stewart, who may have believed it, told them that we were big-time radio coves from the UK. Before you could say 'BBC licence fee', the waiters had whipped out a large camera and were demanding that Danny and I say cheese. Our likeness, they insisted, would that very day be part of the pantheon with which we found ourselves surrounded. Only one problem: there was not a single vacant space left on the wall. In this circumstance, they reckoned, the tradition was that the new inductees chose whose picture would be taken down to make room for theirs.

Did Stalin himself ever wield such power? Does Simon Cowell ever exert such influence over the strings of show business fate? As we peered up and down the rows of grinning greats, did two such undeserving small fry ever feel such a delicious sense of mischief? Eventually, giggling like giddy girls, we made our choice. I will not tell you, now or ever, what caused us to pinpoint our victim. I'm not sure I entirely remember. Or ever knew. Others might, I guess, have been tempted, for a laugh, to decommission Frank Sinatra or Ed Sullivan, but that was never going to be our chosen road. Suffice to say that, for whatever reason, the waiters were soon taking down, with due ceremony, the black-and-white likeness of... why?... our fellow Radio 1 DJ Steve Wright.

I've never returned to that eatery (where, no doubt, we ourselves have now been displaced by Vanilla Ice or the lawyer from *Scrubs*), but I've occasionally wondered if Steve Wright has ever drifted back there and searched forlornly for his cheery old mug. 'I'm sure it used to be over there, somewhere near Harry Belafonte and... who's that?... those two idiots.' Wondered but never worried. For reasons I've never quite been able to pin down, that final bit of nonsense was the most glistening of cherries on top of the most fabulous knickerbocker glory of a weekend that I've ever known. Sorry, Steve. Sorry, Steve's many fans.

## Baker & Kelly at the World Cup 1998

*Baker & Kelly search for 'somewhere better', get embroiled in international politics and fail the gay cool test.*

**DK remembers.** I know what you think. Because of Jonathan Ross, Terry Wogan and Mark Pougatch, you believe that all radio presenters are brought to work each day in a solid-gold sedan chair pulled by a dozen oiled and perfumed peacocks. Once at the radio station three recent Miss Worlds, you reckon, accompany the haughty talkers to their suede-upholstered La-Z-Boy in a studio decked with antique Arabian silk wallpaper. Finally, the director general himself offers the DJ some Earl Grey in a Ming vase, then checks to see that his darling's panda-skin cushions are properly plumped up, before leaving, walking backwards, gaze to the floor. And that, truthfully, is exactly how it is. At the BBC.

At commercial radio stations, where money has to be prised from the cold, hard earth of commerce rather than pickpocketed at knifepoint from the hapless taxpayer, things can be rather different. By the time the 1998 World Cup in France rolled around, Danny and I were doing some of the best work of our lives on the old Talksport radio, when it still had its studios on Oxford Street. We had a Saturday show split into two parts – two hours before the football matches, then two further hours after them. In the gap we'd repair to the Bathhouse boozer in Dean Street for a couple of frosty ones. Thus the two parts of the show were often very different, the first a whirlwind of wit and conversation that would have graced the Algonquin round table, the second two tipsy blokes tittering at one another and shouting at the callers. Talksport, to give them their due, loved it, let us get on with it and just sat back and waited for the awards to coming rolling in.

They liked it so much they wondered if we'd like to go to France. Course we would. Pick a tie from the group stages. Only one possible choice, we chimed. No, not a match involving England or Brazil or even the Reggae Boys of Jamaica. No, we'd like to cover the game that promised to be the nuttiest encounter in World Cup history. Somehow, during those endless and rigged draws for the group stages, somebody (probably Pelé) messed up and didn't keep the hot and cold balls apart. Thus it was that the two nations most obviously at daggers drawn, most certainly heading for a dust-up, had been drawn together. Yes, we said, we'd very much like to go to France and cover the encounter between those giants of the global game, the United States and Iran.

Thus it was that a few weeks later we found ourselves in the main square in Lyon, preparing for our first broadcast task – to describe the vast battalions of English, Scots and Norwegian supporters that had gathered in France's second-largest city, which was serving as a kind of central staging post for all the matches in the south of the country. In the ordinary way of radio, described above, we would just have left our eight-star Starck-designed megatel, got an army of flunkies and paid admirers to assemble a large mobile studio in close proximity to the people we needed to talk to, and then wheeled in the supplicants.

That's the BBC. Our hotel was fine – clean, anonymous, no complaints there – but we were severely lacking, our engineer informed us, the kind of gear with which one might ordinarily essay an outside broadcast. As if either Danny or I had the slightest idea what he was talking about, he sought to confirm this paucity of technology by holding up a mid-blue-and-white-striped Tesco carrier. At first we thought he was attempting to display his allegiance to Brighton and Hove Albion; then we wondered if he was offering us a drink; finally he spoke. All the equipment we had for the whole trip was in the Brighton bag.

Tough times call for the kind of ingenuity that once saw half the Mercator projection coloured British-empire pink. Sadly, due to a recent stocktaking error, we were all out of the kind of ingenuity that once saw half the Mercator projection coloured British-empire pink, and had to settle instead for Lame Plan Number One. So when the engineer bod dialled us into the station 'live from the main fan square in Lyon' we were actually sitting on two single beds either side of a coffee table in my room.

In order to achieve the Jasper Maskelyne-style illusion that we were in fact among a teeming torrent of humanity (or at the very least outdoors) we had hung the effects microphone out the window and down a couple of storeys so that it hung just above the quiet thorough-fare below. From there it picked up the vague hum of a city, the occasional backfire of a moped and the equally irregular conversation of passers-by. To most of Talksport's listeners it might just have passed muster as two men talking on a continental street corner. To anyone who spoke French the experience must have been nothing short of surreal, with our intense banter about the unfolding tournament punctuated by conversations from passing locals completely uninterested in the football and the football fans gathering some miles distant...

'So, Dan, a sunny day here in Lyon, perfect for these armies of fans as they anticipate all the World Cup action.'

'That's right, Dan, and what a day it promises to be for the Scots.'

(*Background, in French*) 'Have you seen the price of sprouts, Pierre? It's a disgrace.'

'Yes, I'm not going to buy them. We'll have a salad with vinaigrette instead.'

'No news on the fitness of Robbie Earle yet, Dan?'

'No Dan, the Jamaican camp are playing their cards close to their chest.'

(*Background, in French*) 'Emile, do you think this Christmas will see another shortage of Tracy Island toys?'

'Claudette, I've told you not to bother me with all that American imperialist horse manure. Now run along home and get my dinner on.'

'We're Baker and Kelly, live in Lyon. Here's the news…'

Following the success of Lame Plan Number One, we had several hours to kill before the match. With a sense of duty that hasn't always been our hallmark, we actually wandered down to the vast square, where swathes of fans of many nations were gathered, singing, chanting and drinking the nearby bars pumice-dry. In the normal course of events Dan and I are pretty keen on meeting the listeners; we might even buy them a pint. But that's a couple of blokes in a West End hostelry. If things get frisky, excuses can be made; escapes can be accomplished. What we were here confronted with were thousands of Scots, many without trousers, drinking steadily in preparation for their vital match against Morocco. In three days' time. Discretion, we decided, was the better part of valour. One of them was bound to start asking us awkward questions about Culloden or the where-abouts of the Stone of Scone. Drunk Scots always do, and in that situation no amount of smart quips about Ken Bates seems to suffice as an answer. No, we'd go back across the river in search of 'somewhere better'.

Ah, 'somewhere better'. 'Somewhere better' is the curse of the Baker–Kelly relationship, the one flaw in our otherwise finely honed, brilliantly streamlined modus operandi. Whether it's a bar, restaurant or record shop, we are never content to go into the one outside which we are currently standing. Always – around the nearest corner, down the parallel street, over the distant horizon – is, we firmly believe, 'somewhere better'. So off we trudge in search of this mirage, this pipe dream, this chimera. And the more unfamiliar the town or city, the more certain we are that the very next *Strasse* houses 'somewhere better'. I have sometimes held my head in my hands and wept bitter tears at the thought of the amount of energy we have put into fruitless treks in search of 'somewhere better'. Not to mention what used to be called shoe leather, but which is in our case trainer rubber, enough easily to keep an entire African village in Pumas and Reeboks.

So, we crossed the river in search of 'somewhere better'. It was the usual directionless trudge (think Beavis & Butthead when they decide to trek across the desert in search of New York – 'the sun sucks'), but in the middle of it I at least managed to buy my greatest ever World Cup souvenir. It was in the window of a shop, just asking to be purchased. Quite how we got round the traditional problem of deciding not to buy it there and then (because there must be 'somewhere better' nearby) I don't now recall. All I know is that I was soon inside the emporium and handing over the readies. In return – and in a country obsessed by World Cup security, World Cup violence and World Cup nutcase Brits – I received my World Cup lock knife. That's right, lock knife. Eight inches long when fully extended, sharp as a cute girlfriend's tongue and with the official WC logo stamped on the four-inch blade. In case you're still not convinced, the box features the cute World Cup mascot Footix (a blue cockerel) proclaiming that you have indeed just nabbed yourself a chunk of *produit officielle*. I love that lock knife and I still have it.

Lock knife safely in pocket, the Lyon death march continues, until even we begin to admit that there may not actually be 'somewhere better'. At which precise moment God, in his infinite mercy, takes mercy on his wandering sons. We find ourselves outside a small, dimly lit bar-cum-coffee house. There is nowhere better. We go in, thirst-slakeage at the very top of the agenda. The place is quiet, with just a few lonely figures hunched over glasses and cups; the silence is broken only by the hissing of a giant old-fashioned Gaggia coffee machine. As we approach the counter, it's from behind the gurgling Gaggia that mine host, with an athletic skip to his left, suddenly appears. He is small and lithe, beautifully coiffured and dressed from head to foot in clinging black polo neck and slacks. Around his neck hangs a massive gold pendant. He is, whether he knows it or not, the exact spitting image of Carmen Ghia, the uber-queeny assistant of director Roger De Bris in the original film of *The Producers. Deux bières, s'il vous plaît.*

Back at our table, the penny finally drops. The reason why this bar isn't filled with bellowing Highlanders – the reason why all those heads in the dark recesses of the Stygian gloom are now turning surreptitiously toward the fine figures of men that are myself and the Baker – is that it is Lyon's most clandestine homosexual pick-up joint. This should have been no problem. We are men of the world. We are from swinging London, where everything goes except the Northern Line. We don't have a homophobic bone. Baker's mad about Danny la Rue. And yet. Maybe it's because we're in a foreign land and don't understand the codes. Maybe it's because we feel like we've invaded a private (oh dear) members' club. Maybe we're just not ready to don Nazi regalia and sing 'Springtime For Hitler'. In any event, we are soon wordlessly agreeing to put into operation Lame Plan Number Two. Our beers are skulled with indecent haste, an overly generous amount of cash is left on the table and we bolt for the sunlight and sexual certainty of the outside world.

In a few short hours we have broadcast a blatant lie back to our native land, taken possession of an illegal weapon and flunked the gay cool test. Lesser men might have been discouraged. To the stadium!

The Stade Gerland has seen many remarkable things in its nearly 100 years, including the local side winning seven successive French championships between 2002 and 2009. But nothing could have prepared it for the events of the evening and night of 21 June 1998. The rhetorical war between the USA and Iran was in full swing and France was the epicentre of the Iranian resistance movement. And, everybody knew, this football match was the place where all these poisons would somehow or other hatch out. The night promised to be terribly serious but, as is always the case when people with very strong beliefs gather to shout at each other, very funny too.

We were not disappointed. On arrival at the ground it soon became obvious that Danny and I were the only neutrals. A small knot of American fans huddled behind one of the goals. Every other person in the place was Iranian, either there to protest against the revolution and the ayatollahs, or members of the Iranian secret service, there to spy on and disrupt the dissidents. One very helpful gent put us right on who was who: clean-shaven equals protester, huge bushy moustache equals secret service.

Those without facial fungus all seemed to have another thing in common: on a sultry night all of them were wearing jackets; and all the jackets were closed. The reason for this became clear only after the teams had entered the arena and the national anthems were being sung. As the PA struck up the Iranian hymn, about 25,000 people whipped off windcheaters and blazers and blousons to reveal a mass of white T-shirts, each one emblazoned with the face of the young would-be shah of Iran, the man they wanted restored to the Peacock Throne.

Then, as the captains shook hands, a balloon about the size of a spacehopper, with yet another picture of the proto-shah attached to it, floated across the pitch, right over to the skippers, right into the hungry lenses of the TV cameras. This was too much for the regime in Iran. While they had managed to just about avoid the great divesting of a few minutes earlier, there was no way they could ignore or tolerate this latest image. So they cut off the television pictures to the entire country, and 70 million people were told that there'd been a power cut in France.

Once the game started (and, it should be said, the actual match was played in an exemplary spirit) it soon became obvious just how complex this whole situation was. Many of the non-moustaches around me and Danny were chanting, 'Iran!...USA!...Iran!...USA!' They supported their country but also wanted to give a boost to the only nation on earth they thought might overthrow the regime they despised. To this already Byzantine brew was added further complication when a group to our left started augmenting the chant we'd only just got our head round: 'Iran!...USA!...Danny Baker!...Iran!...USA!...Danny Baker!' Turned out they were from Eltham.

In the midst of all this hullabaloo the teams played out a pretty decent 90 minutes. Very close to where we were standing Iran's defensive midfielder Hamid Estili sent a great header past the helpless Yank keeper Kasey Keller; Mehdi Mahdavikia got a second a few minutes from the end; the last-gasp American goal by Brian McBride (lately of Fulham) was mere consolation. At the end the players made a genuine effort to be civil, and the match was later said to have greatly improved relations between the two nations.

Outside the stadium after the final whistle, though, it was bad-tempered business as usual. The anti-revolution faction had gathered for a great march around the stadium. They formed up in disciplined rows across the main road, perhaps twenty abreast. As is always the case with these sorts of things, they had a large banner covering the whole width of the front row of the marchers. With loud ululations and clenched fists aloft, they set off, TV news camera crews and Iranian secret service men filming their every step.

Danny and I were watching all this from 200 yards away. As the screaming stream of humanity drew ever nearer we had yet another brainwave. Nay-sayers and party-poopers might well identify it as Lame Plan Number Three, but that would be too harsh. Because in similar circumstances what red-blooded male could resist the temptation? So at the exact moment the procession drew level with our spot on the pavement, we ran out in front of it, assuming a position at its head. For 50 glorious yards, with balled fists held high and fierce cries of 'Up the Lions!' and 'Come On You Spurs!' we actually led the parade.

Afterwards, when we tried to explain to each other why we'd done it, the best we could do was some hokum about hoping our loved ones would see us on *News at Ten*. And many times since that night my mind has wandered to the forbidding Teheran headquarters of the Iranian security services. In a cinema full of men with immense moustaches, a flickering film of that night is shown over and over again. The moustaches call for freeze-frames and close-ups. They howl in exasperation as the video once again focuses on two unidentified bespectacled gents of jaunty step defying the revolution and everything for which it stands. 'Who *are* those guys?

About a year after the match in Lyon I was interviewing the charming and intelligent Kasey Keller on my TV show *Under the Moon*. I told him that the last time we'd been in close proximity, he'd been beaten by a fine header by an Iranian midfielder. He was slightly amazed. 'You were at that match?'

Indeed I was, I replied, though I thought better of telling him that I'd also led a major political demonstration afterwards. I remarked on the extraordinary atmosphere that had prevailed in the ground that night, and asked him, in all seriousness, 'Have you ever kept goal, Kasey, in a more nutty, ferocious, hostile, crazy madhouse of a stadium than that?'

He fixed me with a look, shook his head slightly, then replied in a voice which suggested I had just asked history's dumbest question, 'Are you kidding? For three years I played for Millwall...'

# What is the most fabulous player name to ever grace a World Cup?

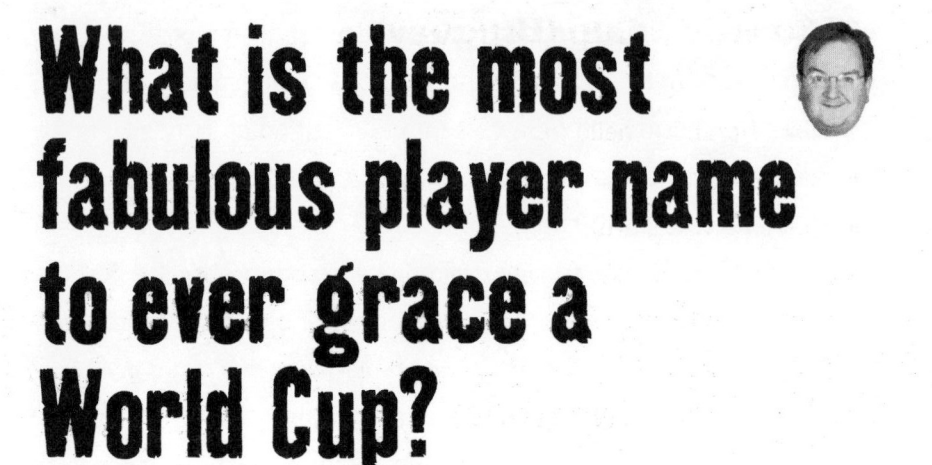

**_'And that is a simply stunning finish by Philibert Smellinckx!'_**

Let's get one thing straight right from the get-go. This list is not designed just to make fun of foreigners' funny names. Well, it is... but it's very gentle fun. And we've included a couple of Irishmen. Plus we are fully aware that this sort of thing happens all over the world, in every culture. Thus in the Nigerian edition of this book we've included the fact that speakers of the Yoruba language find themselves reduced to helpless tears by the names Stewart Downing and David Bentley. Equally, in the Korean edition we've revealed that Michael Carrick translates as 'germs in my cake', while Newcastle United sounds, in colloquial Korean, like 'bison-strong buttocks'.

Having assured you, then, that our intentions are beyond reproach and entirely comedic, B&K are proud to present a list of the players who, over three quarters of a century and nearly a score of World Cups, have had the most marvellous monikers. Serving suggestion: this definitely works best when you read them out loud.

# 1930 World Cup (Uruguay)

A debut World Cup hello to...
- Poly (Brazil)
- Jorge Pardon (Peru)
- ...and Belgium's Nic Hoydonckx (of course Nic Hoydonckx!)

# 1934 World Cup (Italy)

Say *buongiorno* to...
- Antonin Puc (Czechoslovakia)
- Jakob Bender (Germany)
- Sandor Biro (Hungary)
- Knut Kroon (Sweden)
- Einarr Snitt (Sweden)
- Kick Smit (Holland)
- Puck Van Heel (Holland)
- ...and Belgium's Philibert Smellinckx (of course Philibert Smellinckx!)

# 1938 World Cup (France)

A big *bonjour* to...
- Pal Titkos (Hungary)
- Tim (Brazil)
- Daaf Drok (Holland)
- Piet Punt (Holland)
- G.H.V.L. Faulhaber (Dutch East Indies)
- ...and Dutch East Indies' Bing Mo Heng (of course Bing Mo Heng!)

# 1950 World Cup (Brazil) – only 13 teams

A hearty post-war hiya to...

- Adolphe Hug (Switzerland)
- Vladimir Firm (Yugoslavia)
- ...and Paraguay's Pablo Centurion (of course Pablo Centurion!)

## 1954 World Cup (Switzerland)

Say hello in three (or is it four?) languages to...

- Pinga (Brazil)
- Svatopluk Pluskal (Czechoslovakia)
- Marcel Flückiger (Switzerland)
- Gilbert Fesselet (Switzerland)
- Denis Houf (Belgium)
- ...and Belgium's Hippolyte Van Den Bosch (of course Hippolyte Van Den Bosch!)

## 1958 World Cup (Sweden)

A broad grin in the general direction of...

- Roy Rae (Northern Ireland)
- Wilbur Cush (Northern Ireland)
- Sven Axbom (Sweden)
- Ken Leek (Wales)
- Tom Baker (Wales)
- ...and Czechoslovakia's Titus Bubernik (of course Titus Bubernik!)

# 1962 World Cup (Chile)

Just loving the chosen appellations of...

- Igor Netto (USSR)
- Srboljub Krivoku a (Yugoslavia) (Oh come on – Srboljub!?!)
- Jorge Toro (Chile)
- Jiri Tichy (Czechoslovakia)
- Lajos Tichy (Hungary)
- Ivan Ivanov (Bulgaria)
- ...and Argentina's Vladislao Cap (of course Vladislao Cap!)

# 1966 World Cup (England)

Not everyone was called Ray Wilson...

- Hansruedi Führer (Switzerland)
- Werner Leimgruber (Switzerland)
- Roberto Hodge (Chile)
- ...and The USSR's Valeriy Porkujan (of course Valeriy Porkujan!)

# 1970 World Cup (Mexico)

A high-altitude hi to...

- Gennady Logofet (USSR)
- Mario Monge (El Salvador)
- Roland Grip (Sweden)
- Shraga Bar (Israel)
- Driss Bamous (Morocco)
- ...and Peru's Hector Chumpitas (of course Hector Chumpitas!)

# 1974 World Cup (West Germany)

*Guten abend!* to...

- Peter Duck (East Germany)
- Uba Kembo Kembo (Zaire)
- Pleun Strik (Holland)
- Aldo Poy (Argentina)
- Wilner Piquant (Haiti)
- ...and Poland's Zbigniew Gut (of course Zbigniew Gut!)

# 1978 World Cup (Argentina)

Wave a cheery welcome to...

- Dominique Dropsy (France)
- Eric Beer (West Germany)
- Ronald Worm (West Germany)
- ...and Argentina's Daniel Killer (of course Daniel Killer!)

# 1982 World Cup (Spain)

Wow! Look over there. It's...

- Vladimir Bigorra (Chile)
- Gerónimo Barbadillo (Peru)
- Fathi Kamel (Kuwait)
- ...and Brazil's Roberto Dinamite (of course Roberto Dinamite!)

# 1986 World Cup (Mexico)

Open your hearts and minds to...
- Huh Jung-Moo (South Korea)
- Tomas Boy (Mexico)
- Greg Ion (Canada)
- Albert Rust (France)
- Mustafa Merry (Morocco)
- Joel Bats (France)
- Vasiliy Rats (USSR)
- ...and South Korea's Cha Bum-Cun (of course Cha Bum-Cun!)

# 1990 World Cup (Italy)

A huge cheer for...
- Silviu Lung (Romania)
- Danut Lupu (Romania)
- Bismarck (Brazil)
- Gu Sang-Bum (South Korea)
- Danny Blind (Holland)
- ...and Holland's Adri van Tiggelen (of course Adri van Tiggelen!)

# 1994 World Cup (USA)

A giant howdy to...
- Marco Sandy (Bolivia)
- Stefan Kuntz (Germany) (Had to be done!)
- Choi Moon-Sik (South Korea)

- Alexis Alexiou (Greece)
- Ola By Rise (Norway)
- Roar Strand (Norway)
- Danny Boffin (Belgium)
- Mahi Triki (Morocco)
- ...and Cameroon's Rigobert Song (of course Rigobert Song!)

## 1998 World Cup (France)

*La plume de ma tante! Les noms magnifiques...*
- Youssef Chippo (Morocco)
- Mini Jakobsen (Norway)
- Bernard Lama (France)
- Doctor Khumalo (South Africa)
- Andy Williams (Jamaica)
- ...and Mexico's German Villa (of course German Villa!)

## 2002 World Cup (Japan and Korea)

*Banzai!!* (only Japanese word we know)...
- Gao Yao (China)
- Torsten Frings (Germany)
- Justice Christopher (Nigeria)
- Wellington Sanchez (Ecuador)
- Wesley Sonck (Belgium)
- ...and Senegal's Omar Daf (of course Omar Daf!)

# 2006 World Cup (Germany)

A no-nonsense Teutonic hello to...

- Lebo Lebo (Angola)
- Love (Angola)
- Loco (Angola)
- Brian Ching (USA)
- Jerko Leko (Croatia)
- Hakan Yakin (Switzerland)
- ...and Ivory Coast's Gilles Yapi Yapo (of course Gilles Yapi Yapo!)

# Who is the greatest footballing dad?

How girls get into football is a mystery, as unfathomable as the mountains of Mars or Jonathan Woodgate choosing to look like an extra from *Dawn of the Dead*. With chaps, it's an altogether more straightforward learning curve – they pick up their passion for football from their fathers.

Which got us thinking – inevitably, since we had to fill these pages with something, anything – about football and dads. And, to be more specific, who is the greatest footballing dad of all?

The answer, it turned out, came in seven parts. Strap yourself in therefore for The Top Seven Footballing Fathers...

## 7. Papa Bouba Diop (Lens, Fulham, Portsmouth and Senegal)

The wardrobe-proportioned midfielder is the only player whose name has actually got a fatherly ring. Unless you count Papa Kouli Diop, his countryman currently plying his trade (*see* Stuff People Only Say When Talking About Football, page 194) with Gimnastic de Tarragona in Spain. Anyway, Papa's in.

## 6. The daddy of the Sodje clan

Obviously, Mrs Sodje should also be given her due, but we really must toot a very large horn in the direction of the tireless Mr Samuel Sodje, who came to these shores from Nigeria, settled in the leafy London Borough of Greenwich (nowadays home to the Bakers and pronounced by all locals 'Grinnidge') and fathered ten little Sodjes. Of these, no less than four have gone on to play professional football.

Sam Jnr has done his stuff for Brentford, West Brom, Charlton, Watford and Leeds and is these days on the books at Reading; he's also had a couple of games for Nigeria. Akpo, the youngest of the Sodje swarm, has turned out for Huddersfield, Darlington, Port Vale and Sheffield Wednesday. Efi is a real nomad, having sported the colours of Macclesfield, Luton, Colchester, Crewe, Huddersfield, Yeovil, Southend, Gillingham and his current employers, Bury. Steve, clearly the runt of the litter, has kicked around the semi-pro game and is now playing for Ashford Town.

It should also be noted that yet another brother, Bright, is a professional rugby league player, with the Sheffield Eagles.

Old Sam himself has no doubt that the boys inherited their prowess from him. In a BBC interview in 2005 he recounted that back home in the Nigerian town of Warri he was a more than useful player, glorying in the nickname of the 'Wizard of the Field'

## 5. Footballing dads 'n' lads

Neither Baker nor Kelly has any formal training in the fields of medicine, biology or genetics. Despite this, they were (with their paper 'Towards an Understanding of Generationally Transmitted Footballing Skills', first published in the *Lancet* in 2001, now a major motion picture) the first people to notice that blokes who were good at football often sired offspring who were also decent manipulators of the old spheroid.

The idea initially occurred to Danny Kelly as he watched Tottenham (managed at that time by one George Graham, *see* Judases and Lion Judases, page 284) beat Leicester City in the 1999 League Cup final at the old Wembley. Between bouts of chanting, 'Bloke in a coat and his blue-and-white army!' – the Spurs fans' affection-filled acknowledgement of their manager – Danny noticed that no less than five of the Tottenham squad on that day – Stephen Clemence, Ramon Vega, Ian Walker, match-winner Allan Nielsen and Steffen Iversen – were the sons of ex-pros.

**Slight detour.** Steffen Iversen's dad, Odd (Yes, Odd. Deal with it) was a goal-scoring legend in their native Norway, breaking all sorts of national records. These feats were made all the more remarkable by the fact that they were achieved despite a very serious drinking problem – Odd is now, thankfully, sober – and has perhaps the biggest ears ever to feature on a professional footballer. (Go on, look at http://www.geocities.com/thomsof/landslaget/players/pics/oddiversen.jpg if you're in any doubt.)

Months of feverish research followed. Tottering towers of yellowing programmes were perused. Those DNA models that look like that wind-activated sculpture thing on the South Bank were examined with a jeweller's eyepiece. Micrometers were used to measure the features of Harry and Jamie Redknapp. When all was ready, our great discovery was unveiled. Yes, footballers were breeding more footballers but, oddly, the new generation were not as good as their fathers.

In pop music this latter phenomenon is known as the Dweezil Zappa principle: the sons and daughters of pop stars who have a go at the music thang produce mostly lamentable results. Dweezil Zappa is not as good a musician as his dad Frank. That's clear. Julian Lennon is a hideous shadow of his father, the sort of thing you might hire from a lookalike agency for a giggle. Sean Lennon is also a musical dud. Brian Wilson's daughters Carnie and Wendy were two thirds of Wilson Philips but failed to write 'Good Vibrations'. Bob Marley's enormous brood have made, in various combinations, over 3,000 records, just one of which (*Welcome to Jamrock*, by Damian) is, by some monkey-typewriter magic, any good. And so on.

With the footballers, it's not quite so clear-cut in favour of the older generation. Judge for yourself from this list of famous football dads and lads...

| Dad | Lad | Verdict (Who's better?) |
| --- | --- | --- |
| Peter Schmeichel* | Kasper Schmeichel* | Dad, obviously |
| Frank Lampard Snr | Frank Lampard Jnr | Young Frank |
| Cesare Maldini | Paolo Maldini | Paolo, just |
| Les Allen | Clive Allen | Les (won the double, 1961) |
| Steve Bruce | Alex Bruce | Pops |
| Johan Cryuff | Jordi Cryuff | Duh! Johan |
| Harry Redknapp | Jamie Redknapp | Jamie |
| Brian Clough | Nigel Clough | Brian |
| Mike Walker* | Ian Walker* | Ian |
| Miguel Reina* | Pepe Reina* | Pepe |
| John Bond | Kevin Bond | Too close to call, both average |
| Alex Ferguson | Darren Ferguson | Too close to call, both useless |

* Lots and lots of goalkeepers. Danny Baker's wife, the lovely Wendy, is currently working up a PhD on this phenomenon.

## 4. The ultimate footballing dad 'n' lad

The most remarkable trans-generational pairing is undoubtedly that of ex-Chelsea and Barcelona forward Eidur Gudjohnsen and his pop, Arnor. On 24 April 1996, in Tallinn, Estonia, they played international football in the same side. Arnor started the match; Eidur came on as a sub – for his father!

In truth it should have been an even more remarkable achievement, but the whole thing got messed up by someone who later pitched up in English football to equally unhelpful effect. Eidur and Arnor should have been on the field *at the same time* but the then-head of the Icelandic FA, one Eggert Magnusson (yes, him with the bald pate and huge overcoat at West Ham, before Iceland went out of business) told coach Logi Olafsson not to pick them because he wanted the historic father-son-same-pitch thing to happen on home turf, against Macedonia two months later. All very well, but in the meantime seventeen-year-old Eidur broke his ankle, and it took nearly two years to heal. By the time he'd recovered, Arnor had retired. Both men have publicly stated that they are still bitter they were denied such a unique opportunity, and are joining the long line of West Ham fans queuing to give Magnusson a good slap across his pasty dome.

## 3. They're creepy and they're kooky, mysterious and spooky, they're all together ooky, the Allen Family

And it's definitely genetic. How else would you explain the Allen family? Brothers Les, Dennis – I know, Les Dennis, but the other brother's called Ron, and Ron Dennis is just as confusing. OK, let's start again. Brothers Ron, Les and Dennis Allen (ha!) came out of Dagenham in the 1930s.

Two of them became professional footballers, Les a legend at Spurs, Dennis making hundreds of appearances for Charlton, Reading and Bournemouth. The three brothers then spawned four pro players. Strikers Clive and Bradley Allen are Les's sons; current Cheltenham manager Martin is Dennis' boy; former West Ham and Tottenham stalwart Paul is the offspring of Ron. It goes on: Clive's son Oliver was a promising striker at Barnet before injuries forced him down the leagues.

## 2. Danny Kelly's dad, as remembered by DK

My father, Andy, who died in 2006, was a wonderful man. A teetotal Irishman, gentle and quiet yet murderously funny, he worked like a husky to keep a family of six in spuds and school uniforms. He cared passionately about only three things: his family, his garden and sport. It's from him that I've inherited my love of the latter. I owe him big time for that, and for everything.

He is central to my very first memory of sport. The 1964 Olympics were held in Tokyo. We had no telly; my dad listened to them on a red transistor radio that he took with him on his long work trips as an attendant on British Rail's overnight sleeper services. On one of the few days he wasn't away from home, he and the seven-year-old version of me lay on his bed and listened to the BBC commentary on Abebe Bikila's incredible barefoot triumph in the marathon. This was exciting enough, but what I really remember was the almost infinite patience with which he explained to a small boy what the marathon was, where Ethiopia was, how a man with no shoes could win, and how great it was for an African to win the gold medal. I was hooked.

Two summers later we bonded further. Spurred on by the Bikila epiphany, I had become a very strange nine-year-old. My contemporaries spent their pocket money on Bazooka Joe bubble gum and *Man from UNCLE* picture cards. With my daily fortune of 6d (two and a half pence in modern parlance) I bought the *Mirror* and read the sports pages till my eyes bled. As the 1966 World Cup rolled around the whole Kelly family decamped to a tiny caravan in Felixstowe, then a stony beach at the end of the A154 onto which crashed bone-crushing break-ers. Now a bustling container port, the Visit Felixstowe website struggles to make the town sound like an East Anglian Monte Carlo, promising, as its highlights, 'the only fort in England to have repelled a full scale invasion attempt – see the 12.5 and 10 inch Rifled Muzzle Loaded guns', and 'migrant birds'.

All I really remember about the holiday was that the football was happening and I was missing it. After the semi-final, I must have read the *Mirror*'s report on England's triumph over Portugal (complete with a picture of Bobby Charlton's winning penalty that I can still see today) about 200 times. Eventually, my mum, not a woman much given to sensitivity over sporting matters, cracked. On the eve of the final she sideways-glanced my dad and, pointing rather disdainfully at her eldest son, sighed, 'I suppose you better take this one home to see the match.'

What a joy! What a thrill! This was in the days before wall-to-wall sports coverage, and before hoverjets linked all our cities. Instead we survived the rattly train back to Liverpool Street – it took about four hours, maybe more – and then the bus to our basement in Islington, where the newly rented Ekco TV stood ready. The streets were genuinely deserted. In the end we learned a valuable lesson about the young Kelly. When West Germany scored first, I stropped out of the room, tears popping out of a beetroot face, vowing not to return until England had equalised at the very least. It's a feeling I often revisit at White Hart Lane. My dad, having made such a special effort to allow me to see the wretched game, just chuckled indulgently. He knew then that whatever other qualities his firstborn might bring with him on life's mystery tour, being a good loser was definitely stamped 'Not Required on Journey'.

In the end we only ever went to two matches together, one a brilliant eye-opener, the other an unmitigated disaster for which I still probably should get therapy. The first was the climax of a magical trip, the like of which should only really happen in boys' comics. As previously mentioned, my father was an attendant on the sleeping cars that British Rail ran through the night from London to Fort William, Penzance and Plymouth. These were essentially rail-bound business hotels, and his job was to check the travellers in, make sure they got to their cabins and, in a pantry/kitchen about four feet by eight, wait for them to ring a bell to order tea, snacks and those little bottles of whisky. That's how it worked. In theory. In fact, Dad felt that, having paid all that money, the passengers ought to get a good night's sleep. He also felt that as he had a second job doing decorating and odd jobs, he really needed all the shut-eye he could get too. The solution was simple; just disconnect the bell. Presto! The punters could wait till morning for their coffee and shortbread; their attendant, stretched out on the floor of the pantry, got some well deserved zzzzs. One passenger once took this whole hotel thing a bit far and, as the train pulled out of Paddington, left his shoes outside the door of his cabin, presumably for the atten- dant to polish. Dad set his little alarm clock for half past four in the morning, knocked up Mr Shoes and told the poor, blinking sap 'I think, sir, these must be yours.'

If the trick with the bell was a flagrant violation of modern health and safety standards (Back off, Brussels!), what he did with eldest offspring would nowadays be the cause of a parliamentary inquiry. Just twice the lovely father wondered if his son – maybe eleven or twelve years of age – would like to come to work with him. Let's go through those words. Would a twelve-year-old boy like to go with his old man to Paddington station quite late at night? Then get on a train pulled by one of the most powerful diesel engines in the world? Then hurtle through the middle of the night to parts of the world he had never even heard of? Yeah, that might be, like, y' know, OK and that.

Thus it was that I got to go deep into the bowels of a mainline rail terminus, where I saw grown men, who I naively thought might be working, smoking roll-ups and playing rummy. Then I got to be stowaway on a train hammering through the darkness. Then I went to Penzance (which might as well have been Ulan Bator, such was its strangeness to me) and ate shark on the sea wall. Finally he took me to Home Park to see Plymouth Argyle play. They wore green shirts. Nobody wore green shirts! It was the most exotic thing I'd ever seen. And, with the exception of a particularly eventful trip myself and the boy Baker made to an establishment on New York's 42nd Street, it remains the most exotic thing I've ever seen.

The second and final match we attended as father and son was no less eventful, though rather less rosy in retrospect. It was 15 February 1969 and I had persuaded the old fella to take me to see my beloved Spurs at Queens Park Rangers. I was 12 and it was the first time I ever saw the Lilywhites play away from White Hart Lane.

In many ways it was an extraordinary day and a remarkable match, overflowing with oddities. A week before the game Tottenham had paid the then-princely sum of £100,000 for the Rangers winger Roger Morgan. He thus made his debut against both his old team, and against his identical twin brother, Ian, who also played on the wing. Plenty of scope for 'Oooh, we've bought the wrong one here...' Equally strangely, Spurs that year were wearing navy-blue shirts as their away strip, which meant that for the very first time anyone could recall the referee wore red and the linesmen green. Nowadays we're used to the officials peacocking around in every conceivable hue, but back then people were utterly shocked –

you'd have thought the Queen had turned up for the state opening of Parliament in just her vest and knickers. And, a few yards in front of me, my hero Jimmy Greaves scored Spurs' goal in a 1–1 draw with a breath-takingly blatant handball.

Yet the most amazing thing about the day was the cold. Man, it was bitter. That iron, determined, urban cold that defies all attempts at insu-lation. Did I mention that the hand with which Greavsie so casually turned in the ball was swathed in a fawn, fingerless glove? All the Totten-ham players wore them, while their QPR counterparts sported fetching yellow efforts, another first on an English field. Even before we'd finished queuing to get in, my father was ostentatiously stamping his feet and snarling, through chattering teeth, 'Never again...'

And it was my own efforts to keep out the raw, biting chill that day that led to the entire event being so unforgettable, and scarring. The match, you see, also saw the proud debut, and tragic finale, of My New Hat. My mum had knitted My New Hat. It was a navy-blue-and-white-striped bobble hat, quiet like a million others worn by football fans every-where. I say 'quite like' because clearly something had gone hideously wrong at the planning stage. In the traditional bobble hat the hat itself is, obviously, the size of a human head, and the bobble, perched atop, about the size of a plum. I don't know what my sainted mother was thinking, but mine was different. Sure, the hat part was traditionally proportioned, snugly bounding the crew-cut Kelly cranium. But the bobble – if indeed such the word can be legitimately employed to describe the monstrosity beneath which I found myself tottering – was nothing less than a huge volcanic explosion of navy and white yarn. It was significantly bigger than my actual head. By the time I discovered that My New Hat was some sort of atomic mutant it was too late to do anything about it, and I made my way down the South Africa Road sway-ing drunkenly from side to side as I tried to balance the mighty orb on top of my noggin. African women carrying vast jugs of water back from the river to the tribal kraal would have sympathised...

Which is more than my schoolmates did. I mentioned that I was just a few yards from Jimmy Greaves' controversial goal, didn't I? Well, the following afternoon the incident was shown over and over and over again on *The Big Match*. And there, in the middle of the TV screen, his frozen face now wreathed with a smile, was a skinny Herbert wearing the biggest bobble – oh hell, it was a pom pom! – in the history of the western world. Everybody saw it.

My mum later trimmed the monster down to a more acceptable scale, but the damage was done. The bobble hat was quietly consigned to some uncharted cranny of the garden shed. My classmates taunted me until some other kid turned up with a boil or BO or some other weakness that could be leapt upon to make them blub. And my father retired to his armchair, to watch thousands of games in comfort, his view unhindered by a New Hat the likes of which would these days be picketed by ecologists worried about the global wool shortage.

Back in Ireland, Dad saw out his remaining days tending his garden and watching football. We spent many a happy hour together banging on about the latter. I tried to persuade him that the current game is brilliant, fast and powerful and skilled. He felt that Dave Mackay might have beaten several of today's Premier League teams 'by himself'. When he died, people, knowing of his passion for the game, came gravely up to me and asked, 'So, who did your father actually support?' It afforded me one last opportunity to recall one of his greatest, and most practised, idiosyncrasies. Whenever he was asked, 'So, Andy, who do you support?' my pop would begin an elaborate performance of demanding that he be brought that day's newspaper, preferably the very latest edition. He would, with great ceremony, spread the paper out on the table, turn very deliberately to the sports section, carefully peer at the top division league table and, in answer to the original question, firmly reply with the name of whichever club was currently top. Over the years he has therefore mostly supported 'Leeds!' 'Manchester United!' 'Liverpool!' 'Brian Clough!' and 'Arsenal!' Sadly, he shuffled off this MC as a fan of Chelsea.

Nowadays when we visit his resting place outside the windswept little chapel at Ballymurphy, my mum always makes up bunches of flowers from his beloved garden to lay on the grave. Red and white ones from my siblings, who mostly follow Arsenal. And navy-blue and white ones from me.

## 1. Gordon's dad. He made Gordon a wooden bow tie, you know.

It seems incredible that anyone could be a better football dad than Andy Kelly. But, friends, such a one exists. A few years ago B&K were doing a show where we were asking the usual load of questions about spotting players in mundane circumstances, and about old football memorabilia listeners had lying round the house. It was all going along swimmingly – a titter here, a tear there – when a Scottish voice, calm and unprepossessing, was put through to air. It was Gordon. He had a story about football and his father. What followed was the funniest phone call ever on British radio. The printed word cannot readily do justice to the mixture of disbelief and helpless mirth that ensued, but give it a try. In any event, it's all over the Internet.

**Scene.** Saturday afternoon, Broadcasting House. Baker & Kelly are packed into the smaller of the old Radio 5 studios. They are enjoying their work. Danny K quaffs tea. A new caller is put through.

**Gordon:** Hiya, Danny.

**Danny Baker:** Who is this?

**G:** I've got football memorabilia and I've got a footballer in a supermarket.

**DB:** Okay, go on.

**G:** The football memorabilia is when I was about nine. I'm now about fifty-odd so it's going back a bit...

**DB:** Yeah.

**G:** I asked my dad if he'd make me a bow tie—

**DB:** Hang on, hang on, hang on. No, hang on! Just say that again.

**G:** I asked my Dad if he'd make me a bow tie.

**Danny Kelly:** The first time ever on Radio 5 Live the sentence, 'I asked my dad to make me a bow tie.'

**DB:** This is already my favourite call ever. Kids, you asked your dad to make you a train, a ship, a boat, some kind of railway station... You asked your father...

**G:** Well it made a difference from a scarf, right. I wanted something with my team's name on it.

**DK:** What team is that?

**G:** Dundee United.

**DB:** OK. Cool. It's great. Go on.

**G:** But they're just called United. So he made it, and it was wee black triangles, you know at the pointy bit, and it was white across the middle and it had UNITED written across the middle...

*(Howls of laughter from DB & DK)*

**DB&DK:** A bow tie!

**G:** ...but it was made of plywood!

*(DB & DK laugh hysterically. Danny Kelly's tone is already arriving at a pitch only normally audible to humming birds)*

**DB:** *(on the verge of tears)*: This is too good. We'll have to play an advert. We're going to have to play an advert.

**DK:** *(squeaking)* We're going commercial... There'll be an advert for the next 20 minutes.

**DB:** *(gasping)* I'm sorry, Gordon... As you know, we usually plough on, but you're wearing a plywood bow tie with Dundee United on it?

**G:** ...and it was two feet wide!

*(DB & DK are now literally screeching with laughter)*

**G:** ...and it was tied round my neck with a big leather strap.

*(The howling chuckles are now interspersed with choking and shortages of breath)*

**G:** ...and by half-time I was Quasimodo.

**DB:** and what did you say when he handed you this thing?

*(Fearful laughter)*

**DK:** Here you go, son. Here's your bow tie.

*(The painful laughter begins anew. Danny Baker is now clutching his heart)*

**DK:** Clank! Clank! Clank! And here's the big leather strap to tie it to your neck.

**DB:** Oh my God!

**G:** It weighed about a stone and a half...

**DK:** You must have ended up with curvature of the spine?

**G:** ... but he saw the error of his ways. So next week...

**DB:** *(weeping)* There's more?

**G:** He produced a big pole...

*(Insane cackling)*

**G:** ... and I went away to the match like a Roman centurion, you know?

**DK:** What was the pole for, sorry?

**G:** *(deadpan)* The bow tie was strapped to the pole...

*(The laughter is now just a helpless wheezing)*

**G:** ...like a Roman standard?

*(Danny Baker thumps the table – crump! crump! crump! – in desperation)*

**DK:** *(barely able to speak)* Like a Roman standard? You're making it worse... don't keep doing that.

**DB:** Gordon, this is my favourite ever, and I've been doing this a while... Sorry, I've gone...

**G:** ...and another quick thing is...

**DB:** No, no, hang on just a minute... You don't have to fill the space... Sometimes it's good to have dead air. Just going back, why did you want a bow tie?

**G:** Why does anybody want anything?

**DB:** No, no, no, seriously... A rattle, yes! A banner, yes! A scarf, as you say... a hat...

**G:** I already had a rattle...

**DB:** Ooooh! Aah, I'm afraid, Gordon, we're going to have to keep your number and have you tell that... I may have to ring you up when I'm at parties and I can't quite remember all the details... Good old Gordon!

**DK:** Wherever tards and retards meet...

**DB:** A two-footwide bow tie

**DK:** And one with a big leather strap the first week, and, on the second week, carried into the ground like a Roman centurion.

**DB:** The thing to do is stick it on a pole. Well, don't feel intimidated by Gordon's call. It may be the best, but please ring.

**DK:** You only have to do better than that and you're on the air!

# I'm 27 and really want to get into footy. How do I start?

Some time in March 1988 it was necessary for Millwall to play at Bournemouth. The game was of supreme importance to Millwall as victory would take them clear at the top of the old Second Division with but a handful of games to go. Bournemouth, always to my mind an anaemic and nervy team, quaked at the prospect of hosting such an important fixture and set about imposing a series of ridiculous restrictions on the visiting fans lest they cause trouble. Now I freely admit that Millwall supporters are perfectly capable of raising hell but that is not the point here. It was Bournemouth's outrageous flap that we must focus on .

One idea they hatched, I recall, was that every Lions fan who travelled that day ought to pay twenty pounds instead of five for their terrace standing ticket but, if the match passed off without incident, they could claim the extra fifteen pounds back after completing the necessary paperwork. This along with several other panic conditions were all eventually vetoed by various authorities, leaving Bournemouth naked and shivering with only a last-ditch attempt at an inconvenient kick-off time to bolster their wobbly knees.

This they eventually squeezed through the proper channels, and the match was switched from a regular Saturday-afternoon slot to one that would start promptly, if curiously, at 6 p.m. on a Wednesday evening.

6 p.m.! Presumably somebody at the club had heard that working-class Londoners are not allowed to put down their shovels, picks and chimney brooms until at least 5.30, so Bournemouth could get the fixture under way with nobody in the ground bar the usual crowd of old ladies, funeral directors and gouty shopkeepers who always attend their home games.

Of course by 2 p.m. on the afternoon of the match Bournemouth town centre was *crawling* with Millwall fans – thousands and thousands of them all demanding chips, ale and seaside rock in the shape of ladies' legs.

An hour before kick-off the siege of the ground was in full swing with access to Dean Court grindingly slow because the police were thoroughly searching absolutely everyone. Or *almost* absolutely everyone.

My father had travelled with us.

As we inched towards the gates, a copper doing the patting-down looked up at my dad and said, 'It's all right, Pops. I won't bother with you. You can go in.'

The old man's eyes flashed and his fists clenched by his sides. Then he exploded. 'Pops? POPS! You saucy bastard, I *demand* to be searched.'

My father was a big bloke. Sort of Bernard Bresslaw with Bob Hoskins overtones. He was the blueprint of the classic Millwall-supporting London docker. It was at his side at five years old that I had been exploded into the screeching Hogarth sketch wired to the National Grid that was match day at the Old Den. No warning, no training, no choice. Delivered from sitting on the couch watching *Bill and Ben* to the howling full-on foul-mouthed mob almost overnight.

We beat Newport County 4–0 in that first match. As we left, my hand reaching up into his, a dozen or so of his dock mates all smoking and jabbering at once in the fizzing lights under the arches of Cold Blow Lane, he shouted down to me, 'Enjoy that, boy?'

Enjoy it? I haven't stopped shaking since.

He felt the call of the club deep in his bones even as it pulsed close to his skin. Millwall as a thing, a manifestation, walked with him always, making it part of who he was. Millwall was a trenchant symbol of his class and his struggle – as arcane as that might sound these days, so much of football's tribalism is still rooted in such heartfelt identity. In their embarrassment at such unmanageable passions, modern football and mass media will seek to decry and disperse these feelings and ideas. But you cannot wipe out history through something as shallow as branding.

Such a personal identification made him wildly overprotective toward *his* club, and down the years he had chalked up a remarkable record for being ejected from many grounds, including the Den. As a small child some of my earliest memories are of being beside the old man as we noisily departed various stadiums long before the final whistle – usually with several stewards or sometimes an actual policeman showing us the way.

One Sunday in 1965 a local copper came to our door and asked to see the old man. Their talk was friendly and at its completion some money changed hands. The exact sum was two pounds ten shillings and it was for the policeman's helmet that my dad had crushed in the melee as he was thrown out of the home game against Coventry the previous day. In those days if a policeman lost or damaged any part of his uniform he was liable to pay for it unless a felon could be produced. Not wanting to arrest my father – the Den police knew most of the more volatile dockers in those days – he simply called round the next day for his fifty bob. With a hangdog apology my dad was more than happy to pay up.

Gillingham, Oxford, Southend, on at least two separate occasions at Selhurst Park and, most vivid to me, a 6–1 defeat at Loftus Road, also saw my dad assisted to exit early amid a flurry of flailing arms and bad language. I would certainly never class Fred – and yes, my dad was actually called Fred – as a violent man. He was not dangerous. But he was big. And noisy. And came from a generation who thought honest 'right-handers' were a legitimate part of everyday robust discourse among men.

I remember once, after I had received the latest in a long line of stinker reviews for whatever rotten TV series I was currently involved in, Dad wondered what I was going to do about this latest example of what he saw as liberty-taking abuse. I said that it just came with the territory or something equally craven. He weighed this. Then, turning the page of the newspaper, he said wearily, 'Couldn't have gotten away with that in the docks. The trouble with your game is that there's not enough right-handers dished out.'

To this day I have not heard a better summation of the bogus, simpering, duplicitous stew that is life in the UK media.

Indeed, once, early on in my career and after a particularly snide commentary on whatever my latest offering was , he offered 'to go up after' the journalist in question. I, of course, talked him down from this position. Looking back, I now think I was too precious by half, and what grand fun it would have been to have let him loose. You wouldn't have seen many more negative reviews of my act. *Pets Win Prizes* would still be running, I promise you.

Rather unfairly it was only comedian Harry Enfield who ever truly experienced the bite behind my old man's protective bark. I was hosting a late-night talk show at the time and Harry was one of the guests. I cued him up to talk about some of the new characters he was working on for his upcoming BBC series, and in response he unfortunately chose this opportunity to premiere his soon-to-be-famous man who takes umbrage at all celebrities. The one who might hear the mention of, say, David Beckham, start by praising him and then gradually get up a head of steam until exploding, 'I'd say, "Oi! Beckham! No! You might be an international brand with a marriage that is constantly the focus of the world's media but if you won't pass me those peanuts like a normal bloke then I will have to smash this table over your perfectly coiffured mane that has beguiled us all with its many extravagant reinventions over the years..."' You know the one.

Anyway, to illustrate the sort of thing this character would be saying over the upcoming weeks Harry started ad-libbing, using me as the subject. 'Oi! Baker! You may be a poncey talk-show host using his gift of the gab to win over butterfly-brained actresses from *Casualty* on a weekly basis, but to me you are still a mouthy bald cockney wang-ka!' Cue huge laugh and spontaneous applause

Now, as was his wont, during the show my dad had been sitting backstage in the green room nursing a Guinness and must have sort of drifted off for a bit during the early part of Harry's chat. He was only snapped out of his reverie when the volume of the burble coming from the TV monitor suddenly increased. All he hears is Harry's character unleashing invective at me followed by the rattling approval of the gathered masses. Putting down the glass in his hand, he now ominously rises and makes for the studio.

By the time he arrives at the studio doors Harry, fresh from his triumphant spot and flushed with success, is just coming out.

'Just the person I want to see!' booms the old man. He then grabs Harry Enfield by the throat, holds him against the corridor wall and through gritted teeth hisses, 'Now him. He's not like me. He's a good kid. But I'm his dad. And if I ever hear you say anything like that to him again I'll chuck you straight out that f***ing window, got it?'

Coming down off the wall, Harry legs it down the corridor with my old man shaking a fist and bellowing after him, 'His mother could have been in that crowd tonight!'

Even today, whenever I meet Harry he always starts by asking, 'Your dad's not with you, is he?'

All my friends loved it when Fred came with us to away matches; his presence was huge. The volume, the storytelling, the inevitable songs (and he really could sing), the generational legitimacy he brought to our support. I think they particularly liked the way he made me – a big-time Charlie from the media – look disappointing and meek by comparison. Their faces would fall as I turned the corner to meet the coach and it became clear I was alone.

'Where's your old man?' they would say aghast.

'He don't fancy it,' I'd bluster back as though it were a small matter.

'But... but... have you *rung* him. *Today*. He might have changed his mind...'

In later years my father's appearance on these away jaunts was decidedly more about socialising than cheering on the Lions on the road. And not necessarily even socialising with us. It took us a while to cotton on to one of his slicker wheezes.

A coachload of Millwall supporters is, you'll be staggered to learn, not every publican's dream. It ought to be, but even our happy party of agreeable men in early middle age, nearly all with children, would sound like a thunderclap over 90 per cent of British boozers once they caught sight of the blue-and-white scarf emblazoned with the dreaded M-word. 'No thanks, lads,' they'd quake, often rushing out to meet the coach in the car park. 'There's another one just down the way...'

Some trips it would be many, many miles between hostelries willing to sell us a few glasses of the life-giving, and so eventually my dad volunteered himself to become our ambassador. As the eldest and ostensibly most respectable member of the group, he offered to go in on his own, playing the poor gasping pensioner, and plead our case with the stern-faced publican while the rest of us waited on the coach for the OK. This seemed eminently sensible and, as a former dock union official, if anyone's considered reasoning could lift the licensee's blanket embargo, his could. Of course they weren't to know that this clubbable old chap in the sports jacket and flat cap was by far the biggest risk among us.

This worked splendidly for a while, though as the season wore on he seemed to lose his winning touch. At pub after pub he'd vanish inside, then, after a couple of minutes, emerge waving his arms saying, 'Nope. No good. They won't have it. Proper ponce that one...'

It was my friend Colin who first saw the smoking gun.

'Your dad,' he said as we waited by the roadside in the rain. 'Watch as he comes out. He's always wiping his mouth. I think he's the only one getting a drink on this entire trip.'

And so it was. The crafty old git had jettisoned both his negotiations and our desperate need in order to operate as a solo turn. While we were often going an hour between refreshments he was getting one in at every pub on the way. Judging by the wait at some of the more picturesque inns, sometimes two.

The last Millwall match my dad and I attended was the Cup final against Manchester United. A good day but hardly the long-awaited vindication of everything a lower-league supporter is supposed to dream about. In fact the old man wasn't much struck by the occasion at all. It seemed false. Silly. Not Millwall at all.

I had been doing some boss-eyed punditry for *Match of the Day* before the match, and after it brought Fred into the BBC green room. There I fell into a nice little session with Alan Hansen and company but Dad hardly said a word. It was not a matter of being overawed – he had always held his own down the years in some very competitive high-profile company, ask Harry Enfield – but this just wasn't his thing at all. Millwall was an enormous part of who he was. Christ, he was actually *from* Millwall, one of twelve children raised in Millwall, worked the Millwall docks, and how many Lions fans can still say that?

In the world of what he understood football to be, what it meant, what it represented, what it said about you, this was simply a room full of tourists. To him the Cup final had been cold. Stage-managed. A show. This was not his Millwall. This was 'Millwall'.

I flinched every time some well-meaning BBC soul asked, 'So, Fred, did you enjoy the big day?'

With a thin smile he would curtly nod.

The big day.

Like all those decades spent shouting and cursing, singing and laughing at the Old Den in storm-battered mud-clogged Division Four fixtures against Crewe and Halifax and Doncaster and Wrexham and Newport and Bradford and Hull were made from lesser days.

Like football was a dream, a show or an aspirational lifestyle. A comfortable seat near the directors' box, good technique with the ball played to feet, and a chance to air your views after on 606. It's footy! Just keep your head down, work hard and even your side can get on and do well! After all there's some good football played outside the Premiership these days. Look, here's Millwall playing Manchester United – *Manchester United* – in the Cup final! A big experience for them to place alongside all those little ones and a great day out for their fans. Why not buy the official DVD, Fred, and keep this precious memory alive forever?

Well, fuck that.

Right, Dad?

Fuck. That.

Here's to you, Fred. And here's to the gift of *living* football that you gave me.

# Twenty facts for your files

**Fact.** When we were very young my sister Sharon once designed a new football kit that incorporated a short silk cape and Donovan-style Breton cap (also in silk). She explained that the cape was purely ceremonial and would be taken off before kick-off but the cap was for match use and could only be removed during corners. To this day she has never actually been to a football match.

**Fact.** The crossbar as we know it was introduced to English football in 1868, thereby preceding goalposts by two years. Nobody today knows how this could possibly have worked.

**Fact.** Before corner flags were standard it was not uncommon to mark the boundaries of the pitch with small fires which were the linesman's duty to keep well stoked and visible. This was in the days when a linesman would signal any infraction spotted by firing off a flare.

**Fact.** What have the following people in common? Julio Iglesias, David Frost, Gordon Ramsey and Fred Flintstone? Answer: They all had trials for Norwich City. (Only David Frost – a goalkeeper – was offered terms.)

**Fact.** At the first modern Olympic Games the football tournament was played on a circular pitch.

**Fact.** At the moment goalkeepers touch gloves as they pass each other, the tradition is for them to shout, 'Fumble.' The one who shouts it first can then choose which type of error he wishes his opposite number to make during the game. (It is thought bad form if something major like throwing the ball into his own net is demanded; however this is not unknown.)

**Fact.** Manchester City did not provide changing rooms for either team until 1955.

**Fact.** First team to officially adopt a nickname? Bury in 1914. The were known as the Undertakers. However, when the First World War broke out this was thought to be in poor taste and so it was dropped. When they revived the name in September 1939 the FA was so outraged it fined them £15,000, docked them six points and forced them to remove a further four letters from their registration. Bury Town became simply Bury overnight.

**Fact.** Under the original rules of Associated Football if a crowd remains absolutely silent throughout the entire fixture including half-time, the result does not stand. Though it remains on the statute book this rule has never been invoked.

**Fact.** Though everyone knows the highest football score of all time was achieved when Arbroath beat Bon Accord 36–0, very few remember that, because of fixture congestion, the game was in fact Bon Accord's fifth consecutive match on the same day. They won all the others.

**Fact.** Peter Crouch was inspired to become super-tall after watching fellow beanpole Tony Cascarino score a hat trick for Millwall against Crystal Palace.

**Fact.** Actress Beryl Reid was the first female spectator ever to be hit in the face with the ball. This happened at the Huddersfield v. Coventry Cup tie in 1972.

**Fact.** The tradition of eating oranges at half-time originated in 1900, when it was believed they contained vitamin C. Before that, thirsty players would suck on the shirt-cuff of the teammate thought to be working hardest.

**Fact.** The name of the BBC football phone-in show *606* comes from the Morse code used when anyone on board an ocean-going ship needs to find out a sporting result. It was first used successfully on the *Titanic*.

**Fact.** Commentator Kenneth Wolstenholme achieved immortality when at the climax of the 1966 World Cup he cried, 'Some people are on the pitch. They think it's all over. It is now. It's four!' However he was later admonished by the BBC when it turned out he had in fact 'borrowed' the phrase from the British wartime comedy *The Foreman Went to France*, starring Tommy Trinder.

**Fact.** In Scotland it is perfectly legal for football players to wear a dirk – the traditional dress short knife – in their sock. The last player to actually do so was Billy Ross of Ayr United in 1962.

**Fact.** Before penalty shoot-outs became the norm in cup matches, teams were required to play each other again to determine who actually was the rightful winner.

**Fact.** Bolton Wanderers were known simply as Wanderers before settling down in Bolton. A rogue element in the squad later revived the old tradition and wandered down as far as Wolverhampton.

**Fact.** Former Arsenal and Scotland defender Ian Ure remains the only top-flight player to ever be 'excused boots'. Upon his 1,000th first-team appearance for the Gunners the FA honoured Ure by announcing that from then on he would be allowed to play any fixture in his street shoes if he so chose. This he did in his final game, against Blackpool in 1974, which Arsenal lost 4–0.

**Fact.** Phil Murray of Shrewsbury Town has a dubious distinction among soccer pros. What is it? Phil is the only player to ever have fallen asleep *during* a match. When Shrewsbury's end-of-season game against Carlisle was held up for eight minutes because of an injury, Phil lay down on the pitch and, while chewing on a blade of grass and shielding his eyes from the strong May sunshine, simply drifted off. When play resumed, Phil went unnoticed until he played Carlisle's Mark Oldstone onside for the visitors' second goal. When roused by furious teammates, Phil claimed to have been elbowed off the ball, but amateur footage shot by a member of the crowd subsequently exposed Phil's crafty nap.

**Fact.** Did you know that football pitches had very different markings prior to the First World War? The most notable divergence from today was the large letter S and the slightly larger N that were painted one either side of the centre circle. S stood for south and N for north. All playing fields in Britain were divided up into north and south irrespective of the direction they faced. Thus teams would call at the coin toss either 'Climb north' or 'Fall south.' This call was far more important than today's meaningless remnant of the ritual because, amazingly, the north side of a pitch was ten feet longer than the south, and drawn games were often decided by the amount of time the attacking teams had spent in the smaller southern section.

Before digital timing this was determined by requiring whoever was on the ball in the south to count aloud thus: 'One inthesouth, two inthesouth, three inthesouth...' and so on. An official would duly note the subsequent period of time to be later awarded. The only other major deviation from today's standard pitch markings was a red rectangular area behind each goal where reserve-team members would act out any incidents in the game that it was thought the crowd would like to see again. This, of course, was long before TV coverage could achieve this instantaneously *and* with the original cast.

The pitch marked out as we know it today was imported from Germany in 1919 as part of reparations after the Great War (*see also* Referee's Whistles, Dug-outs and Retractable Roofs).

# Cosmically bored – adventures with Paul Gascoigne

'What have you done?'

You could tell when he'd done something. He'd disappear for five or ten minutes and then return hopelessly casually, bristling with nonchalance, unable to control the corners of his mouth from turning up and giving off a sort of silent alarm. Also it had been twenty minutes since the last 'thing'.

'Paul, I know you. You've done something. Please don't have done something. This is a great restaurant – I come here a lot.'

'Ha'way man, you're paranoid. I just went for a tab.' And he'd fix you with dancing eyes bursting to let you in on whatever booby trap he'd just set beneath your social standing. This would quickly evolve into a smile that would disappear clear around his jawline. 'What?!' he'd splutter. 'What?! Relax y'old bastard. I swear. I just had a quick puff.'

And I'd receive a concentrated beam of inner hysteria, unbridled laughter in all but sound. Whatever it was this time, he was particularly proud of it and we'd all find out before long.

It could be anything. Paul was very fond of introducing stray cats and dogs to high-end locations. He could be found in the kitchens of unspeakably fashionable eateries searching for 'real bread' in order to make a sudden egg sandwich. Nudity of course was only ever a heartbeat away.

At Champney's health spa in Piccadilly, admittedly an unlikely rendezvous for the pair of us at that time, to the horror of both staff and clientele Paul arrived smoking an enormous Cuban cigar that thoroughly stank up the entire reception area. On being told to extinguish it immediately, he physically jolted at his thoughtlessness, profusely and genuinely apologising. However, in the absence of an ashtray, he then placed the burning tip into the desk fan present, sending not only a thousand shards of stogy into the atmosphere but spreading its hearty smell to hitherto untouched portions of the club.

Going out with Paul Gascoigne was like taking to the town with a case full of wet dynamite. Like promenading with the hybrid of Hunter Thompson and Norman Wisdom. Like nothing mattered.

Everyone at some point in their lives needs to know someone like Paul Gascoigne. Someone reckless, chaotic and utterly magnificent. Someone seemingly raised by lightning. For several years I did intimately, and I cannot think of a period in my life where I've laughed more or felt more alive.

Very few people can literally, as the saying goes, 'stop the mighty roar of London's traffic' simply by appearing on its streets. I know Madonna can't because I've seen Madonna shopping in London's West End and the sight of her pootling along Bond Street barely caused a pizza-bike to backfire. But Paul Gascoigne could.

Shortly before the above-described cigar faux pas I had watched him cross Piccadilly, and every car, every bus, every taxi came to a halt and sounded its horn. People leant from windows hollering jokes and hellos all lost in the swell of the rising din. The tourists knew him; the policemen knew him; the newspaper sellers knew him. The hellzapoppin that followed his every move in the mid-90s was totally genuine. He had no 'people' to organise and manufacture his celebrity, no agenda other than to simply get through the tumultuous daily life that his gift had bequeathed him.

Or possibly gifts. On an early visit to Paul's family home in Newcastle I was shown his trophy room. Though not a large room it was completely shelved, and every shelf was full of cups, medals and prizes. The startling part was that only about a third were for football. Virtually every other mainstream sport was represented there, from cricket to snooker, and very few were silver awards or runner-up certificates. Like Dustin Hoffman's mathematics in *Rainman*, Paul could do sport as easily as draw breath and plainly had been able to do so since taking his first baby steps.

I later found out that his genius for games was so acute that it became difficult for him to find anyone willing to play against him, even among his supposed soccer equals. Thus, at the England training camp, if Paul was playing snooker he was only allowed to hold the cue with one hand. If he played table tennis he would have to put the bat aside and just play with his hands. The only way he could get a game of darts was on condition he threw his arrows with the point facing toward his nose, away from the board. Not only that, but he would simultaneously smoke, talk and keep an eye on the horse racing while playing.

One Wednesday morning on the pitch at St James' Park – we were filming his 'Daft as a Brush' video – I challenged, possibly threatened, him to a penalty shoot-out. I mean, you would, wouldn't you? Anyone can win at penalties. Immediately Paul began compiling a list of handicaps that he would take on.

'Right, you can take ten; I'll just have six. I mustn't have a run-up. I can only kick the ball by putting my right foot around behind my left foot. And I have to tell you in advance where I'm going to put it.'

Now look. I understand that I'm not in Paul Gascoigne's class. I'm not even in Doug Rougvie's. But there is a limit to the amount of patronising tosh a chap can take. But he wasn't done.

'Even better. You can tell me where I have to put it. And on the last one I have to run up backwards and heel it in with me eyes shut.'

It was then it dawned on me that these insane, self-imposed conditions were neither a display of ego nor arrogant grandstanding. They were the only ways he knew of giving these tasks the edge necessary to engage his ferociously competitive drive. Like the chronic gambler who will even agree to sit in on an openly crooked poker game, Paul needed to really stack the odds against himself to feel anything at all from the resultant victory.

Everyday life and action bored him. It always had. The constant need to assuage this gnawing inner ennui was born deep within him. By the 1990s he was attaining the power, freedom and means to temporarily fend off the void by cranking up the heart-stopping risks on a daily basis. Even then he knew it was an addiction that would never be satisfied no matter how spectacular its manifestations became. He knew it would eventually drive him insane. The brighter his star shone the more its inevitable collapse into a black hole haunted him.

On many days, and with growing frequency, I could glimpse the fear of that impending sentence burning wildly behind his always teary eyes. Gazza cried when he laughed and he cried when he hurt. He cried while telling stories and while miles away in thought. There is an argument that he was among the prime movers in making crying such a queasy modern British phenomenon. Yet his were no tears for effect. He simply never wanted any feeling, any fleetingly distracting pulse of experience, to ever stop. The tears marked the moment. He was 'there' then. Soon the restless agonies would swallow him up again, denying him peace, denying him even a few hours sleep.

For a while though, the cures for his pain were both explosive and exhilarating.

I have a huge store of extraordinary stories about Paul, each one presenting a different, unique, astounding, sometimes hilarious, often portentous facet of a personality so huge it eventually obliterated normal everyday function. But let me here simply reproduce one particular sack of monkeys that might help people glimpse what life in his orbit was truly like.

It was the day of that infamous much-reproduced photograph that shows Paul, Chris Evans and myself standing in the reception of the Grosvenor House Hotel London looking like we had been out all night, drinking all day, and had no intention of wrapping things up for at least another 36 hours.

It was actually taken at about midday, and the build-up to it and the events subsequent to its taking pretty much sum up the insatiable circus Paul commanded back then.

The first thing to say is that in that shot we are all stone-cold sober. Not only that, but if you look at Paul, he is frozen to the spot in out-and-out terror. You'll discover why.

The plan had been, hastily arranged via a few phone calls earlier that morning, to go and spend the day at the races. Why, I have no recollection – none of us gambles. Paul was playing for Glasgow Rangers at the time and rarely made it down to London, so probably we were looking for something more to do with his furlough than just watch DVDs with a few Budweisers.

He, Chris and I were extremely close friends then, bonded by our love of proletarian low life laced with liberating high jinks. We had no interest at all in the usual celebrity circuit and its fascination with exclusive media venues like the Groucho Club. Indeed, the fact that when we did have a drink we'd do it openly in ordinary pubs somehow set the tone for the whole 'Three Muska-Beers' tagline that has dogged the three of us to varying degrees ever since.

If we were photographed in a pub on a Monday and then again on a Thursday it was presumed and indeed printed that we had been at it for the whole four days. To be fair, sometimes Chris actually had. (I have never in my life known anyone who could take the almighty pace like Chris Evans but that is truly another story.)

Me? I could indulge in the occasional long day's carousing, but, like most men, not like I could in my teens and twenties. Besides, I had a terrific home life with young children, and though the idea that I was part of some new hell-raising elite could be flattering and amusing in equal part, it certainly did not tally with the middle-aged dad making the school run most mornings. Also my wife is a crack shot with both a handgun and a large-calibre rifle. The question 'Where have you been all night?' would almost certainly be addressed to a smoking corpse rather than an errant latter-day Richard Harris.

Then there's Gazza. Gazza never was and never will be able to drink alcohol. In those days this was true in every sense, literal and physical. Not only would two beers have him swaying on his axis with the world doing a Watusi around him, but he never seemed to really like the stuff and tried whenever possible to actually avoid drinking it.

An early trick I observed, and a common one for men who feel intimidated by the capacity of those around them, was, when sitting with a larger group, to surreptitiously pour booze away when he thought everyone else was distracted. I'd see him take his drink from the table and, while keeping his eyes directly on whoever was talking, slowly drop his arm down by his ankles. The glass would quickly emerge a couple of inches less full. He would then wink at me and mime that I should keep quiet. This, of course, while regularly motioning the bar staff to keep them coming for everyone else. He loved nothing more than being part of, indeed being *the cause of*, a good time. The fact that he was always slightly apart from and outside the euphoria could only be detected through longer exposure to his hosting technique.

In the early days, with just the three of us, Paul would actually seek permission to either miss a round or have a soft drink. 'Lads, I'm lagging; I can't do it any more. Do you mind if I have a Coke or something?' Yet if somebody else joined us he would say he was on the vodka and Cokes and, being bought one, would dutifully drink it down, always in one huge gulp. Never wanting to disappoint, he would slip into the cartoon Gazza of red-top legend.

Later he took to ordering bizarre and comical combinations as if to satisfy both sides of this ludicrous social pressure. If you hadn't seen him for a while it was always intriguing to see what two disparate drinks he had moved on to in the interim. Brandy and 7-Up. Malibu and black-currant. Pernod and Sunny Delight.

'Paul,' I would say, 'that is ridiculous, disgusting. There is no such drink.'

But he would be quite serious. 'Danny, it's brilliant – have one. It gets you blootered but you can carry on drinking it.'

But that desperate ambition to numb himself was still some way off.

Initially, with Chris and I, he didn't need to keep up any act. We were drinkers and he liked that. But the drinking wasn't *why* we all got on so well, and he liked that even more.

In Chris he'd met his restless equal in his need to keep the crack in constant motion. For different reasons Chris lived his life then as a trav-elling circus of possibilities with an ever-changing backdrop of locations and faces. Pubs acted as essential base camps as he mounted that day's sensory Everest. The point was simply to be out, to be doing something, and that dovetailed perfectly with Paul's dread of being alone.

Conversely, in me, or perhaps more pertinently my family, he saw a home. Ours is a huge extended family, and he loved all the kids, the noise, the meals, the motion, the neighbours, the permanence. On the many times when he came to stay and all that was planned was a big dinner and a night in, he would lie full length on the sofa repeating over and over to himself – all who know Paul will attest he continuously carries on a personal mumbled monologue – 'This is it. Staying in. Stay in. Door's shut. Fook off, that's me in now. Done. Door's shut. Telly's on. Love it. In. *In.*'

None of this is to say that there weren't times when Paul, Chris and I would get pleasantly lit up, but to my knowledge none of these excellent sessions were carried out within a flashbulb of a press pack.

So to that Tuesday morning and the phone ringing.

Peculiarly, the agreed rendezvous was a pub in Shepherd's Bush, a part of town only matched in its lack of promise by its inconvenience for all three of us. The meet was set at eleven-ish, and upon convening, with all three of us husbanding a soothing freezing cold half, it soon became clear that leaving the bustling metropolis and going to some racecourse to slog it through seven wallet-sapping races was something that only maniacs might consider progress, so what were the alternatives?

Now here I should perhaps recap how well-known a tabloid trio we were at this point. Yes, even me.

I had just the previous week been noisily fired from BBC's *606* for suggesting on air that appalling refereeing is a constant threat to law and order, and should a mob one day decide to go to a referee's house with lighted torches and form some sort of picket, I could totally understand their ire. The fallout made both the front pages of papers and even the nine o'clock TV news.

Chris was quite simply the best-known media personality in the UK. Host of the hugely successful and impossibly hip *TFI Friday*, he was also the controversial kingpin of Radio 1's breakfast show.

And Paul was, well, Paul at the height of his pomp, one of the most famous people in the whole world and, as it turns out, *not even supposed to be in London at all* that day.

So, given all, that it seems an unlikely course of action that we eventually decided upon.

We decided to pitch up at a nearby media awards ceremony.

For those of you who don't live in London you ought to know that award ceremonies are as common in the capital as Gap or McDonald's. Most large buildings are hosting one of these events at any given time, sometimes several simultaneously on different floors.

This one was happening about twenty minutes away and was, I believe, the Television and Radio Industries Club – TRIC – bash. If you are unaware of the TRIC Awards that is perfectly understandable. Nobody has ever referred to the TRIC Awards as 'the traditional curtain-raiser to the Oscars' or even 'an important bellwether for the TV soap gongs'. It is a low-key untelevised industry do that can sometimes be a little undernourished in the high-profile-recipient 'actually being there' department.

Chris's radio show had been nominated for two awards at this affair, and his office had sent a message in reply to the invite saying he would do his best to attend, diary permitting. This is agent-speak for no.

However, as we huddled in that pallid pub mulling the way forward, it did seem like something to do before we decided what really to do. My only objection was that, being grotesquely unshaven and wearing an enormous shapeless World War II navy duffel coat, I was hardly likely to be mistaken for David Niven promenading around Cap Ferrat. Would the TRIC people mind? Chris said that seeing as Paul and I weren't invited anyway we shouldn't let such social niceties cloud our thinking.

And this is where the story really starts.

To get to the hotels on Park Lane from Shepherd's Bush is straightforward and takes about five minutes. Except that it doesn't, because the roads are always so choked with traffic it takes about six months. And on this day it was going to take twice as long as that.

Stuck in the back of a stifling taxi, Paul, as usual, simply could not sit still. He was acting as though somebody had told him Elvis Presley had come back to life, was in London, and if you looked through the right cab window at exactly the right moment, you'd see him. But which window? Then there was the ever-running monologue.

'Shall we get out? Is it far? Shall we get out? Shall we just leave it? I might walk – shall we walk? How 'bout we run through that park? Come on, let's run. Driver! Drive on the pavement, go on! Go through that sweet shop – I'll give you fifty quid. I'm getting out. Look at her in that Porsche. Look at that bloke's tie. I'm going to buy it off him and wear it roond me heed. I'm boiling. I'm gonna take me shoes off. How many legs has that dog got? Is it a dog or a rubbish bin? Look at him! Look at him! Jogging! Ha! Jogger! (*Window down*) Hey mate! Git ya lig o'er! Run, Forest, Run! Ya daft bastard! Come on, let's catch him up. Let's run with him. Driver, have ya got a cigar?'

Now immediately behind us in the stationary parade was a double-decker London bus. Kneeling backwards on the taxi seat Paul, via the rear window, began miming to its driver that there was something wrong with the bus's wheels. The driver wasn't buying it. So Gazza upped the ante and feigned horror because apparently now the radiator had flames coming from it. The driver shook his head but, with a squint, suddenly realised who this antsy alarmist was. He smiled broadly and started applauding.

This was when Gazza got out of the taxi.

Chris and I watched him walk up to the bus driver's window and reach up to shake his hand. In a moment, most of the passengers were leaning out the bus windows and calling his name. Cars in the jam began to sound their hooters in salute. Paul acknowledged all this but was carrying on a pretty intense dialogue about something with the driver. Whatever was under discussion was taking some thrashing out, but all became clear when Gazza grinned triumphantly and hauled himself up into the driver's cab alongside his new friend. The bus driver had to really budge up but soon they were both in there...with Paul's hands firmly on the wheel.

In fits and starts Paul Gascoigne drove that bright red double-decker London bus right along the Bayswater Road. Sometimes he came dangerously close to the rear of the cab Chris and I were still in, helpless with awe and laughter.

When the bus eventually trundled up to Marble Arch junction we figured the fun was over and London Transport would get their bus back. Marble Arch is as dangerous a circuit as the capital has to offer. Vehicles are coming at you from all angles. You have to be completely on your toes when negotiating Marble Arch. It is not for skylarking amateurs.

Arriving at the intersection, our taxi awaited its chance before quickly accelerating out into the mayhem. We turned to see what the bus was going to do...and, Sweet Mother of Mercy, there it was, still right behind us, picking up the pace and honking its horn. Paul, still at the wheel, was shouting something at us, clearly pantomiming an irate motorist. As the bus careered across the junction he even shook his fist. As in a movie, Chris and I both gasped, 'Oh no...' and shut our eyes.

Let me say this. Whenever I have told friends this story I inwardly wonder whether, like most men's tales, it has become polished and embellished over the years. But it hasn't. With Gazza stories you don't need to. Paul Gascoigne really did drive a London bus full of people around Marble Arch in broad daylight. And *still* he wasn't done.

He brought the bus to a stop about 50 yards into Park Lane, where the traffic had once again solidified. Jumping down from the driving seat, he pumped his sponsor's hand and then stood, arms spread wide, in front of the cheering passengers – none of whom I believe had any idea that he had actually been driving the thing and dicing with their very lives for the last ten minutes.

▲ A youthful Danny Kelly talks a half-time break on Hackney Marshes. Note variety of 'dark blue shorts' and slight air of homoeroticism.

◀ Danny K on the morning of the 1982 League Cup final. Note 'lucky' face paint and 'lucky' baby sister Joanne. Spurs lost.

▼ A raffish Kelly receives the North Middlesex League Cup. (Legal note: In reality, DK's side lost the final 5-0; the trophy is for 'Most Sporting Team'. Snigger.)

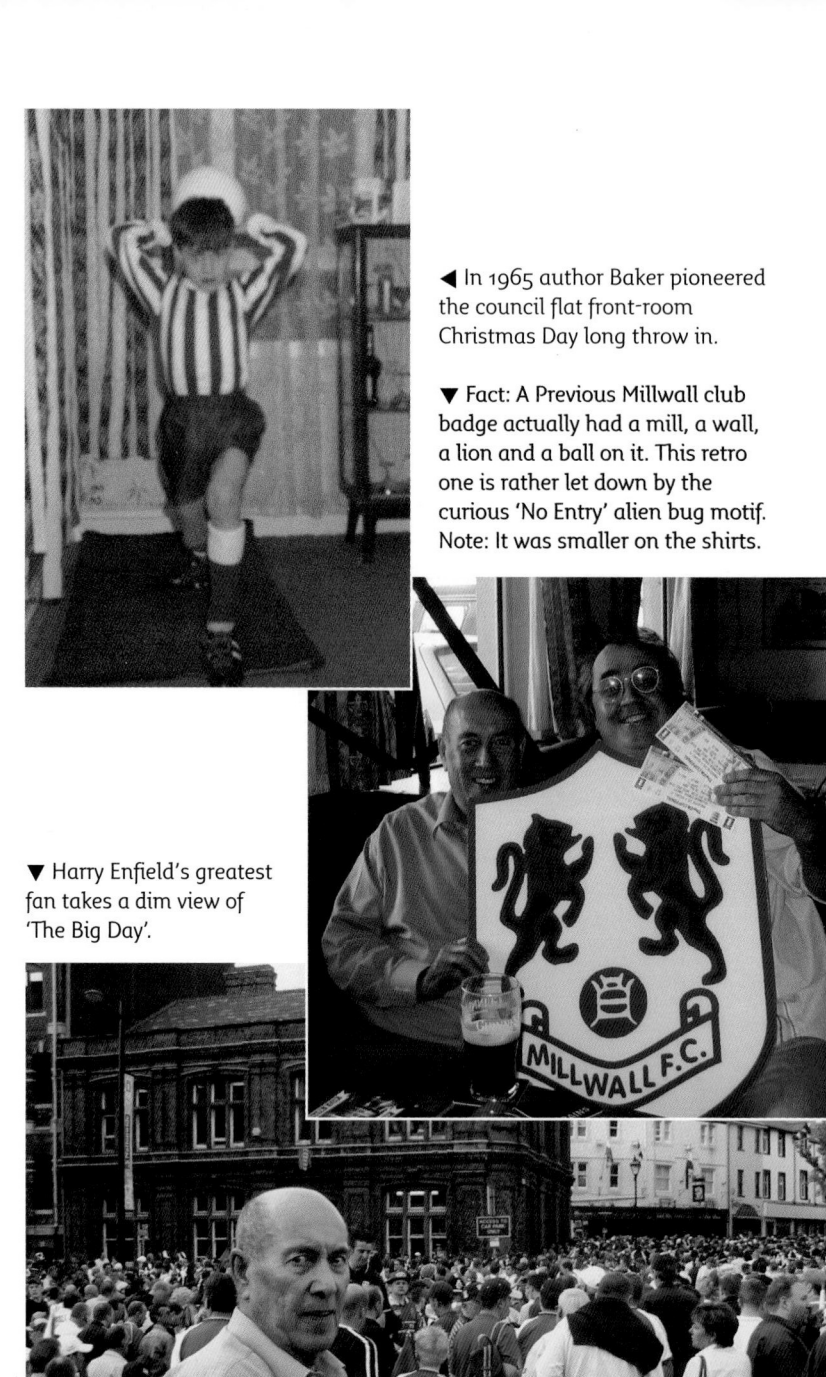

◀ In 1965 author Baker pioneered the council flat front-room Christmas Day long throw in.

▼ Fact: A Previous Millwall club badge actually had a mill, a wall, a lion and a ball on it. This retro one is rather let down by the curious 'No Entry' alien bug motif. Note: It was smaller on the shirts.

▼ Harry Enfield's greatest fan takes a dim view of 'The Big Day'.

▶ The last time I saw Paul. I guarantee he would say he looks fat in this photo. Completely ignoring the fact he is standing next to Oliver Hardy.

▲ Danny Kelly doubting whether a Newcastle supporter could ever really be elected to high office.

▶ 'Sure, Liam, that's right. One day Man City really will be the richest club in the world...' DK patronising a rock star.

▲ Danny Kelly, Sardinia, Italia '90. Once again, the budget didn't run to actual hotels.

▶ Stadio Sant'Elia, Italia '90. Danny K looking forward to seeing George Graham held at gunpoint.

◀ Spot the author. DK in the crowd for Italy v England, Rome 1997. Top right.

▲ Baker and Kelly outside Giants Stadium, New Jersey, for Ireland v Italy, World Cup 1990. Hordes of screaming girls not pictured.

▼ Italy v Ireland again; oblivious to the football, Danny Baker applauds the arrival of another round of ice-cold lager.

◀ Germany 2006. The authors set out on the 600 km trip to Cologne. En route they would be joined by Dawn French and Robbie Coltrane who would help pass the hours with music on the tuba and double bass.

▶ Tickets to all the England matches at the World Cup. We were, of course, getting paid for this. Oh and they give you free beer before during and after the games. And gift bags. On balance, we'd do it again.

◀ In between the great matches and the free stuff, the Germans provided giant screens and special limited edition beer flavoured with lemon. Note to new Ebury Press employers: yep, we'd *definitely* do it again.

▶ At first glance these two pictures featuring the world's oldest football may look identical. But, in fact, there are six crucial differences in the shots. Can you spot all six?

▼ The FA Governors' meeting at Lancaster Gate.

◄ Before the goalposts as we know them were standardised, many varying designs were attempted. This outlandish arrangement, used during a Lincoln v Exeter fixture in 1902, confused both the players and the small crowd. The match was eventually abandoned with the score unclear.

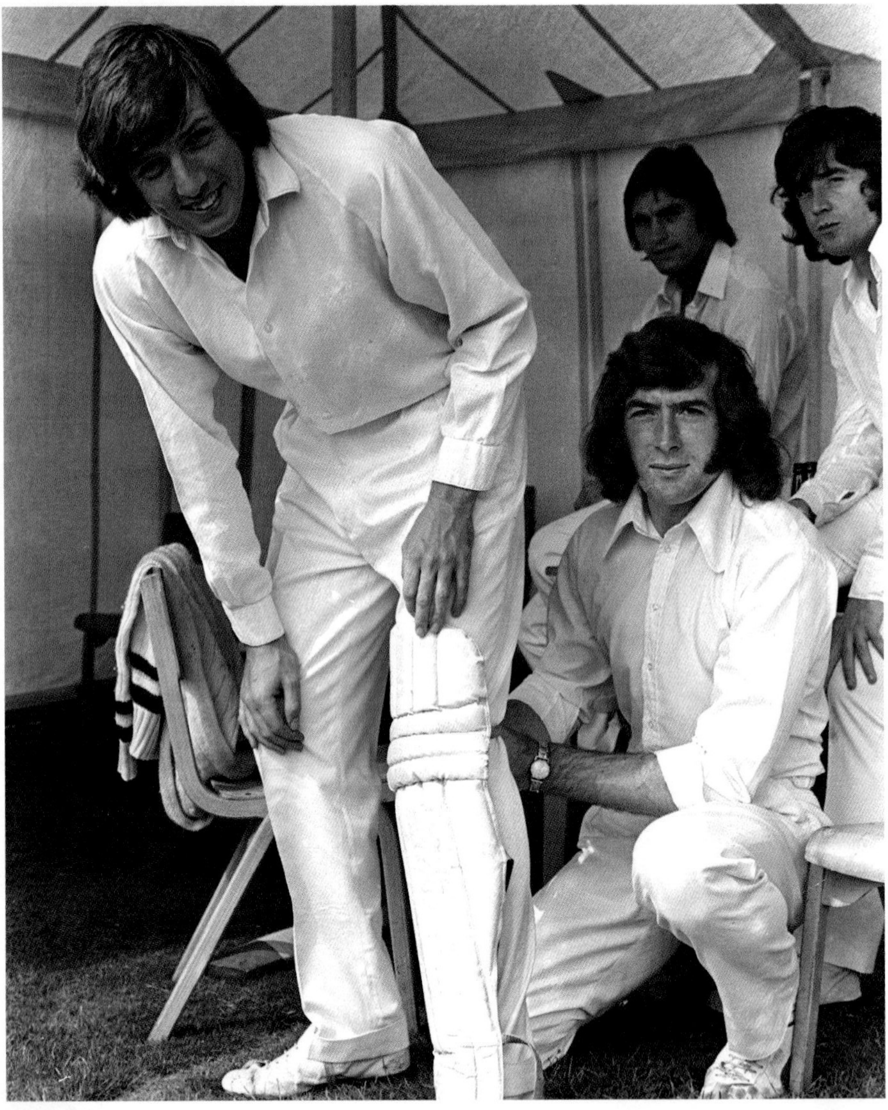

▲ Legendary players Martin Peters and Pat Jennings – Danny K's all-time fave footballer – try out cricket gear (insert own 'fine leg' joke here). More to the point, who's that, far right? Only a hairy Joe Kinnear!

Jumping back into our cab, Paul's face was now giving off sparks. It was clear the world had become his playground and that he hadn't felt so alive in ages. We all spoke at once, but within seconds he was suddenly off once more, this time exiting through the other door.

What he had seen was a gang of council workmen digging up the pavement.

The group greeted him explosively and Paul quickly outlined to them his latest idea. After a brief consultation, on went a high-visibility vest and ear-protectors, and one of the chaps hauled a huge pneumatic drill his way. Thundering the thing into life Gazza began randomly digging up sections of London several feet from where work had actually commenced. It was pure Harpo Marx. In a communal panic the men eventually guided him towards the area that actually needed excavation and for a couple of minutes Paul concentrated intensely on his task.

He stopped. Chris and I, still watching breathlessly from the sluggish cab, thought this might signal his return to us. It didn't. Gazza was merely negotiating a cigarette. One was provided, lit, placed between the lips and he was off drilling again. Gas mains would have to look out for themselves.

It was here, for the first time, that the driver of our taxi remarked upon the surreal events unfolding behind his back. 'Your mate,' he said drily, 'he's not all there is he?' Then narrowing his eyes toward the drilling he confessed, 'You know, that's the one thing I've always wanted to do – what he's doing now. Fair play to him.' Plainly the bus episode was a bit downmarket for a cabbie.

Deciding to walk the rest of the way, we paid him off and crossed to the far pavement, where Paul was still jack-hammering away. The watching workmen proffered both myself and Chris some power tools too but we politely declined.

'What shall we do now?' Paul said after curtailing his shift. We reminded him of the awards-show-thing. 'How far's that?' he then asked as if it the idea was a recently hatched strategy. We pointed out the hotel – about a quarter of a mile along Park Lane.

'How're we getting there?'

'Walk.'

Paul's face registered that he felt this answer was a complete abdication of the better and readily available options.

'Howay!' he announced and strode out into the traffic again. What had caught his eye was an enormous old-fashioned Rolls-Royce, the type you can still see decanting out brides at weddings. We called after him but it was no good.

He strode up to the car and tapped on the darkened rear passenger window. It opened a little. A conversation ensued. Then the door open and Paul disappeared inside.

Amazingly the traffic immediately began to loosen up a little and so began a farcical period wherein Chris and I, now walking towards our destination, were continually parallel to the Rolls with Gazza at its window smiling and waving, heckling the pair of us as 'peasants' 'riff-raff' and much worse. An elderly man and woman sitting alongside him found the gag as hilarious as Paul did. Only he could have managed this.

Thanks to some aggressively red traffic lights we arrived at the hotel just ahead of the Rolls. What happened next we should really should have predicted. Instead of stopping and allowing its stowaway off, it simply glided on past us and off towards distant Piccadilly, Gazza's hand regally twirling away in our direction.

Now what?

Chris and I sat down on a patch of grass and waited for our careering loose cannon to return. Or not.

About fifteen minutes later he was back, this time in a Toyota, driven, he informed us, by an 'Everton supporter called Tom'. He'd asked Tom to join us at the awards but Tom had had to get back up north.

And so, at last, in we went and...flash! Something approaching pandemonium broke out.

If you study that photograph you can see that both Chris and Paul have simultaneously realised what a terrible idea it was. I am actually in mid-sentence saying to one of the photographers, 'Snap away, matey. You've missed the scoop. You should have been with him in the last half an hour...'

Paul had by far the most to lose by being seen seemingly lotus-eating the day away at some free booze-up in the West End. He was supposedly injured. He was supposedly in Scotland. He had promised, *promised*, his boss Walter Smith that he was going to stay at the lodge house by the lake that Rangers billeted him in, doing nothing more physically stren-uous than channel-hopping.

All of this he was muttering to me through a rictus grin as he stood poleaxed in the reception area of the Grosvenor House Hotel having the life papped out of him.

As a table was made available and we shuffled our way towards it Paul kept up his self-berating dialogue, albeit with several bursts of cathartic laughter. 'I'm finished, I'm finished,' he spluttered. 'I'm dead!'

At one point he grabbed a waiter and told him that on no account must there be any alcohol visible on our table. This was done. However, never underestimate a good Fleet Street photo editor. What there was on the table were several bottles of Highland Spring water. With a little cropping of the shots, the distinctive green-glass tapering tops of these bottles looked an awful lot like the shoulders of white-wine bottles. Boom! No further questions, your witness...

Within five minutes of sitting down and with every camera still trained on the table, it was Chris who saw the way out. Literally. 'There's the way out,' he said. 'We have to go.' And so we did. We pretty much legged it outside, where for once Gazza's magical ways of persuasion with car drivers had a practical edge. Trotting up to a waiting chauffeur whose client was obviously inside for the duration he quickly negotiated our getaway.

In the back of the commandeered Bentley – and by the way don't ever try this method of getting around town, it is exclusively a Gazza thing – Paul, as usual, while looking out the window, mentally miles way, let us all in on his continual inner dialogue.

'I'll ring Walter. Ring him. I'll say I had to come down to give you an award. Charity. You'd asked special. Presenting an award. Forgot to tell him. You'd asked me and I flew down on the spur of the moment. Just for the morning. Flew straight back...'

This he would go over and over until he'd convinced himself the scenario sounded totally plausible.

'So do you want to get to the airport?' I asked eventually.

Paul snapped his head towards me and gave an astounded look as though he had no inkling of how: a) I could have possibly heard him; and b) I could have even arrived at such a fantastic idea.

'Do I fook – I'm starving! Where's that hamburger place we went to with your kids that time?'

And so to Ed's Easy Diner on Old Compton Street, Soho. A glass building that might have been made with the paparazzi in mind. I think it was here, but I can't totally swear to it, that he took a swing at one photographer and chased another one up the street.

After an hour of this – with Paul asking me to order extra food so it was placed in front of me and him taking very swift and guilty bites – we decided to cut our losses and go back to my house in Deptford. Chris opted to stay in Soho, where his choices were still varied and appealing.

The rest of the day was blissfully and thankfully mundane, with Paul, shoes and shirt off immediately, small-talking with my family and neighbours, doing magic tricks and gags for the kids and making a series of long calls to Walter Smith until he felt he really had it all smoothed out. He slept as he always preferred to – on the sofa. That way he could keep watching TV all night with a few fitful bursts of escape until the sun came up again. As soon as it did he'd stand on my doorstep smoking, having long and lively conversations with every early-morning mover who passed by, offering and cadging further smokes. Once, before I was up, he rode for a few streets with the milkman, making deliveries alongside him.

The morning after the day described, photographs of the Three Muska-Beers were in every paper alongside tales of long thirsty sessions and all-night hullabaloo. Chris was seen leaving a bar at 2 a.m., and the clear insinuation was that he had left Gazza inside. That same morning Paul went with me when I took my son, then eight or nine, on the morning school run. Photographers outside my house took their shots, and when they appeared Paul was invariably described as 'bleary eyed'.

And Paul would see every one. He was incapable of passing a tabloid newspaper without vigorously leafing through the pages to search out his coverage. Then, settling on it, he would read it in a see-sawing mutter, as though he were being nagged, punctuating it with his own oaths, curses and threats. Invariably the rag would end up in a crushed heap several feet away.

Chris and I soon tired of pointing out the cure for such self-torture.

'I have to,' he'd argue, 'All of it. I have to know what they are saying. The lads will slaughter me when I go training so I've got to know what they'll be talking about.'

How much of a footballer's inner life is governed by the pin-headed psychological peer pressure within the changing room – itself puppeteered by the press – has never been properly examined. Pat Nevin once told me how he had to hide his copy of the *New Musical Express* when he bought it en route to the Chelsea training ground because if the lads had seen it and discovered just how interested he was in 'different' music and culture it would have triggered off months of knockabout abuse and several new nicknames. When a copy of the *NME* was eventually ripped from his kitbag amid howls of derision, Pat had to come up with a new strategy. So, from then on he would buy two *NME*s every week. One would be left lying in plain sight so his teammates could gleefully take it, tear it up and throw it in the showers, and the other copy, tucked under the lining at the bottom of the bag, would survive till he was alone at home to safely digest another 3,000-word think-piece about Echo & The Bunnymen.

I don't doubt for a moment this same harsh and scrupulous watch for any minor deviations from the pack are today just as ubiquitous from Stranraer to Stamford Bridge. It may have been typical of Paul, so acutely aware of his otherness and sense of isolation, that he created the mother of all red herrings in offering up his prankish ringmaster of a public personality. I promise you, the gurning bloke you saw wearing the plastic boobs on the open-top bus was not Paul Gascoigne. That was Gazza.

So what happened?

How did the hype and prophecy come to be so shockingly fulfilled? How did the cartoon tabloid Gazza become the actual Paul Gascoigne?

Well, the Italian period didn't help. Signing for Lazio was very serious. Grown up. The big room. But they wanted Paul Gascoigne, footballer, full stop. This was entirely reasonable. Lazio were splashing out a huge fee on the greatest property in the world. Somehow though, they failed to notice that the house was on fire.

For Paul just being a footballer was OK up to a point. The football part that is. When he was on, in the theatre, he was just fine. But football as a culture, as a discipline still bored the living bejesus out of him. He couldn't help it. To be building a career, mixing with the elite and moving up the ladder simply didn't interest him that much. He loved Italy and the Italians and learned Italian within a couple of months. He found learning a new language both a challenge (at last!) and thoroughly absorbing. However, once again I noted that he would grade his fluency depending who was at the table, always wary of another pro chiding, 'Ooh listen to you...'

When the injuries started piling up though, so did the calls begging friends to come out and stay in the big empty house on the Tiber. Despite Jimmy 'Five Bellies' Gardner's Herculean sacrifices – and Jim had always been a totally loyal Jeeves to Paul's Bertie Wooster – sooner or later Paul would be simply alone in Rome. A now-physical isolation to accompany the emotional one. It was in Rome that Paul discovered wine, which he also began to learn like a language, and from wine the numbing 'benefits' of getting sloshed alone.

Back at Rangers, I think Paul realised that his use for football and its use for him had reached a plateau. Sporting genius, his one great ally in staving off the everyday was beginning to come adrift.

He was still a tremendous asset to any club, but whereas other pros might enjoy the later rich seasons of industry respect and entitlement, Paul could see nothing but the yawning abyss of decline. He started to talk more of the frightening and unmapped years beyond. When the world no longer wanted Gazza they would have to accept Paul Gascoigne instead, and Paul believed that that incarnation of himself would not be acceptable. He would disappoint. Be found out.

That dreaded moment finally came, in Paul's mind, when, in what remains for me one of the most notorious and stupid decisions ever managed by an eclipsed former star seemingly hell-bent on salvaging his own reputation, the then England manager Glenn Hoddle inexplicably decided to leave Paul Gascoigne out of the England 1998 World Cup squad, a side that everybody else, including the rest of the players, knew he had every right be part of. It was a vile and personal decision that utterly destroyed Paul's confidence and allowed his most destructive inner demons to gain the whip hand.

Even though Paul's very greatest playing days were behind him at the time of France 98 there simply wasn't a team in the world who, had the scores been level with 15 minutes to play, wouldn't have drawn breath had they seen Gazza warming up at pitch-side ready to battle against them. Purely from a morale point of view he should have been in the squad – the sight of Paul Gascoigne running onto a pitch sent an electric charge through crowds and fixtures the world over. But it was clear to those close to Paul that Glenn Hoddle wanted to make his splash. In the event it turned out to be just the latest in a line of managerial belly-flops and one with catastrophic repercussions for the player.

After that, very slowly, Paul's off-field stunts became more implosive, the self-loathing blossomed and his obsession with stopping the clock filled his every action.

Never quite having the faith in himself to buy into life when he was a global success, when ruin became an option he embraced it like his destiny. He had been the greatest triumph in the world; now he would show how good he could be at failure too.

Failure. Why not? It's something to do.

Over the last few years there has been no shortage of people willing to 'cure' the bad Paul 'Gazza' Gascoigne – the broken person Paul has always thought he must be – and Paul has been an attendant and, I suspect, lucrative patient.

Pyschobabble and clichéd self-discovery have become his new Italian. My phone number has never changed and yet, for the last few years, he hasn't called. The last time we met up we went to a restaurant near my home and, while he didn't exactly wolf down his steak, he looked good and drank nothing but water. I drank wine and told him how sweet it tasted. His eyes twinkled because he knew how wrong – and therefore how appropriate a joke – that was. An appalling jest that only very close friends can dare. The sort of joke nobody says around him any more because he has supposedly become a tragedy, a walking cautionary tale. Except he hasn't quite, thank God.

That night I brought my son, who was now old enough to hear and understand Paul's unexpurgated stories, to witness his wilfully silly stunts and japes directed at those on surrounding tables. All these facilities were still present and correct, and Sonny laughed, I noted, like nobody else – and I have to include myself here – has ever made him laugh. The kind of laughter when breath becomes exhausted and you make a genuine request for your tormentor to stop.

That is what, still, in my life, only Paul Gascoigne can do.

More than anything in this world now, I wish Paul would get well and once and for all realise how widely loved, respected and important he is.

You did it, Paul. You made it. The hard work is finished now, so just sit back and bask in the glory. Enjoy, once again, the applause of the earth.

You are Paul fucking Gascoigne, for God's sake.

Nothing more to live up to and certainly nothing whatsoever to live down.

Just live, Paul.

Live.

# Nine names of imaginary women who don't like football but happen to be footballer's sisters

Michelle Drogba

Tina Eto'o

Nicola Pelé

Lulu Cantona

Joycie Cruyff

Pat Platini

Diane Zoff

Val Valderrama

Bobbie Charlton

# How can my club save money?

In these days of immense fiscal stricture, when all of us are walking around without shoes and wearing cardboard belts, what can we prune from our football clubs to make them more cost-effective?

Now may the record show that I am the last person to wish to see anyone thrown out of work, but I think I have someone that all clubs could lose and not miss at all. The person on the stadium PA system. The announcer. Your in-house match-day host. Are any of them worth keeping? Indeed is there a maverick among them?

A good friend tells me that very recently at half-time at QPR their own terror at the tannoy actually played Johnny Winter's obscure 1970 classic track, 'Rock and Roll Hoochie Coo' .

OK, we'll keep him then.

But the rest of them? I can't think of a single reason they're needed these days, and since the advent of instant information outlets like Twitter and Gumby do we really need a live human being to boom, 'Substitution for Torquay. Coming on for number 3 Whettleton is number 16 LaPoot,' or, 'We extend our thanks to the match sponsors today, Geldray's Liver-Flavoured Toothpaste for Dogs'?

And for the away supporter, is there anything more likely to incite a murder than when the home side's gormless Uncle Fun at the mike, immediately after they have taken the lead, says in a rising honk, 'First goal today for the Shrimpers scored by Vic Bottomley!!!!!' Then, when you equalise, this same formerly freewheeling wretch intones with all the warmth of a suicide attempt at Lenin's tomb, 'Goal for Kettering scored by Mark Larkstrum.'

No, I say replace them with pre-taped stock phrases read by a famous actor. I mean, who wouldn't much rather have John Hurt or Bette Midler tell them the officials have decided there will be four minutes added time than some nasal drone who drives a taxi the rest of the week.

# Is being a football pundit as easy as it looks?

Absolutely. There are just two rules: 1) before a match explain exactly why a team cannot possibly lose; 2) after the final whistle explain exactly why they did.

Boom! You're a pundit!

# Which country's supporters save the most money on lettering for replica shirts?

It's tough if you are a follower of Poland or Sri Lanka. Then you're endlessly forced to pay a great pile of euros or rupees to get names like Baszczynski, Kaczmarek or Kazmierczak (all current members of the Polish squad; the latter's forename is, incidentally, Przemyslaw), or Thilakaratne, Samarasekera or Pushpakumara (all competing for places in the Sri Lankan starting XI*) splashed across your back.

Much more economical to be a fan of the perennial world champions Brazil. They don't go in for long monikers. Indeed the XI on the page opposite is made up from players (in their proper positions) who have represented the Samba Boys in World Cup finals. And just wait till Jo (the multi-million Manchester City misfit) plays up front in 2010; one of those pesky four-letter strikers will be gone. Anyway, here it is...

The Brazilian World Cup Monosyllabic XI

Leao

Jau    Rai    Juan    Kris

Tim    Jair    Joel (1930)    Gil

Fred    Joel (1958)

*Someone needs to explain why the Sri Lankan team is nicknamed the Brave Reds. Their home kit is yellow; away, they wear blue.*

# Do club shops cover all your supporting needs?

The problem with club shops is that they sum up all that is cynical, dull and grasping about football. It is as if all club shops are centrally stocked from a huge depressing hangar somewhere in Coventry and managed by disappointed people whose only incentive is the promise of an occasional free seat to a midweek reserve game. I mean, babies' bibs. Key rings. Cheap semi-cotton baggy ladies' briefs with slogans on them. Football shops appear to simply hoover up all the tat left over after fifth-rate travelling funfairs have taken what they need to offer as prizes on the stalls. And the atmosphere in those places! Artificial lighting battles the drone of distant convector heaters to see which can more quickly suffocate the human spirit. Two paces inside even a Premiership merchandising shop and you soon realise that, by comparison, the ambience in your local British Home Stores is like New Orleans during Mardi Gras.

Quite why club shops are necessary is a modern mystery on a par with crop circles, the whereabouts of Lord Lucan and why today's comedians think twelve episodes of a sitcom takes the characters 'as far as they can go'. (Good job *Bilko* didn't end in such a precious panic, eh? Or *Seinfeld*? Or even *On the Buses* come to that. It's called imagination, lads!)

The hopeless junkie–pusher relationship between fans and club shops can be directly traced back through the decline in teaching traditional skills in schools. For example, my brother actually *made* his own rattle at school, in woodwork. A solid chunky proper old-fashioned racket-making rattle. I've still got it and it works thunderously. Of course you can't take such items within ninety miles of grounds now, presumably for fear you will mow down rows of opposing supporters after adapting it to operate like some sort of Gatling gun on the Somme. But it is a beautiful piece of handicraft.

Between we two brothers, Mike, the elder, had all the traditional male skills like making things from trees and thumping blokes he disagreed with, whereas I was lightly gifted in the cerebral – and according to my wife – less useful muses.

Nowhere was this gulf between us better illustrated than with Mike's rattle. This sturdy and exam-winning creation was plainly the work of a good craftsman. He even painted it superbly – all clean strokes and tastefully blue and white, something I would be at a total loss to do. However, it was when he came to inscribe the finished masterpiece with a suitable legend that he really should have consulted me.

Michael was a Millwall supporter. If anything, more rabid than I am. So naturally when he came to adorn his rattle he wanted his allegiance to be unequivocal and plain. He wanted to use words that anybody could understand. That here was the rattle of a fan of the mighty Lions.

But, as I say, I hogged most of the literary light from our parents' gene pool, and even though I can certainly see what Mike was aiming at, it has to be agreed he fell a bit short.

What he actually wrote – in bold white gloss paint – all along one side of his hand-made rattle was, UP THE LOINS.

Up. The. Loins. He didn't even notice until the paint was dry and I came in from school. With some nervousness I pointed it out. This was where his other great skill – the thumping of blokes he disagreed with – was given an airing.

All these 40-plus years later I still wonder how on earth UP THE LOINS could have possibly been my fault.

# Are English referees the best in the world? Or… English referees are destroying the World Cup!

I know. I know. The very idea! But there was a time, not that long ago, when the English media genuinely used to stomp about the globe wearing a sandwich board bearing the legend SEE US, WE'VE GOT THE BEST REFEREES IN THE WORLD. In recent years, of course, one simple technological development has quickly and thoroughly disabused all and sundry of that notion. Namely, the arrival of Sky TV, with its twenty-plus prying lenses, all of them, it seems, specifically designed to demonstrate that the man with the whistle is a cross-eyed poltroon incapable of seeing an ankle tap from four feet away. But in truth our referees have always been rubbish.

We should have known that something was up right from the game's first dawnings. As early as 1878, the FA Cup final was reffed by one Mr

Bastard. For the record, Mr S.R. Bastard was, by all surviving accounts, a pretty decent sort of cove who combined his refereeing career with a parallel life as a player (he actually refereed an international – England v. Wales in 1879 – a year before he played in one – England's 5–4 defeat against Scotland). He also owned a racehorse. Imagine Mark Halsey turning out for his country, or miserable Mike Riley peering at the 4.15 at Wincanton through binoculars (insert own ref/ocular instrument joke here) to see if his nag is taking closer order with the early leaders.

And the greatest demonstrations of our referees' haplessness have come on the biggest stage of all, as English (and, to be scrupulously fair, Welsh) officials have set out to... destroy the World Cup!

## The 1954 World Cup – the Battle of Berne

In the quarter-final of the 1954 World Cup in Switzerland the two best teams on the planet, Brazil and Hungary, perhaps understanding that this was really the final, took something of a dislike to one another. To express this mutual distaste, they decided to kick, hack, gouge and bite lumps out of one another. The match became known as the Battle of Berne, and was certainly the dirtiest match in World Cup history. Three sendings-off, four bookings, two penalties and 42 free kicks were liberally punctuated by bouts of fisticuffs, pitch invasions by Brazilian officials and journalists and interventions from the Swiss police, whose previous most stressful day had involved someone whose library books were nearly a fortnight overdue. Overseeing this mayhem? The cream of English officialdom, Mr Arthur Ellis.

Old Arthur might have got an inkling of what was about to occur as early as the third minute, when Hungary's inside forward Nandor Hidegkuti (who twelve months earlier had scored a hat-trick as the

Magyars famously mashed England 6–3 at Wembley) opened the scoring. The Brazilians tore off his shorts. From then on the game was essentially a series of running battles (on one occasion Djalma Santos chased Czibor, Benny Hill-style, for over 100 yards), controversial decisions and sendings-off. After Nilton Santos and Boszik were given their marching orders, they refused to budge; only the arrival of the Berne constabulary on the greensward persuaded them to depart the stage. Plod was back on later when assorted South Americans tried to get the game abandoned. Eventually Hungary won 4–2.

But there was more. Much more. After the match the Brazilians waited for the celebrating Hungarians in the tunnel, turned off the lights, then jumped them. The resultant brawl spilled into the Hungarian dressing room; fists and boots flew; furnishings were turned into weapons. The victorious coach, Gustav Sebes, needed four stitches after he was hit by a broken bottle. After some semblance of order was restored, Brazil complained to FIFA that Mr Ellis was part of a plot to aid Soviet-bloc Hungary; as he left the stadium, his car was spat at by yellow-clad supporters shouting 'Communista!'

Of course West Germany won the World Cup, beating the Hungarians 3–2 in the final, having lost to them 8–3 in a group match.

In 1956 Arthur Ellis went on to referee the first European Cup final, and then replaced football infamy with entertainment immortality when he became the main referee of *It's a Knockout*.

*Note.* In 2003 Sonke Wortmann made his film *The Miracle of Berne*, a stunning and inspiring drama about how Germany's victory in the 1954 World Cup helped heal the wounds of World War II. You should see it.

# The 1978 World Cup – Brazil's lost winner

Clive 'The Book' Thomas was Welsh but spent his refereeing life marching sternly about the upper echelons of English football. In 1978 he scarred the World Cup in Argentina with one of the most bizarre, and daft, decisions in the history of a tournament pocked with such aberrations.

The Group 3 match between Sweden and Brazil was meandering to a 1–1 draw when, late in injury time, Brazil, favourites for the title, gained one last corner. When the ball came across, the great Zico rose on the edge of the six-yard box and headed the winner. Or so he (the rest of the players, the assembled media, the vast crowd in the Mar del Plata and millions of TV viewers worldwide) thought. In fact, the only person on the planet who didn't believe that Zico had scored was Mr Thomas. As the Brazilians danced their traditional samba around the crestfallen Swedes, the Welshman was busy tooting his whistle over and over again and making vast sweeps of his arms to indicate 'No goal.'

In an unprecedented piece of pernicketyness, Clive had decided that the game had ended some time during the two seconds it had taken the ball to travel from the corner flag to Zico's noggin. Or during the one third of second it took to travel from Zico's head to the back of the net. Nobody was sure. They still aren't. All that's certain is that it was, and remains, one of the silliest pieces of refereeing ever seen on a football pitch. One that wouldn't be repeated for another 28 years...

*Aftermath.* Brazil, it turned out, were hopeless pretenders and the Argentinian hosts won the Cup. Clive Thomas went on his merry officiating way: as recently as 2002 the old boy was made High Sheriff of Mid-Glamorgan.

# The 2006 World Cup – our man goes tonto!

Graham Poll has an A level in mathematics and so might reasonably be expected to be able to count to three. He was also, to my mind, one of the most self important referees ever to pull on a jersey in the Premiership. In Germany in the summer of 2006 he spectacularly dynamited a career that many good judges expected to end with him peacocking his way through the World Cup final itself.

In many ways, the Group F match between Australia and Croatia was the most exciting and combative of the whole tournament: great play, tough tackling, a 2–2 draw and a dramatic ending, all taking place against a backdrop of a refereeing performance of comical eccentricity.

It's recent enough in the memory to need only the highlights repeating. Poll booked Josip Šimunić twice but failed to send him off. Then, incredibly, he repeated Clive Thomas's piece of tomfoolery from almost three decades earlier, blowing the final whistle even as the ball was crossing the Croatian line, and the Australian scorer, Tim Cahill (used to play for Millwall, you know) was spinning away in triumph. And in the lunacy that followed the last kick the poor boob found himself giving Šimunić yet another yellow card, his third, and a red one. It was chaos and it was farce. It was also the end of Graham Poll's hopes of scaling the refereeing equivalent of Everest. He was sent home a few days later with the flotsam and jetsam of global officialdom, leaving the reputation of English arbiters in tatters.

*Aftermath.* First, Mr Poll did that most modern of toe-curlers, the tearful TV confessional. There was a certain weirdness in his thought that the worst thing about the entire fiasco was that he wouldn't be able to dangle his grandson on his knee and tell him that his old granddad had reffed the Big One. Nothing about spoiling a major game or threatening Australia's World Cup campaign then, Graham? Eventually, a couple of years ago, he chucked in the whole thing a year early and can now be hired – as an, erm, inspirational speaker. For between one and three of your English grand.

# The 1974 World Cup – the exception that proves the rule

In the days before they became pros, referees turned up for big games from their day jobs. Even so, it's hard to believe the quote from Jack Taylor (the only Englishman to ref the world's biggest match), who said, 'I literally did swap my butcher's apron for the whistle to take charge of the World Cup final.' In 1974 Wolverhampton butcher Jack was the only Englishman in Germany, the national side having failed to qualify. He beat off competition from Scotsman Bob Davidson to take the final between the hosts and Holland.

If you watched British TV, you'd have thought that the final was between the 22 players and the brave man in black. On ITV they mentioned 'Jack Taylor' by name no less than 43 times! In truth, 'Jack Taylor' had a great game. Alone among 100,000 people in the stadium 'Jack Taylor' noticed, as kick-off approached, that there were no corner flags. In the opening minute of the game 'Jack Taylor' gave the first ever World Cup final penalty... against the home team... before they'd even touched the ball! ('You are an Englishman!' hissed the highly unimpressed Franz Beckenbauer). Twenty minutes later 'Jack Taylor' awarded one against Holland. Both were correct and 'Jack Taylor', unlike his colleagues Ellis, Thomas and Poll, was foot-perfect throughout. Well done, 'Jack Taylor'.

*Aftermath.* 'Jack Taylor' is still alive and kicking. Good old 'Jack Taylor'.

# Which is the dirtiest team of all time?

## Champions of violence, treachery and theatricals

Lies, damn lies and statistics. It's hard to believe, but it's possible that the filthiest team ever is one managed by a bookish thinker with a reputation for producing sides that play the game with a silky flourish. The statistics indicate that the all-time dons of dirt are Arsène Wenger's widely conquering **Arsenal** team of the last ten or so years. For all the flowing football and fawning praise, no less than 73 blood-red cards are splattered all over Wenger's CV, and from a formidably wide variety of sources. In Arsène's time (deep breath) Steve Bould, Tony Adams, Ian Wright, John Hartson, the surprisingly spiky Dennis Bergkamp, Jason Crowe, Emmanuel Petit, repeat offender Martin Keown, even more repeat offender Patrick Vieira, Lee Dixon, Ray Parlour, Gilles Grimandi, Nelson Vivas, Freddie Ljungberg, Thierry Henry, Oleg Luzhny, Ashley Cole, John Halls, Giovanni van Bronckhorst, Sol Campbell...

Hold on, the keyboard's overheating. Let's give it a little rest to cool down... *tick tock... tick tock...* There, that's better...

Kolo Touré, Pascal Cygan, Francis Jeffers, Lauren, Robin van Persie, José Antonio Reyes, Gilberto, Cesc Fabregas, Jens Lehmann, Philippe Senderos, Emmanuel Adebayor, Denilson, Nicklas Bendtner, Emmanuel Eboué and Abou Diaby have all made early use of the dressing-room soap, some of them multiple times. The truth, though, is that, with the exception of their ludicrous assault on Ruud Van Nistelrooy at Old Trafford, they were never proper nutters; the modern game just doesn't allow the kind of mindless brutality that we're looking for here. And, in all fairness, Arsenal have largely cleaned up their act.

For real thuggery we have to look a little further back in time, and a little further afield. The hideous Argentine sides that competed (yes, that's the word, competed) for the World Club Championship in the late 1960s would be on most people's dirty dastards shortlists. In 1967 Celtic took on **Racing Club of Buenos Aires** in the Intercontinental Cup (now the World Club Championship). The three games – one in Glasgow, one in BA, and a play-off in Montevideo – further damaged the transatlantic wound hacked open by the previous year's World Cup clash between England and Argentina. In the first two legs Racing players kicked and gouged, spat and acted to such spectacular effect that their efforts have gone into legend, and print. *Tears From Argentina* is Tom Campbell's book about the ill-starred series, while poet Daniel McDonagh has also tried his hand at describing the hideous events. The play-off was a farce, with the Celtic players, fearing for life and limb, deciding that attack was the best, maybe only, form of defence. Six players got red cards, including four Scots; Racing Club won the trophy. The headline in *Miroir du Football*, the French pro-South American magazine, told the story best: RACING CLUB OF BUENOS AIRES, CHAMPIONS OF VIOLENCE, TREACHERY AND THEATRICALS.

Over the next three years **Estudiantes de la Plata** took on Manchester United, AC Milan and Feyenoord in the same competition, displaying such mastery of football's dark side – including smashing opponents' spectacles and spitting into wounds they'd already inflicted – that the 1971 European champions, Ajax, refused to take part in the ongoing farce of Argentinian teams turning soccer matches into lawless knife fights.

At national level, twice World Cup winners **Uruguay** had a reputation for fearsome violence that long overshadowed any excellence they might have brought to the game. By far the tiniest country to ever win the world's leading tournament (their population of four million is dwarfed by the size of the next smallest winners, Argentina, with 40 million), Uruguay relied on 'commitment' and 'effort' to make up for their lack of a talent base. For decades it worked, as football's authorities turned a blind eye to their meaty excesses. Gradually, though, the laws caught up with Uruguay, and their power in world football ebbed away. Perhaps the tipping point was their 1986 World Cup match against a talented Scotland in Neza, Mexico, the last hurrah of the old style. The Uruguayans set out their stall with an organ-rattling tackle by José Batista on Gordon Strachan after... *peep!*... a few seconds. Less than a minute gone and – to their evident and genuine bewilderment – the South Americans were down to ten men. They still clung on for a goalless draw though. Nine years later Uruguay won the South American championship. One of that team's best players, Gus Poyet, recently told one half of B&K that this was a critical win, proving to the players that they could win without war. The rest of his countrymen, he said sadly, remain stonily unconvinced.

Back in Europe, there will be votes for the **Italy** team of the 1930s, who dictator Benito Mussolini ensured were beyond any sanction when playing at home; also for the **Real Madrid** side of the 1950s, who were similarly protected by Franco; the *catenaccio* **Inter Milan** team of the mid-60s stretched the rules until they squealed; Don Revie's **Leeds United** firm, while pretty decent at the actual game, took a belt-and-braces approach by also being the unchallenged kings of snidey anti-football at a time when such antics were the norm in England; and **Wimbledon**'s so-called Crazy Gang of the 1980s managed to lay a gauze of rose-tinted romanticism over what was, let's face it, barely legal skulduggery. All very, very bad boys, but still not quite evil or crazy enough.

The runners-up in the dirtiest team category were not really all that dirty. Just girder-hard and cuckoo-crazy. The law of averages says that at any given time there must be at least a half a dozen truly granite, slightly off-kilter characters earning a living in English professional football. What was unique about **Birmingham City** of the mid-80s was that they were all playing for the same team.

The side, put together by Ron Saunders – himself quarried from the grittiest marble – was awash with an insane array of boozers, brawlers, ne'er-do-wells and, it transpired, petty criminals. Between 1983 and 1986 the squad included such legendary miscreants and toughies as Mick Harford, Mark Dennis, Noel Blake, Howard Gayle, Tony Coton and Robert Hopkins, the so-called Birmingham Six – that sinister moniker itself borrowed from the IRA bombers found guilty (wrongly, as was later proved) of destroying Birmingham city centre a decade before. On the pitch they were teak-tough; off it they drank like fish who'd been brought up in Scotland, fought the fans of rival teams, grappled with taxi drivers, trashed cars, got run over by buses and ended up in hospital with stab wounds. Their legend as the most frightening team ever to pull on an athletic support endures to this day.

How rough were they? On his TV sports chat show *Under the Moon* Danny Kelly habitually asked every footballer who appeared the same question: 'Who's the hardest player you've ever come up against?' To a man, they replied with some variant of 'You mean, *after* Mick Harford?' How up for it were they? In one notorious incident an armed mob of opposing supporters waylaid Coton, Hopkins, Blake and Gayle. The quartet administered such a terrible beating to their attackers that some of the original aggressors actually complained to the police. Through broken teeth and wired jaws. And how bad were they? They were, it seems, capable of just about anything, including slaughtering some of football's most sacred taboos. Winger Hopkins – though a hard-core Birmingham fan – found himself early in his career playing for the Blues' hated local rivals Aston Villa. In his last game for the club he wore a Birmingham badge over the Villa crest on his shirt. When he went to take a corner in front of the Aston Villa fans, they noticed this piece of sacrilege and began, unsurprisingly, climbing the fences that in those days girded the playing area, clawing desperately at the winger and howling for his blood. Hopkins laughed at them, flicked them a few V-signs, deliberately booted the ball out for a goal kick and ran off. A few weeks later he joined Birmingham (see Judases and Lion Judases, page 284). That, friends of B&K, is baaaad behaviour.

But still not baaaad enough to ensure top spot in this most closely contested of races. And here, in a handbrake turn totally unpredicted by the pundits, we are going to give the dirtiest accolade not to a team, but to an individual. An individual who, wherever his career took him, dragged the name and the game of football into the excrement. Take a bow, **Señor Juan Carlos Lorenzo**.

'Toto' Lorenzo was a good footballer both in his native Argentina and in Spain, France and Italy. While playing in the latter, he came under the negative, defensive, destructive thrall of Hellenio Herrera, coach of the dead-eyed Internazionale team mentioned above. To this already fetid concoction Lorenzo added the cynicism and spite endemic to the game in his homeland. It was a brew that poisoned football the world over for the next decade and was only eventually overcome by the antidote provided by the balletic beauty of Brazil's World Cup winning team of 1970.

To examples. After a thorough schooling in the frenzied cockpit of kick, hold and spit that was the Italian league in the early 60s, Lorenzo brought the Argentinian national side to England for the 1966 World Cup. Their quarter-final against the hosts has gone down in history as one of the bitterest football matches in history, one which soured relations between the major footballing continents for years and was, it does not go too far to say, part of the long fuse that led to the Falklands War.

The facts are well known. On a hot day at Wembley Lorenzo's **Argentina** set about England with a vengeance. The referee, Herr Kreitlein, did his best, booking one son of the pampas after another, all the time getting an earful from the giant Argentine captain, Antonio Rattin. After 35 minutes and yet another booking, Rattin, already cautioned, was finally sent off. A good foot taller than the ref, he just stood there and refused to go. For ten minutes chaos reigned. The South Americans threatened to come off the pitch, threatened the England players, threatened Kreitlein. Only when the Argentinians were warned of imminent expulsion from the tournament did Rattin finally trudge off, Lorenzo's consoling arm around his shoulder. The remainder of the match was a snarling, hate-filled disgrace to the glorious game. At its end England's placid manager, Alf Ramsey, ran on to the pitch and vehemently prevented his players from swapping shirts with their narrowly defeated opponents. In one case he physically tug-o'-warred a jersey back from an Argentinian hand. Worse followed. At the post-match press conference he said the opposition should not behave like 'animals'. The insult spread round the globe like a virus. In Buenos Aires Ramsey was never forgiven, and England were never forgiven. The rest is the Malvinas, the Hand of God, David Beckham kicking Diego Simeone and an ill will that simmers horribly away.

It was a further five years before Señor Lorenzo brought his special brand of magic to our attention again. In 1970/1 Arsenal met his **Lazio** team in a two-legged Fairs Cup tie of unbridled viciousness. After the post-match dinner in Rome the Lazio players laid into their Arsenal counterparts in the street. In the resulting ruckus the Gunners' mild-mannered but ex-army manager, Bertie Mee, excelled himself. Many Goons to this day believe that that punch-up forged an unbreakable bond between the players and their manager, one which propelled them to the double at the end of that season.

After a successful spell back home with San Lorenzo, Toto next appeared on British radar as the manager of the **Atletico Madrid** team that met Celtic – yes, poor old Celtic again – in the semi-final of the 1974 European Cup. It was to be his finest display of the black arts. One commentator mused that in recruiting his team Lorenzo had clearly scoured the jails and dockyards of the Hispanic world to produce a swaggering posse of cut-throats, brigands and cock-droppers. On the eve of the game in Glasgow the Atletico players warmed up by booting the tripes out of each other; fights broke out on the training pitch.

The match itself was a madhouse. Ruben Diaz, who seven years earlier, playing for Racing Club, had kicked Jinky Jimmy Johnstone to the point of unconsciousness, picked up exactly where he'd left off. Inside the first 20 minutes the referee had booked three Atletico players – this, don't forget, in an era where you had to cut someone's head off with a rusty hacksaw blade to even begin to incur the wrath of the officials. The first Madrid villain was finally sent off midway through the second half. Hearing the crwd roar, Celtic's Dixie Deans, soaking his bruises in the bath after being substituted, assumed there had been a goal and rushed from the tub to the corridor to get confirmation. For his trouble, and clad in just a hand-towel, he received a swift kick to the trossocks from the dismissed Spaniard.

Back on the Parkhead sward, the assault and battery continued, with special treatment being meted out to Johnstone, David Hay and the emergent genius of Kenny Dalglish. By the end Madrid only had eight players left on the pitch; of these five had also been booked, including the goalkeeper. Among those sent off was the Rapunzel-tressed Argentinian Ruben Ayala, in theory their most creative player. But Lorenzo and his gang got what they wanted – the game ended 0–0.

The game ended; the shenanigans did not. In the tunnel Jimmy Johnstone was ambushed yet again. The Celtic players, no longer bound by the laws of the game, waded in. The resultant Wild West-style bar-room brawl only ended when Strathclyde police appeared mob-handed.

Atletico won the return 2–0, the Celtic players no doubt cowed by the death threats received by Jinky Jim. Eventually EUFA fined Atletico £14,000, and six of their more obvious psychopaths were banned for a couple of games. In the European Cup final, despite the suspensions, they came within one minute of winning the trophy. Thankfully, God intervened: Bayern Munich equalised and flayed the men who put the mad in Madrid 4–0 in the replay. But not even that defeat could rob Juan Carlos 'Toto' Lorenzo of his crown as the master of the dirtiest football teams in history. And we, slightly afraid of a kicking he's organised from beyond the grave, salute him.

# Which footballing folk could hold their own in the squared circle?

*'And...in the blue corner...weighing in at 87 kilos...all the way from Dagenahm, east London...the fighting pride of the football association... Please welcome Trevor 'Sweet Left' Brooking!!!'*

A few years ago there was a craze for celebrity fighting. Ricky Gervais boxed Grant 'Mr Anthea Turner' Bovey. In America Danny Bonaduce (Danny, the ginger one out of *The Partridge Family*) won fights against both Donnie Osmond and Barry Williams (Greg from *The Brady Bunch*) before getting an honourable draw against José Canseco (the steroid-quaffing baseball legend outweighed Bonaduce by 100 pounds!). Why has this malarkey largely dried up? One senses the dead hand of the Health and Safety gang. Back off, Brussels!

Baker & Kelly would love to see – no, Baker & Kelly demand to see! – the return of celebrity fighting, but always involving at least one contestant from the puffed-up world of football. Boxing, mixed martial arts, all-in wrestling... we don't care as long as the great and the good of football are in there swinging.

Here are just some of the bouts we'd really like to see. As men of compassion and lovers of justice, you'll note that we have always tried to match people of roughly equal weight and age. So, picture the scene: half-time, an octagonal cage on the centre circle, well-known football folk in sequinned shorts and big gloves, and the crowd at Old Trafford, Gresty Road or Love Street baying for famous blood...

- Arsène 'The 'Ammer' Wenger v. Sir Mick 'Stunning Stone' Jagger
- Mark 'Lights Out' Lawrenson v. Michael 'Awight?' Barrymore
- Jose 'The Milan Mauler' Mourinho v. Lewis 'Hands of Stone' Hamilton
- Cristiano Ronaldo v. Craig Bellamy (Two footballers, sure, but come on...)
- Dimitar 'The Battling Bulgar' Berbatov v. the Archbishop of Canterbury
- Rafa 'Fists of Fury – Fact!' Benitez v. Gordon 'Eye of the Tiger' Brown
- Birmingham CEO Karen 'Bunch of Fives' Brady v. Hillary Clinton
- Diego 'The Pampas Pudding' Maradona v. 'Punchin'' Peter Shilton
- Fightin' Mohamed Al Fayed v. Peter 'Rocky' Ridsdale
- 'Bish Bosh' Posh Spice v. Russell 'The Muscle' Brand
- Big 'Sam' Allardyce v. a Kodiak bear
- Didier 'Dive! Dive! Dive!' Drogba v. Gordon 'Endive! Endive! Endive!' Ramsey
- Jimmy 'Over the' Hill v. Dot 'The Walford Widow Woman' Cotton
- Harry 'Code' Redknapp v. Richard 'Victor' Wilson
- Roy Keane v. Audley Harrison
- Jimmy 'Raging' Bullard v. Noel 'The Beast with the Beard' Edmonds
- Darren 'Handy' Anderton v. Shelley Duval, wobbly Wendy from *The Shining*

- Ian Dowie v. Roy Keane's dog Trigger
- Sven Goran Eriksson v. Joanna Lumley

## Two-man tag matches

Dennis Wise and Mike Ashley v. Phil and Grant Mitchell

Roman Abramovic and Peter Kenyon v. Lennox Lewis and Sir Alex Ferguson

## Three-man tag match

Alan Green, John Murray and Jackie Oatley v. Borat, Azarmat and Borat's bear

## Five-woman tag match (book Wembley!)

Charlotte Mears, Danielle Lloyd, Chantelle Horton, Chanelle Hayes and Abbey Clancy ('The Wrangling WAGs') v. Girls Aloud

# Is it too late to introduce new language into football commentary?

Absolutely not. Indeed new phrases are being cautiously piloted all the time. In 2009 FIFA asked the Bolivian FA to roll-out the term 're-equalise' in their national match coverage under a pilot scheme.

To 're-equalise' means to snatch back the lead just moments after the opposition have levelled the score. So a commentator might say, 'Stoke fans were still noisily celebrating Taylor's equaliser for Stoke when LeBoyer dramatically re-equalised for Bury, bringing the score to 3–2.'

Results on this term are due back from Bolivia in 2011, and a decision whether to officially introduce it globally will be made some time over the next 50 years.

# Does luck actually exist?

The answer here is no.

Football supporters think it does, but then again they are notorious and downright shameless hypocrites. I know I am.

So are you.

Constantly on the cusp of being exposed as having no more knowledge about the Great Truths of the Game than a Basildon lady-chav's big hooped earrings, football supporters will wriggle, flip-flop, dodge, duck and plain outright lie whenever cornered about any one aspect of the sport. And the very last resort of the bamboozled pundit is that wicked old MacGuffin, luck.

Fans will see luck – and more often bad luck – anywhere and everywhere during a match, and will use this insane concept to explain Why Things Are in a way that is simply never applied in their wider lives.

Look at it this way. When a ball hits the bar it wasn't because of either good or bad luck. It hit the bar because it wasn't struck low enough to go in the goal or high enough to go over it. It just hit the bar.

After all, the big old goalmouth itself is what everyone's frantically aiming at in every single fixture so, when you think about it, the ball's bound to hit the bar at least a couple of times per match. But no. Not according to supporters. That's the gods that is.

Hitting the bar – particularly when coupled with that other mystical element 'in the last minute' – is always deemed by football fans to be an infallible barometer of where luck currently stands. 'On another day that would have gone in,' they will say as though the very earth on which we stand physically rolls and undulates according to Fate's whim. I know of several people who think hitting the bar or post really ought to count as half a goal.

You weren't unlucky; you just got beat. Suck it up, Cicero.

# Then is superstition 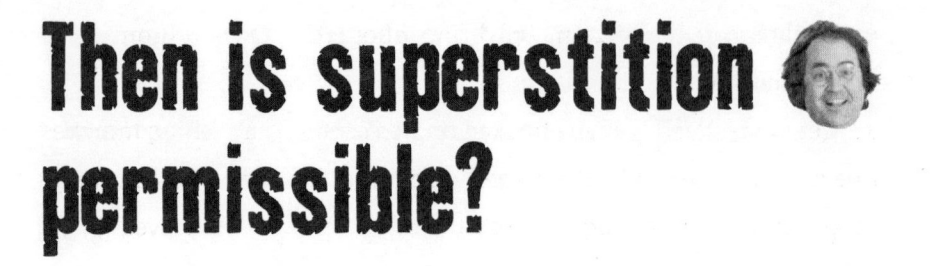 permissible?

If luck is our mumbo then superstition is our equally prevalent and fictitious jumbo.

Glenn Hoddle was soundly castigated during his tedious reign as England manager for many things but mainly because he introduced into the England camp the fabulous Eileen Drury. Ms Drury, broadly speaking, was one of those slapstick mental turns who believe that trees have spirits, kites are good for the soul and all of us have a protective colour, or aura, around us that not only guides our lives but contains magical properties far beyond those of the BBC iPlayer. She was, to all Hoddle doubters, an absolute gift.

However, not content with the fabulous comic potential of such quackery, football fans became dangerously righteous in pursuit of exposing Ms Drury's spiritual claims. Instead of celebrating an era when it seemed England's players might have to sleep inside pyramids, they became rancorous and sour, saying what they heard coming out of the England training camp was frankly preposterous and in danger of harming our boys at a fundamental level. What, they demanded, had football come to, with all this talk of karma, healing and vibes?

Well I ask you? This from a breed who sincerely believe that as long as four friends all sit in the same seats each week their team's good home form will continue. That humming a certain tune will make a man miss a penalty. That keeping a precise number of shirt buttons undone and rubbing a lucky coin will bring about the rejuvenation of an outclassed squad.

Let me be frank. I am as hooked on this as anybody. During matches I never look away from the digital clock until it shows at least one 5. I promise you. If I manage to miss the all-important time played 55.55, I consider the game as good as lost. During televised games I know that if I leave the room to get a cold drink it will cause something important to happen. I make myself do this, with alarming frequency, during most internationals. In my memory it has never failed but I'm sure it must have.

Now nobody was a more pragmatic no-nonsense type than my dad. He was a big man, a docker. Yet in the front room, during high-tension TV fixtures, he would sit on the arm of the sofa if, as the game reached a climax, the opposition had a corner or particularly threatening free kick.

Heaving himself off the cushions he would say, 'It's no good, I've got to go up for this one.' And he'd perch on that arm until danger was cleared. Again it really seemed to work, playing a tremendous part in, among other fixtures, Manchester United's 1968 European Cup victory over Benfica. And now, of course, that's exactly what I do.

But it is a meaningless act in a cold and uncaring universe. So why, if I fail to do it, do I think something dreadful will happen. As I said when England went out of the 2006 World Cup. 'I can't help but feel partially responsible.'

Or maybe it was your fault.

# England win the World Cup – in French!

*'Some are on launching. They think it's everywhere.' (points of Hurst) 'It is now!'*

Here is how the Wikipedia knowledge machine describes England's triumph in the 1966 World Cup.

London's Wembley Stadium provided the venue for the final, and 98,000 people crammed inside to watch. After 12 minutes 32 seconds Helmut Haller had put West Germany ahead, but the score was levelled by Geoff Hurst four minutes later. Martin Peters put England in the lead in the 78th minute; England looked set to claim the title when the referee awarded a free kick to West Germany with one minute left. The ball was launched goalward and Wolfgang Weber managed to poke it across the line, with England appealing in vain for handball as the ball came through the crowded penalty area.

With the score level at 2–2 at the end of 90 minutes, the game went to extra time. In the 98th minute Hurst found himself on the score sheet again; his shot hit the crossbar, bounced down onto or near the goal line. Whether the ball actually crossed the goal line or not has been a matter of discussion for decades, and this goal, known as the 'Ghost Goal', has become part of World Cup history. Recent digitally enhanced footage is said to clearly illustrate that Geoff Hurst's second goal did not cross the line. In the last minute it was Hurst again, who dribbled easily through the German half to net his third goal, just as the gathered crowd invaded the pitch to celebrate with the team, thus cementing the victory for England with another controversial goal. This made Geoff Hurst the only player ever to have scored three times in a World Cup final.

BBC commentator Kenneth Wolstenholme's description of the match's closing moments has gone down in history: 'Some people are on the pitch. They think it's all over.' *(Hurst scores)* 'It is now!'

England received the recovered Jules Rimet trophy from the Queen and were crowned World Cup winners for the first time.

In honour of old Jules Rimet himself... England win the World Cup – in French! Here's the same report, fed into an English–French translation machine, then translated back into English. For best results, read out loud.

London; the stage of South Wembley provided the place of appointment for the final, and 98,000 filled people with l' interior with the watch. After 12 minutes 32 second Helmut Haller had put the Germany ahead, but the points were levelled by Geoff Hurst four minutes later. Martin Peters put l' England in the wire in the sixty-ten-eighth minute; L' England looked at to claim the title together when l' referee allotted a free blow-of-foot in Germany with a left minute. The ball was goalward launched and Wolfgang Weber managed to push it through the line, with l' England launching a call in vain for the handball because the ball came by the tight sector of penalty.

With the level of points to 2–2 at the end of 90 minutes, the play went at extra time. In the ninety small Hurst is found on the sheet of points still; its projectile struck the transverse bar, rebounded downwards or close to the line of goal. That the ball crossed the line of goal or not was really a question of discussion during decades, and this goal, known under the name of 'Goal phantom', part become d'history of World Cup. In of last minute; was Hurst still, which streamed easily by the German half to take its third goal, just as crowd collected invaded launching to celebrate with l' equip, of this fact cementing the victory for l' England with another discussed goal.

It encouraged in Geoff Hurst the only player never to have marked three times in a finale of the World Cup. Commentator Kenneth Wolstenholme of BBC; description of the match, the closing moments of entered l'downwards history: 'Some are on launching. They think it's everywhere.' (points of Hurst); 'It is now!'.

L' England received the recovered trophy of Jules Rimet of the queen and gaining them was crowned World Cup for the first time.

In honour of the famous linesman... England win the World Cup – in Russian! Translating the match from English to a language that uses the Cyrillic alphabet, and then back again, sheds further insight onto the proceedings...

London: the stadium of Wembley supplied place for the final examinations, and 98,000 people of those crammed inward watch. 32 seconds of Helmut Of Haller placed West Germany forward after 12 minutes, but calculation was evened Geoff Of

Hurst of 4 minutes more late. Martin Peters it assumed England into the management into 78th to minute; They looked that complete set claimed England the name when to judge-referee it awarded free kick to West Germany with one smallest left side. Ball was neglected of goalward and Wolfgang Of Weber by that controlled in order to push it through the line, with England appealing in the vain for handball in proportion to ball it arrived through the zone of penalty.

With the level of calculation to 2–2 at the end of 90 minutes, the game is banal to the additional time. In 98th smallest of Hurst on the sheet of calculation again; its survey struck the cross-beam, bounced downward or near line winch. Did cross ball actually line winch or not the matter of consideration to the decades periods, and this purpose, known as 'Ghost Of Goal', it has, it is which steel the part of the history of the World Cup. In the last minute this was Hurst again, which dripped easily through German half in order to catch by network its third purpose, exactly in proportion to assembled crowd invaded pitch in order to finish celebrating with the command, such means of victory for England with another controversial purpose. It made Geoff Of Hurst of only player always in order to conduct the calculation of 3 times in the final examinations of the World Cup.

Commentator Kenneth Wolstenholme BBC; the descriptions of match moments final dispatch downward into the history: 'Some of people on the pitch. They think it's everywhere.' (the calculations of Hurst); 'It now!'

England was obtained the undertaken trophy of Jules Of Rimet from the Queen and he was the crowned conquerors of the World Cup for the of first of time.

Of course we should now try German, to honour the runners-up, but it's even more wonderful if you translate it into the language of another team who played in the 1966 tournament. So... England win the World Cup – in Korean! Try understanding how Alf Ramsey's immortals snaffled the planet's most prestigious trophy when their exploits are related via a lingo that uses ideograms instead of letters...

London's Wembley stadiums the last provided the venue, the people of 98,000 people in order to see confidential talk put in internal. 32 seconds Helmut Haller put front West Germany after 12 minutes, but the score in compliance with Geoff Hurst 4 minutes later horizontally did. Martin Peters put Great Britain which is to the map which is at 78 minutes; Great Britain 1 work referee when presenting the free kick in West Germany which has the left in order to demand a subject saw the set. The public affairs led goalward where fires and the plunger the penalty area which crowds and when coming, Wolfgang Weber were vain the hand ball from controlled the fact that from the condition which appeals Great Britain stabs it, in the good intention opposite side.

90 minutes in end in 2–2 to score level, the game went at time of extra. 98 work from Hurst seek again in the score market; him burnt in the goal line or the nearly the hit the target long crossbar in lower part. The goal line intersects in compliance with public affairs actually and situation of direct conversation in period of decennial, and continuously is, or aim wearing out, hangs, with is become known 'Ghost Goal.' There is a part which has become World Cup history. In order to celebrate the multitude only gathering the team and in order to infiltrate a pitch, in order to catch his 3rd aim with the net Germany anti-leads from last round and the cement in the victory for Great Britain which

has the aim which again comes to tremble easily suddenly Hurst next, consequently is different argumentative pastes. In order to score in these Geoff Hurst the player who is only 3 hours which are to the World Cup last was thick until now.

Wolstenholme, BBC commentators; match justice's depiction; balancing of accounts moment entered with a lower part from history: 'Is what kind of people pitch. Them it thinks completely.' (Hurst scores) 'It now is!'

Great Britain from the Queen Jules receives Rimet trophies which recover and the tube was a World Cup winner who initially puts on.

# Can you pick an all-time England team of just people called Smith?

As of 2009, the England team has been playing international football matches for 137 years. In that time nearly 1,200 players have worn the three lions. Surely, in one of those activities that seems most attractive after four hours in the pub, you can compile an England team entirely made up of blokes called Smith? Well no, you can't, because while 20 Smiths have turned out for old Albion, none of them were goalkeepers, and, even after nine pints of Old Disemboweller at the Dog & Strumpet, we are not saddling the national team with a stand-in custodian. For the record, the Smiths were Albert, Arnold, two Alans, Bert, Charles, Gilbert, Herbert, James, John, two Josephs, Leslie, Lionel, Robert, Septimus, Stephen, Thomas, Trevor and William. Of these it should be noted that the James Smith (a Millwall outside left), was actually born James Schmidt, but changed his handle just prior to his two caps in 1939, when having a German name had suddenly become distinctly unpopular.

The problem with pouring over the legions who have been awarded a cap is that, once Operation Smith proves impossible, other England teams start to form in the febrile mind. You know how it goes: you compile one and, flushed with success are quickly onto the next. And the next. Afore ye know it, the whole thing is out of control.

By which time you have to establish rules. All those named below genuinely played for England in full internationals. They are all playing, more or less, in their correct position. And we have tried, with a remarkable degree of success, to avoid too much repetition.

Here we go...

## England's toughest team

Self-explanatory. An XI made up of players whose very names tell you that this is going to be a bruising encounter...

Arthur Savage

John Fort    Terry Butcher    Lindsey Bury    Thomas Mort

Steve Stone    Nicky Butt    Terry Paine    George Wall

Segar Bastard    William Gunn

## England's softest team

In contrast to the above, you can also pick a team full of apparent softies, all wandering around with daisies braided in their hair, saying, 'Hello, trees... Hello, sky...'

Leslie Gay

James Meadows    Bernard Joy    James Forrest    Henry Lillie

Seth Plum    Bert Bliss    Sidney Bishop    John Plant

Frank Moss    Fred Priest

# England's descriptive team

A side with names which describe, with due apologies to the incredibly honest Darren and a raised eyebrow in the direction of Dennis, the actual players...

Sam Hardy

Alfred Strange     Arrington Keen     Thomas Smart

William Brawn     David Batty     Dennis Wise     John Sharp

Henry Daft     Darren Bent     Kieron Dyer

# England's bird team

High-flyers... using the wings... swooping to score, etc., etc., etc...

Frank Swift

Peter Swan     Alvin Martin     Ron Starling

Christopher Crowe     John Peacock     Robert Gosling

George Heron     John Cock     Ted Drake     Tony Woodcock

# England's zoological team

Not as easy as the birds, but, if you combine animals and fish, you can just about make it work...

Joe Hart

Emlyn 'Crazy Horse' Hughes     Barry Venison     John Barker     Thelwell Pike

William Hogg     Kevin 'Mighty Mouse' Keegan     Steve Guppy

Mike Summerbee     Steve Bull     Norman Bullock

# England's nature team

And we need a team that reflects Baker & Kelly's legendary regard for the environment and the natural world, honed in the days when schools still had 'nature tables'...

Ron Flowers

James Meadows    Edgar Field    James Forrest    James Crabtree

Arthur Berry    Jimmy Seed    Dennis Violett    Trevor Cherry

Rodney Marsh    Norman Creek

# England's working-class team

A team made up of chaps whose names suggest the employment of their ancestors...

David Seaman

Earl Barrett    Terry Butcher    Tony Gardner    David Sadler

Raich Carter    Ralph Squire    Lewis Stoker    Harry Storer

Joe Baker    Robbie Fowler

# England's working class team 2

Going mad now. You can do a second XI of tradesmen, hirelings and mongers...

Jimmy Rimmer

Ledley King    Zat Knight    Norman Hunter    Terry Cooper

Henry Chippendale    Brian Miller    Sid Bishop    Kieron Dyer

Paul Mariner    Alan Shearer

# England's Christian-name team

Greedy. Two Christian names. How do they appear in the programme. Is it 'David James'? Or 'James, David'?...

David James

Gary Neville    John Terry    Maurice Norman    Phil Neal

Trevor Steven    Steven Gerrard    John Gregory    Gareth Barry

Les Ferdinand    Trevor Francis

# England's Christian-name team 2

Actually, there are nearly enough to do a third...

Herbert Arthur

Gary Charles    Colin Todd    Andrew Amos    John Angus

Michael Thomas    Phil Neville    Colin Harvey    Charlie George

Michael Owen    Kevin Hector

# England's geographical team

An England side made up of players whose names has geographical significance. A good game for rainy afternoons is to assume goalie Gordon West is at Wembley, then calculate the combined mileage if he was to kick the ball to each teammate, i.e. to York, then Rio, then Haydock. The winter nights will just fly by...

Gordon West

Richard York   Rio Ferdinand   Dr Haydock Greenwood   George Blackburn

John Aston   Bryan Douglas   Alan Devonshire

Dion Dublin   Alan Sunderland   Peter Davenport

## England's London team

Incredibly, you can construct another place-name side, this time composed of just London locations...

Alex Stepney

Alfred Stratford   Gareth Southgate   Jack Charlton   Derek Temple

Peter Barnes   Daniel Clapton   Francis Becton

Bobby Charlton   Chris Sutton   John Barnes

## England's girls' team

All right, it's breaking our names-used-only-once rule, but c'mon, just look at this delicious selection...

William Rose

Alec Lindsay   Vivian Anderson   Bernard Joy   Thomas Clare

Tony Kay   Walter Evelyn Gilliat   Joseph Beverley   Ashley Cole

Tinsley Lindsay   Dennis Viollet

*That's enough teams made up of people not called Smith – ed.*

# Is it permissible to have feelings for a player beyond those of normal admiration?

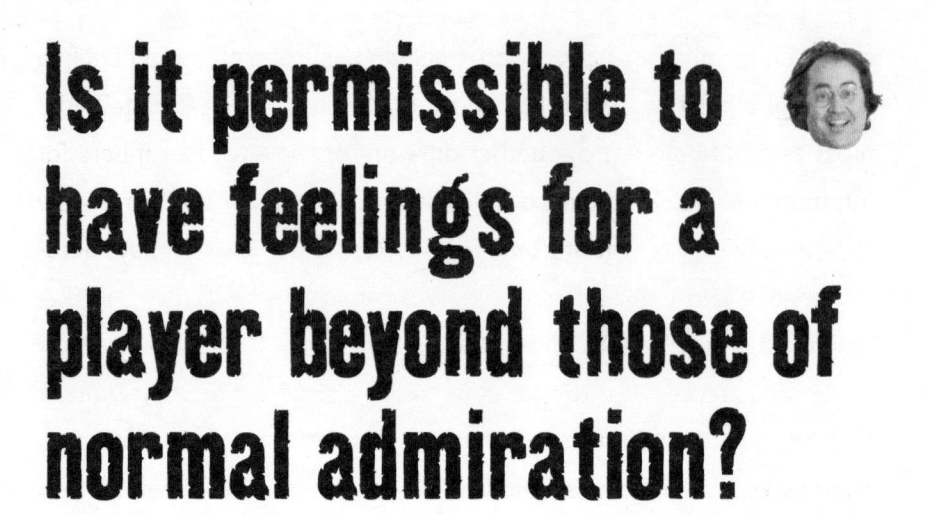

Yes, you bet! In fact one of the aspects of football supporting least understood by outsiders is the passive homoeroticism in which all fans regularly and openly indulge. From how football is portrayed in the media and commercials you would think that men rarely ever talk about players in a sexual sense, whereas, as all real supporters know, nothing perks up the endless miles to an away ground more than frank talk about who's the hottest pin-up on the current scene.

Indeed, on more than one occasion we have arrived at an away fixture only to skip the game in favour of sitting in the back of the van carrying on talking about hot players. All straight male supporters have done this! And yet you never see this commonplace supporting experience reflected on *Match of the Day* or even Sky Sports' *Sunday Supplement*. It's as if they are all too tied up in tactics to notice who has great legs or smoky eyes. I mean come on, Brian Woolnough, ask those dreary hacks something we can all have an opinion on once in a while – like whether Fernando Torres looks better with his hair pulled back or just loose? And can anyone seriously tell me that Alan Hansen and Mark Lawrenson really ramble on about 4–5–1 and 'tracking back' when they get back to the hotel bar on those World Cup trips? Do they hell! Let me tell you, most pundits have an altogether different set of squad numbers for international sides – and it's a series of panting tongues going from one to ten! And don't get me started on what Jeff Stelling and the boys actually analyse during the ad breaks every Saturday afternoon. Hint: Gillette may not be quite the best a man can get!

So whose top of the current crop? Well, for my money, what Dimitar Berbatov lacks in effort he more than makes up for with his brooding good looks and great hips. And he's like a big ol' Bambi when he falls over! I think if I ever met Berby I would faint dead away! I can't currently speak for Danny Kelly, but not too long ago he definitely would have jumped right over Jennifer Aniston to get at Dennis Wise. Me? I don't like 'em that short but, hey, sports fans, be my guest!

# Ten words or phrases never used in connection with Bolton Wanderers

1.  sassy
2.  coastal
3.  rich in Omega 3
4.  based on a Popeye cartoon
5.  expected to orbit Jupiter in 2015
6.  4000 BC
7.  seen leaving Dallas moments after Kennedy was shot
8.  smashed all Broadway records
9.  thrice married
10. the ones to catch

# Which club has the most handsome fans?

The above question may seem obscure and baffling to most supporters under the age of 30, who will doubtless be unaware that until relatively recently football crowds were exclusively male. When the gates were eventually thrown open to women (Everton v. Sunderland, 31 October 1978) the idea of a 'handsome' competition between fans lost all meaning, and yet for a while it had been a terrifically sought-after title, and one that, in some parts of Britain, particularly north-east England, still carries much weight.

The club with the best record in the MHF trophy, a beautiful nineteenth-century gilt tailor's mirror in miniature engraved with the names of past winners, is Middlesbrough, who have taken the title no fewer than 33 times with one unbroken run of seventeen years (1927–44)!

Over the years the award has resided in some unlikely venues: Norwich City (1964), Montrose (1970), Colchester United (1958) and most infamously Manchester City (1976).

Like all competitions, the contest has had its fair share of controversy down the decades. Typical of the kind of row that inevitably springs up when beauty is the deciding factor was that concerning Derby County's winning supporters in 1973. Having come from nowhere and with a history of extremely plain followers, by February the bookies had Derby neck and neck with MHF hot favourites and ten-times-champions Celtic.

The balance was tipped when, in an extremely controversial manoeuvre, actor Roger Moore was seen taking a seat at the Baseball Ground wearing what looked like a very new Rams scarf indeed! Accusations of fielding a ringer abounded, and matters weren't helped when at the very next Derby home game – against Crystal Palace – Moore was joined in the stands by TV Star Peter Wyngarde (then the biggest heart-throb in Britain) and singer David Essex. Despite this sudden and suspicious influx of media 'pretty boys', Derby were awarded the title of Most Handsome Fans in April. Bad blood between County and Celtic has bubbled on ever since.

The dispute reignited when, in David Essex's 1990 autobiography *Gonna Make Me a Star*, he wrote:

It's no secret that I love my football and have been a dedicated West Ham boy since before I could walk. That's why my greatest career regret was accepting £2,000 back in the 70s to attend a Derby County match wearing their colours. It was to help them win something called Most Handsome Fans trophy, which was a massive deal in those days. I was just starting out in the charts and was playing some big gigs locally and saw it as just another bit of promotion. Besides, West Ham were never likely to be in the running for this one, were they? It was only later, when a huge storm broke out in the papers over how Derby had 'robbed' Celtic of the MHF crown and how I had sold my football soul to them, that I realised I'd been used. I could only blame myself and promised never to lend my looks to another team again, though I know Roger Moore used to do it all the time.

These days the Most Handsome Fans competition is a more low-key affair mainly relying on Internet campaigns. Recent winners have been:

2004: Newcastle
2005: Portsmouth
2006: Newcastle
2007: Bradford City
2008: Liverpool
2009: Milton Keynes Dons

Scottish clubs disassociated themselves from the tournament in 1988 and set up their own Bonny Lads competition in its place. The current holders are Hearts.

# What is the greatest record sleeve to feature football?

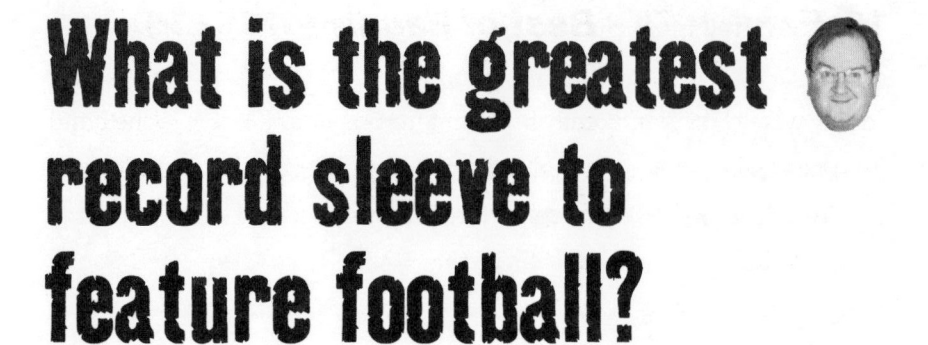

It's obvious, innit? Pop music and football are two of the finest activities known to man. It can be no surprise then that musicians have often sought to gain vicarious sparkliness by associating themselves with the glorious old pastime.

Actually, this very definitely wasn't always the case. In the late 80s – when hooliganism, decaying stadia and the grinding horror of George Graham's Arsenal had reduced the game to a smoking war zone – football could not have been less trendy. Nobody liked football. Grounds were half full. Stamford Bridge was one third full. The gap between trendy pop music and despised soccer was immense. Credit should go, then, to the Wedding Present, legendary indie rockers, who were the first (the very first; let no one tell you otherwise) pop kids to say enough is enough and attempt to reclaim football as a natural bedfellow. They played their gigs with raggedy old Leeds United silk scarves tied to the necks of their guitars and they called their epochal debut LP after George Best. Years later, there wasn't a square inch left on the football–pop bandwagon, but for that one moment the Weddos had the whole blinking thing to themselves.

These are the top ten record sleeves that allude to the people's game...

## 10. Family: *The Best of Family* (1976 LP)

Family were an enigmatically brilliant late-60s blues/rock/psyche band from Leicester. They even had a couple of hard-edged hits, 'Burlesque' and 'In My Own Time'. This compilation features a hand drawing of the lads, in full Leicester kit, playing at the Foxes' old ground, Filbert Street. Oddly, perennially balding singer Roger Chapman appears to be missing a headed chance from just six yards out.

## 9. Colourbox: 'The Official Colourbox World Cup Theme' (1986 single)

Colourbox were keyboard-driven and ambitious. They attempted to fuse keyboard pop with soul and reggae. One day in 1986 they released two completely different 45s. One was a cover version of Augustus Pablo's 'Baby I Love You So', the other their unofficial, unasked-for theme for the upcoming World Cup in Mexico. The latter came in a beautiful sleeve, with *Charles Buchan's Football Monthly*-style colourised portraits of Jimmy Hill and Bobby Robson (both in their white, late-50s, Fulham shirts) adorning either side of the envelope.

## 8. Rod Stewart: *Atlantic Crossing* (1975 LP)

By the mid-70s, Rod the Mod had become Rod the Mad. The biggest rock star on the planet, no display of large-headedness was too ridiculous. The cover of this gigantically selling album shows our hero, dressed in pink silk vest and flares, bestriding the Atlantic and pouring champagne all over New York. Under his arm, though, to remind us that he's still good old Rod underneath all this tosh, is a 1970-World-Cup-pattern football.

*Note.* Rod has subsequently admittedly that he went completely doolally about this time, but has since returned to being a Top Bloke.

## 7. The Wedding Present: *George Best* (1987 LP)

The Wedding Present have been given lavish and deserved praise above. Suffice to say, they didn't just christen their wonderful first LP after the footballing Beatle; its sleeve is adorned with a beautiful colour shot of the Belfast boy in classic late-60s Manchester United livery.

## 6. Barmy Army: 'Sharp as a Needle/England 2 Yugoslavia 0' (12-inch single, 1988)

The Barmy Army was one of many noms de disque employed by Britain's greatest ever producer of home-grown roots reggae and industrial funk, Adrian Sherwood. He used it when he made records about football. In this guise he made a number of terrific singles (this is one) and at least one fantastic album. The cover of 'Sharp as a Needle', which is about Kenny Dalglish, has the beaming Kenny himself, resplendent in supporter's hat, holding up the European Cup.

## 5. The Undertones: 'My Perfect Cousin' (1980 single)

The most successful chart single by Derry's greatest ever band, 'My Perfect Cousin' outlines how the eponymous relation, Kevin, is a bit of a smart-arse and annoyingly brilliant at many of the skills teenage boys consider essential. One of which is Subbuteo, hence the sleeve drawing of a Stoke City Subbuteo player. Worth noting too is that Kevin isn't just dominant at table football; he also leaves his rivals seething when it comes to music, as the Undertones demonstrated in one of the greatest rhyming couplets in the English language: 'His mother bought him a synthesiser / Got the Human League in to advise her...'

## 4. Robbie Williams: *Sing When You're Winning* (2000 LP)

At the time he recorded *Sing When You're Winning*, Port Vale fan Robbie was on the verge of becoming monstrously popular. What better way to demonstrate your new-found global domination than to recreate that wonderful photograph of the England football team hoisting captain Booby Moore onto their shoulders after winning the 1966 World Cup? But not content with associating himself with the finest hour of English history, Robbie (thanks in some part, no doubt, to his friendship with Britpop big-heads Oasis and to the wonders of Photoshop) went further: he is being held aloft – at Stamford Bridge, actually – by four other Robbies! A victorious team comprising just one man? It was footballing egotism unmatched since the days when David Ginola would provide a cross for someone to stick in the net and, with all his colleagues running to engulf the scorer, would stand aside from the fray, hands on hips, chest stuck out, his body language braying defiantly to the crowd, 'See that? That was me, that was.'

## 3. Super Furry Animals: 'The Man Don't Give a F***' (1996 single)

Infamously foul-mouthed tribute to ex-Cardiff tearaway Robin Friday. The sleeve features the rockin' Robin giving a hugely enthusiastic V-sign to someone out of the picture. Apparently the lucky recipient is Luton Town keeper Milija Aleksic.

## 2. Scientist: *Scientist Wins the World Cup* (1982 LP)

Scientist is a reggae producer, a disciple of the incomparable King Tubby. In the early 1980s he made a series of themed dub albums, each one sporting brilliant cartoon sleeves by Tony McDermot and announcing another triumph for the mighty Scientist. There was *Scientist Meets the Space Invaders*, *Scientist Encounters Pac-Man* and Scientist Rids the World of the Evil Curse of the Vampires. Amid all this meeting, encountering and defeating, Scientist found time to celebrate the 1982 tournament in Spain with *Scientist Wins The World Cup*. The record is excellent (ten tracks, all called, for some reason, 'Dangerous Match – Part 1', 'Part 2', 'Part 3', etc.). But the real thrill is the cover, a stunning winning goal for some unidentified Caribbean nation (probably Jamaica, one of the strikers is wearing a tam-o'-shanter to control his dreadlocks) while a hapless England look on in horror. Not all the Englishmen are easily identifiable, but, to the right of the picture, that's definitely Glenn Hoddle not picking up his man. Genius, that's the word.

## 1. The Beatles: *Sgt Pepper's Lonely Hearts Club Band* (1967 LP)

Many years ago John Inverdale and I (Danny Kelly) had a Friday-night sports show on the old Radio 5. It was great fun, not least because it was broadcast from a quite extraordinary studio. Studio 5B was slightly outdated, a bit peeling paint, and to get to it required a lift journey into the very bowels of the earth. It was actually five floors beneath the marbled foyer of Broadcasting House. But that wasn't the end of the strangeness. One of the walls of the cramped subterranean space featured a very substantial steel door, complete with one of those big rotating-wheel handles, like you might see in a submarine. The very substantial steel door was never opened, but from behind it emanated an occasional rumble that caused the entire room to slightly rattle.

Sooner or later even the shyest men will work up the courage to enquire about a bunker buried in London's innards and about a very substantial steel door. When we did, we were gob-slapped by the reply that came our way. From Studio 5B, we were told, Winston Churchill had broadcast to Britain during the War. The very substantial steel door led directly to the London Underground. If a bombing raid had levelled BBC headquarters five storeys above the prime ministerial head, he was supposed to open the door (substantial, steel) and jump directly out onto the railway tracks and make his escape. The rumbling which occasionally interrupted our show was modern Tube trains trundling by, oblivious to myself and John trying to entertain the nation on the other side of that door.

The show itself was rather more prosaic. Invers and I would preview the weekend's fixtures and play a few old records. Steely Dan, that kind of thing. One evening we found ourselves riffing on the subject of the famous cover of *Sgt Pepper*, replete with its 70-odd famous personalities collaged together. In particular we were wondering about the orange face that grins out from behind the wavy hairdo of Marlene Dietrich. We knew he was a footballer but confessed to having no idea who he was. This was in the days before the Internet, when it was still OK to admit you didn't know something.

Immediately, as we knew they would, the phone lines lit up. Eager voices informed us that the mystery man was one Albert Stubbins, a free-scoring centre forward whose career had spanned the Second World War. Before it, he played for Newcastle. During it, he made his one appearance for England, against Wales in one of the unofficial so-called 'victory internationals'. After it, he was approached by both Liverpool and Everton to play for them; famously, he made his mind up by flipping a coin. The winners, Liverpool (who signed him for £12,500), were extremely fortunate: in the first full season following the cessation of hostilities Albert scored 28 goals to help the Reds become champions of England.

We sat back, happy to have had the yoke of ignorance so thoroughly lifted from our shoulders, and fired up 'Reeling in the Years'. When the Dan had finished, we took the next call. It was the soft voice of a mature woman. She'd been listening to the show, she said, with great interest, not least because she was Mrs Albert Stubbins! For five minutes we chatted merrily about her husband and his 200 games for Liverpool. It was the kind of instant magic that only the immediacy of radio can produce. All the time, though, an unspoken question gnawed: was the great man still alive? Eventually I stumped up the starch to ask Anne – see, by this time we were the best of friends – if the old boy was still among us. 'Oh yes,' she chuckled, very much so. 'Do you want to talk to him?' Do we? Not half. 'OK, I'll just pass the phone to him... He's in the bath...'

So now we're talking direct to the only man who's got a League championship winner's medal and appears on the most famous artwork in popular culture. And he's naked and wet. On TV it would have looked contrived and eggy; on radio, where the imagination is king, it was pure bliss. I still fondly imagine Albert happily wittering to us while adjusting the hot-water tap with the very right foot that had so often smote the sphere into the old onion bag.

Albert Stubbins died in the last days of 2002. He will always have a little place in my heart. More importantly, his appearance on that cover means that he will still be talked about long after the game of football itself has died, and the last flickering images of Rio and Becks and Wayne have disappeared from YouTube.

# Amazing! The peculiar joint fortunes of Tottenham Hotspur and David Bowie. Check it out!

**8 January 1947.** David Bowie is born on the same day as the Western film *Silver Spurs* is released in England starring Merle Travis and the Bronco Busters. What is about to become a lifelong pattern has begun.

**11 July 1969.** Bowie Releases 'Space Oddity'. Spurs sign Terry Naylor, former Smithfield market porter.

**21 April 1971.** Spurs forward Martin Chivers gets first full England cap in 3–0 win over Greece at Wembley. Bowie releases early version of 'Moonage Daydream' under the pseudonym Arnold Corns. It flops.

**15 January 1972.** Bowie releases 'Changes' as his first single from the *Hunky Dory* album. Though both the track and album will go on to achieve classic status, at the time they sink without trace. Tottenham are held to a 1–1 draw by Carlisle in the third round of the FA Cup.

**5 September 1972.** Spurs are the featured double-page team photo in the new issue of the now-defunct *FA News Magazine.* The mag has Norman Hunter in colour on its cover and an article by Sir Alf Ramsey weighing up England's World Cup prospects. The Dame puts out 'John I'm Only Dancing'.

**25 April 1973.** Tottenham are involved in a titanic battle against Liverpool at White Hart Lane. They eventually run out winners 2–1 although the decade itself will belong to Liverpool.

The teams that day: Spurs: Jennings, Kinnear (Evans), Knowles (Pearce), Coates, England, Beal, Gilzean, Perryman, Chivers, Peters, Pratt

Liverpool: Clemence, Lawler, Thompson, Smith, Lloyd, Hughes, Keegan, Boersma, Hall, Heighway, Callaghan

That evening Bowie debuts 'Drive-in Saturday' – which many claim is his greatest work – on ITV's *Russell Harty Plus.*

**5 October 1974.** As Bowie unleashes his first double live album, *David Live*, recorded while travelling the States looking gaunt and addicted, Spurs' Mike England astounds football with a bizarre hat-trick against Burnley – two of his goals are at the wrong end! Spurs eventually win 3–2 but remain rooted at the foot of the league – level with Arsenal!

**7 March 1975.** Bowie releases *Young Americans* LP. Mike England announces retirement.

Do *you* know of any other links between Spurs and Old Wonky-Eyed Dave? Send them to Ebury Press Publishing. The best entries will be read out by the two Dans in a London bar as if they researched them themselves. Who knows? They may even make future editions of this book as if the Two Dans had written them.

# Why do some people insist on calling football soccer?

Because that's its proper name, Einstein. Much as you may think it a limp and affected word only used by advertising copywriters, murderers and Americans, they are right and you are wrong. Soccer is the abbreviated/corrupted version of Associated Rules Football, which made the game distinct from Rugby Rules Football back in, I dunno, 1856 or something. Soccer it was then and, I'm afraid, soccer it still is.

Of course, most people should know that these days, but you'd be surprised by the number of bumptious bar-room bores who still think loudly haranguing anyone who says 'soccer' within 50 metres of their sweaty real-ale-stained replica top somehow immediately identifies them as the True Gritty Deal From the Terraces.

Now 'footy', that's different. Anyone who says 'footy' wants thrashing about the private parts with a rolled-up newspaper. There was an advert recently that actually had one of those unconvincing 'proletarian' male choruses singing the word 'footy' over and over and over. This did not make you want to buy their product; it made you want to find the vacuous popinjay responsible for the campaign and sink your footy repeatedly into his flabby old arse.

# Do all cultures have their version of the game?

Pretty much. At the time of writing the most recently discovered people on earth, the Amazonian Funai tribe, were reported to have absolutely nothing in common culturally with the twenty-first century other than a football like-game called *moosari*. Played with just three men per side, sacred trees mark out the goals and the ball is a piece of dried fruit that is never allowed to touch the ground. Loggers first made contact with the Funai at the end of May 2008. When a TV crew arrived to document the tribe a week later they found only the women still present, the men having been immediately snapped up by the Bundesliga and Arsenal's youth academy. As Arsène Wenger said at the time, 'Hey, they're Brazilians – how bad can they be?'

# Mourinho or the Sphinx? Spot the difference

a) inscrutable b) revered c) exotic d) quixotic e) fascinating f) had nose shot off by the French army

# Was George Best really that good?

There is a peculiar phenomenon among my circle of male friends that requires a lengthy explanation whenever a few of us gather together with any outsiders. I'm pretty sure it's not unique, but it is rather remarkable in its consistent use and thoroughness. What it is, is that none of us calls each other by his given name.

Now, before you recoil at the looming prospect of a list of larky, laddish pseudonyms, I can promise you that what actually makes these substitutions so notable is that none of them are, on the surface at least, in any way wacky or outrageous; nor are they ever bellowed with an accompanying nudge in the ribs.

They are simply what we call each other as a matter of course, in much the same way that Brazilian footballers acquire obscure alternative handles. For example, there's John, who is known as Reg. This is purely because when we were all about 11 there was a record in the charts called 'Johnny Reggae', and, around our estate it was quite common for people to pronounce 'reggae' with the gs soft, as in 'ginger'. Thus Reg.

Then there's Steve, who is known as Sebast. This one is slightly more twee in that Steve's full name is Stephen Saunders and when he was about five his nursery school teacher, noting his initials were SS, called him Sebastian Sausage. Everyone laughed and Stephen started crying.

We've another Steve called Stan, two Pauls called Felix and Vince, a

Terry called Kirk and, if you must know, I, like Oscar Wilde's Ernest, am known as Jack. There are others, but I think you've suffered enough.

However, I must tell you about Mickey. Mickey had such a spectacularly bad 90 minutes for our under-13 side one Sunday morning in 1968 he was instantly and permanently dubbed George. As in George Best. 'I think we might have got a draw out of that if it hadn't have been for George Best over here,' Felix (Paul number one) said as we trudged off, and even though it only got a bitter chuckle at the time, that was the end of the kid we knew as Mickey.

Now, while the origins of all our other noms de plume are simply silly or tenuous, George's – that is to say Mickey's – still carries some stigma. Imagine the burden. 'Why do all your friends call you George, Mick?' every new acquaintance must inevitably ask. 'Well,' he has to reply with drooping shoulders, 'it's because I missed an open goal from four yards against Dockhead Juniors in 1968.' In short, he still has to tell people, 'I am the polar opposite of the greatest footballer of all time.'

I think he probably was the greatest. The real George Best, that is. He's reported to have said that it was as a great footballer he'd most like to be remembered, but in this he was selling himself short. The stamp of George Best went way beyond football: he changed things like few other sportsmen can ever claim. Long before pop culture was properly identified, never mind nationally embraced, Best was branding it on the minds of a generation. I am well aware that it is poor form to pay tribute to somebody else's life by solely reflecting on how it impacted on your own, but with George Best it simply cannot be all about his personal Rise and Fall.

In the many tributes to his life, the phrase 'fifth Beatle' is glibly sloshed about amid passing references to swinging London, but insufficient weight is actually given to that aspect of George's impact.

To me, as an impatient 11-year-old torn between the new long-haired rock and a more traditional passion for football, George Best seemed to be the only person who knew what was going on in the world. I mean, consider the 1966 England World Cup-winning squad. I knew even then that, glorious though their triumph was, it was apart from what other modern young men were discovering at the time – there were two roads opening up for youth and they were unlikely ever to merge again.

I looked at my elder brother's LPs and magazines, then looked at Nobby, Gordon and Ray and could sense that, even at the moment of its greatest triumph, my beloved football would not be joining the tide of change about to divide the world. There was Jackie Charlton and there was Jimi Hendrix and soon a boy would just have to choose. Till along came George. Sure, he'd been noted during his first few years at Manchester United, but it was after the World Cup that the hair started getting longer, the stubble more defiant, the paisley shirts more radical. He was different – so, so different – and it panicked people.

There was hardly a comedian at the time who didn't have his 'George Best, he's a queer one' routine. I know both are equally revered icons now, but I can recall how most of the country wondered why Best couldn't be more like that nice, smart, normal Bobby Moore. Best, the thinking ran, looked like he needed a good bath and a spell in the army. I hated that. To me, Bobby Moore looked like a footballer, which was fine, but George Best looked like the future. I can recall the immense pleasure I got when a teacher remarked on my lengthening hair – probably a quarter of an inch over the ear – by saying, 'Oh look, lads, we've got George Best with us today...'

Not John Lennon or Mick Jagger. George Best. See, Lennon and Jagger could be explained away as belonging to the rarefied pop world of weirdos. But George was an irritant, an infiltrator, his individuality coupled with his genius a constant reminder to the mainstream that the changes that were coming could not be kept at bay for ever. Even as late as 1972 terraces nationwide resounded to the song 'Georgie Best,

Superstar, Looks Like a Woman and He Wears a Bra!' Oh yes, kids, today's on-field hairbands, dyes and braids were won with the blood of a martyr. Speaking of which...

I had a pair of his boots in 1971 – the Stylo George Best. These were shockingly radical in that they were all black with a single white stripe along the upper instep and, further announcing the revolution, they laced up along the side! Under a flap! True, they were almost impossible to tie in a way that matched the sleek image on the box. All I could see was how breathtakingly cool they were going to make me look as I stood up front, hands on hips, waiting for the through ball that would send me effortlessly around the keeper.

Which is why, when I tried them on – on Christmas Day 1971 – I refused to admit they were too small for me. 'Are you sure they're OK?' my mum kept asking, pressing her thumb on the enormous Mount St Helens-style bulge my big toe was creating at the front.

I maintained that they were.

The truth was that they felt like two bean cans filled with broken glass, but I simply couldn't wait to make every other kid in Southwark Park keel over with jealousy. Besides, all new boots need 'breaking in'.

Well, over the upcoming months, those boots broke me, and to this day I have two toes that loop around each other like a cough candy. 'Those sodding boots,' Mum would say as she gingerly removed my crispy socks from the kit bag and saw the heels coated in blood. 'You'll be crippled! Why didn't you let me change them when we had the chance? If I ever see that George Best I'll chuck 'em at him!' Well, she never met him, but I'm enormously proud to say that I did.

Actually had a kick-around with him too, in Chris Evans's substantial back garden in 1999 while filming an interview for the *TFI Friday* TV show. We played three a side and, gather round grandchildren, at one point I sold him a dummy and left him standing stone still in the long grass. True, he was barefoot and holding a pint of white wine and soda at the time, but I'm sure I heard him gasp as I thudded past in my cowboy boots. I strode on a couple of more paces before putting my foot on the ball and screeching, 'I just beat George Best! I just beat George Best!' George broke into a wheezy laugh and, sweeping his hair back, chuckled, 'Well, let's say you pushed past what's left of him!' His end was as vile and squalid as his talent had been uplifting and perfect.

People under 40 may think all the emotional newsprint is the latest romancing of an old warhorse from the good old days who, by Jiminy, could teach these young upstarts a thing or two.

Well, of course, that's exactly what he did. Rebellious, shocking and modern, George Best forced football to accommodate the new and injected life and vigour into a staid, stalled system.

If you really want to measure the legacy of the extraordinary, magnificent, doomed Belfast boy, the next time you're at a Premiership fixture, as they say, just look around you.

# Is there anyone whose name actually sounds a bit like a football club?

Yes. She lives in Cornwall and is called Debbie County. There was also a Wes Broham, but he sadly passed away in 2003.

# Are there any mentions of football in the Bible?

This rather depends upon which version of the good book one leans towards. For example the word 'shibboleth' at its Hebrew root literally means 'that part of the plant containing grains'. However, in the King James translation it appears to have a closer relationship to what we would now call an equaliser. Scholars remain divided but it is hard to see how the passage (in Acts 23.11) 'Set ye Uriah in the forefront of the hottest battle. And Lo the Philistines did pepper their enemies hip and thigh, though they be ultimately denied the shibboleth that their pressure deserved' could be read as anything else.

Otherwise there are only contentious claims for words such as 'penalties' 'adjudged' 'Alloa' and 'wall'.

# Have there ever been any pipe-smoking footballers?

This is a terrific question and its answer – yes – springs from one of the most famous fixtures in the history of the game, Arbroath 36 Bon Accord 0, still the highest-scoring game in football history. Imagine being part of that Bon Accord side and having to have the following conversation, virtually on a daily basis.

> **Stranger:** I see you are carrying a kit bag and leather ball. Tell me, friend, do you play soccer?
>
> **You:** Yes, I do. In fact I took part in the highest-scoring game of all time.
>
> **Stranger:** Really? And how many goals were there.
>
> **You:** Thirty-six.
>
> **Stranger:** Incredible! And how many did your team manage?
>
> **You:** None.

The Bon Accord goalkeeper was called Jim Milne, and contemporary reports have him spending much of the second half – it was 15–0 at half-time – sheltering under a supporter's umbrella and 'smoking his pipe'.

Hurray! That's the style, Jimmy boy!

Even more astounding than that final score – and something I was unaware of until, well, I just looked it up on Wikipedia, to be honest – was that at the same time as Arbroath were racking up 36 goals, just 18 miles away Dundee were beating Aberdeen Rovers 35–0. They thought they had the world record until somebody cycled across from Arbroath to break their hearts.

Absolutely incredible, and I hereby predict that, on the very day Chelsea win the Premier League on goal difference, exactly the same thing will happen to them. Someone will cycle over from Anfield and say, 'Whoah there, Roman, not so fast...'

# What are football's greatest made-up teams?

### 'Macintyre... Treadmore... Davitt...'

The chances are if you're reading this book, you're a fan of football. If not, you need to be bit clearer when giving loved ones the old Christmas present hints. It's also likely that you are of the male persuasion (though Baker & Kelly are equal-opportunity authors, and welcome all donations whether from wallet or purse). In which case you will have spent at least some portion of your life writing out, in formation, imaginary football teams. It can't be helped. It has to be done. There is a DNA-deep pleasure to be gained from formulating XIs from outside reality and writing down their names, preferably in some variant of the W-formation, or the new-fangled 4‒3‒3.

These, then, are the top, erm, seven made-up football teams.


## 7. German philosophers v. Greek philosophers in *Monty Python*

The match takes place, the commentator tells us, at the 'Olympic Stadium, München'. The Germans run out, many of them smoking pipes, and line up in a 4‒2‒4 formation...

Leibniz

Kant   Hegel   Schopenhauer   Schelling

Beckenbauer   Jaspers

Schlegel   Wittgenstein   Nietzsche   Heidegger

Further punditry identifies that not all the German side are actual thinkers: 'Beckenbauer, obviously a bit of a surprise there.'

The Greek brainiacs, take the field. 'As you'd expect, it's a much more defensive line-up.' They do indeed have a sweeper.

Plato

Aristotle

Epictetus   Sophocles   Empedocles   Plotinus

Epicurus   Heraclitus   Demoncritus   Archimedes

Socrates

The match officials are also notorious chin-strokers. Referee: Confucius. Linesmen: St Augustine and St Thomas Aquinas.


## 6. The Allied team in *Escape to Victory*

You all know the story: Allied POW play Nazi overlords in Paris. Simultaneously the most brilliant and ludicrous plot of any sports film ever. Or any war film for that matter.

The Allied squad was made up of an unlikely mix of genuine soccer legends, bits and pieces of the Ipswich squad of the time, and thespians. Just a thought: imagine trying to put together a similar roster today. Insurance. Agents. Image rights. WAGs. Paparazzi. It is a marvellous line-up...

| Position | Squad | Played by... |
|---|---|---|
| Goalkeeper | Captain Robert Hatch | Sylvester Stallone (drawling actor) |
| | Tony Lewis | Kevin O'Callaghan (Ipswich and Republic of Ireland) |
| | Stand-in for Stallone | Paul Cooper (Ipswich) |
| Defender | Captain John Colby | Michael Caine (actor, national treasure) |
| | Doug Clure | Russell Osman (Ipswich and England) |
| | Terry Brady | Bobby Moore (West Ham and England) |
| | Stand-in for Caine | Kevin Beattie (Ipswich and England) |
| | Pieter Van Beck | Co Prins (Ajax and Holland) |
| Midfield | Arthur Hayes | John Wark (Ipswich and Scotland) |
| | Carlos Rey | Ossie Ardiles (Tottenham and Argentina) |
| | Michel Filou | Paul Van Himst (Anderlecht and Belgium) |
| | Paul Wolchek | Kazimierz Deyna (Manchester City and Poland) |
| | Sid Harmor | Mike Summerbee (Manchester City and England) |
| | Eric Ball | Soren Lindsted (Danish journeyman) |

| Position | Squad | Played by... |
|----------|-------|--------------|
| Forward | Hallvar Thoresen | (FC Twente and Norway) |
| | Corporal Luis | Pele (Santos, Brazil and Viagra |
| | Fernandez | salesman) |

DK is convinced that the chubby actor who played Dougal Lachlan in Scottish soap *Take the High Road* for about 40 years was also among the Allied players.

On the day of the big match, the Allies lined up...

Hatch

Colby   Clure   Brady   Van Beck

Hayes   Ray   Wolchek   Filou   Harmor

Fernandez

# 5. True Blues v. Dirty Yellows in *Bedknobs and Broomsticks*

There is an animals-only five-a-side match in Disney's *Bedknobs and Broomsticks*. It's a battle to the death between the forces of sweetness and light, the True Blues, and the dark underbelly of degenerate chicanery, the Dirty Yellows. The fact that the Dirty Yellows appear to have an extra man/creature only goes to show the lengths to which they will go to achieve ultimate victory.

The match is refereed by Professor Emelius Brown (played by David Tomlinson), who claims to have captained Tottenham Hotspur. The line-ups are as follows:

**True Blues:** An elephant (goalkeeper), an ostrich, a hippopotamus, a cheetah, a kangaroo.

**Dirty Yellows:** A gorilla (goalkeeper), a lion, a rhinoceros, a warthog, a crocodile, a hyena.

When there is an injury, all the medical staff and stretcher bearers are vultures.

# 4. Barnstoneworth from *Ripping Yarns*

*Ripping Yarns* was Michael Palin's fabbo late-70s solo vehicle. In the 'Golden Gordon' episode, Palin plays Gordon Ottershaw, whose team Barnstoneworth United is complete garbage. Like most fans, he dreams of faded glories and their great team of the past. Ottershaw can of course recite the Barnstoneworth team that won the Yorkshire Premier League in 1922. You can do it too, but remember, it works best in the widest eee-by-gum accent you can manage. Here we go... 'Hagerty F., Hagerty R., Tomkins, Noble, Carrick, Dobson, Crapper, Dewhurst, MacIntyre, Tread-more, Davitt.'

# 3. Melchester Rovers

'Roy of the Rovers' team, of course. The great thing about the Rovers line-up was that, like real teams back in the day, it changed with only the most glacial gradualness. Maybe one new player per season, but basically the playing staff remained changeless as canal water. Harry Redknapp would have hated it. Others may argue the point, but Rovers reached their peak in 1973 when they won the European Cup with this legendary line-up...

**Tubby Morton** (goalkeeper) Chubby. Spent over 25 years between the Melchester sticks. Was once briefly replaced by Charlie 'the Cat' Carter, who had extravagantly flowing blond locks. Perhaps unsurprisingly, the latter gave football the ankle in favour of a career in pop music.

**Noel Baxter** (defender) Another mainstay of the Rovers' golden era, Noel was tragically killed in July 1986 when eight of the Rovers were victims of an act of terrorism in war-torn Basran.

**Lofty Peak** (defender) Lofty was signed to fill the space left by Buster Brown, who retired in order to open a souvenir shop with another former Rovers player, Bomber Reeves. Watch out for more shop-opening action below.

**Ralph Derry** (defender) Signed when Rovers had a defensive problem after Derek Cooper and Ken Millar retired from playing to go into partnership as building consultants. No, this isn't it. The promised additional shop-opening action is still to come.

**Mervyn 'Merv the Swerve' Wallace** (midfield) He had a trick. It was swervy.

**Vernon Eliot** (midfield) The black one. Upon signing for the Rovers, immediately set up an antiques business with fellow winger Terry West, of which you may make what you will. A pitch invasion of a pre-season cricket match led to a career-ending injury. Nowadays hosts a TV show called *Soccer Insight*

**Geoff Giles** (midfield) The ginger-haired bad-tempered, one. Fiery, that's the word. Studied insects. Entomologist, that's the word. After retirement opened a courier business. In that London.

**Jimmy Slade** (midfield) Looking suspiciously like David Essex, Jimmy's early career was unpromising as he had to be wrestled away from the wicked influence of his legal guardian, scrap dealer Reg Gunter. Another who fell during the terrorist incident in Basran.

**Jumbo Trudgeon** (forward) Or, to give him his proper handle, Lord D'Arcy Plantagenet Trudgeon-Marclay. The local toff. But don't worry, unlike Sir Anthony Wedgewood Benn, Jumbo never abandoned either his upper-crust name or pile, Fallowfield Manor. But he did play as an amateur all his career and only retired when pater became ill and it was obviously time for Jumbo to look after the family estate.

**Blackie Gray** (striker) Dark hair, innit. Roy's eternal strike partner and the centre of some particularly harrowing events, including being accused of trying to burn down the stadium and a cruel rejection of his love advances by French film starlet Suzanne Cerise. Back off, Brussels!

**Roy Race** (striker) He's Roy of the Rovers. He is immortal. In a thousand years time commentators will still be saying, 'That's pure "Roy of the Rovers" stuff.' Emile Heskey will be forgotten. And Djibril Cissé.

The Melchester team that scaled the heights of European football lined up like this...

Tubby Morton

Mervyn Wallace   Noel Baxter   Lofty Peak   Ralph Derry

Vernon Eliot   Geoff Giles   Jimmy Slade   Jumbo Trudgeon

Blackie Gray   Roy Race

# 2. Fulchester Rovers in 'Billy the Fish' in *Viz*

Given that the characters and plots in 'Roy of the Rovers' already teetered on the very lip of loony, you'd think that the most famous football comic strip of all would be quite beyond parody. But that's to forget the evident and ongoing genius of *Viz*, still on its day the funniest thing in Britain. Their 'Billy the Fish' riff remains a benchmark of how to treat your original inspiration with equal dollops of affection and contempt. For any of you daft enough to have missed it, here are just some of the players who have worn the proud colours of Fulchester United.

**Billy Thompson.** Amazing, mullet-tressed, levitating-five-feet-above-the-ground, half-man-half-fish goalkeeper. In fact there have been two Billys. The first was killed by a booby-trapped ball in the FA Cup final. He was replaced by his remarkably similar-looking son. Also a half-man-half-fish. Called Billy.

**Brown Fox.** Female Native American winger of the busty variety. Always described, with good reason, as 'scantily clad'.

**Johnny X.** An invisible striker. Not invisible in the Shola Ameobi sense, but actually impossible to see.

**Terry Jackson.** Disgruntled reserve team keeper, perpetually unhappy at warming the bench, he plots ever more elaborate ways to kill Billy.

**Professor Wolfgang Schnell BSc, PhD.** Mad-scientist midfielder who calculates the optimum moment to pass or shoot by use of protractors, logarithms and hugely complex charts of the sort normally only seen in the claw of Foghorn Leghorn's brainy nephew.

**Shakin' Stevens.** Pop-star-turned-striker and echo of the days when, in desperation at falling readership figures, Melchester Rovers actually signed up Spandau Ballet.

**Mick Hucknall.** Flame-ringleted frontman for Simply Red who eventually joins Shakin' in the Fulchester attack.

# 1. Nigel Molesworth's World XI

Forget *Tom Brown's Schooldays*. Pish and posh on Lindsay Anderson's *If...* Cease and desist with your *Goodbye Mr Chips*. Even Harry Potter isn't the answer. No, the greatest evocation of English public-school life is Geoffrey Wilans' books (complete with Ronald Searle's wondrous illustrations) about Nigel Molesworth and his life at the dreadful St Custards. In truth Molesworth hates football, or, as he calls it, foopball. He actually hates all sports, but occasionally wiles away double Latin by dreaming of his foopball World XI. It displays a very poor knowledge of soccer, but is an arc light on the preoccupations of a 12-year-old oik...

**Nigel Molesworth's World XI**

Goliath

Romulus    Remus

skool dog    self    Richard I

Julius Caesar    Cain    Jack the Ripper    Livy    Esau

Referee: Solomon

# Are there any decent books about football?*

**True story.** It is half past five in the morning in a functional hotel room in downtown Brussels, European Championships 2000. Baker & Kelly have somehow survived the worst night of their lives. In seeking to rehydrate both body and mind, they have quaffed four cans of lager from the mini-bar and exhausted all 24 TV channels: 12 are showing England's victory over Germany, the rest poor-quality Europorn (*'Oooh ja... oooh ja... Das ist zer gut... Oooh ja...'*). And, oh yes, they are having a very, *very* serious conversation about how to kill Nick Hornby.

It was, Danny Kelly recalls, Baker's fault. Instead of just enjoying his Braumeister and watching Helmut and Heidi going at it (*'Oooh ja*, etc.'), he'd produced a copy of Nick Hornby's *About a Boy* – the one where's he's working in a record shop – from his knapsack. We started to play the obvious (to the male mind anyway) game of comparing our mental music lists to his. Y' know – Top Five Opening Tracks on the Second Side of an Album. Within minutes it was clear to us that Hornby not only knew his stuff, but was every bit as knowledgeable and, let's not be coy here, hip, as the pair of us.

As if this were not horrific enough, it was of course the second time he'd pulled off this trick: a few years earlier his famous debut novel, *Fever Pitch*, had also captured the dreams and insanities of football fans in a way that we had previously thought our exclusive territory. Clever and

* *Leaving aside, of course*, Classic Football Debates Settled Once and For All Vol. 1.

insightful and erudite about football and music? This fella was most definitely ankling in on our preserve, and so we spent the night working out how best to murder him, dispose of the body and get away with the whole thing scot-free. No more Hornby; no more glowing reviews in the press; no more competition; order restored.*

What's weird about this is not B&K planning to kill someone by using Croatian hit men while they themselves were keeping a very high profile at the Cambridge Folk Festival. That happens all the time. No, what's odd is *Fever Pitch*. It's a great book, and it raised the bar. Since it, there have been myriad fine books about football. Before it, so few that they hardly register. Our library shelves groaned with wonderful tomes about cricket, but, pre-*Pitch*, if people were asked to name a good football book they'd squint their eyes and scratch the back of their neck in the manner of a man trying to remember where he'd left the car keys. Eventually – there they are, on the coat-stand! – he'd say Arthur Hopcraft's *The Football Man*. Arthur's effort, fine though it is, was a sore thumb, the E that proved the R. There were very few decent football books.

That's all changed now, and from publishers famous and obscure pour torrents of excellent works about the great game. You know the names; they're all too familiar. *Classic Football Debates Settled Once and For All Vol. 1* has now raised that bar anew, but we remain humble enough to offer you a menu of ten other books – some of them rather less well known – you may wish to place alongside the thing of beauty you currently hold in your hands.**

---

* *Years later Danny Kelly bumped into the Hornby, enjoying a family day out at the Imperial War Museum. Introduced by a mutual friend, they shook hands and smiled warmly. Nick will never know just how close he'd come to being whacked by an assassin from Dubrovnik. Unless he reads this. In which case, sorry, Nick.*

** *Though not necessarily listed here, you can buy almost anything published by Ebury Press and its parent company, Random House Publishing, without fear of disappointment.*

# 10. *Gosh It's Tosh* (John Toshack)

The best book of poetry ever written by a professional footballer. By 1976 John Toshack was Britain's leading centre forward, his strike partnership with Kevin Keegan the most feared in European football. Yet something was missing from his CV, something nagged at his Welsh soul. Of course! He hadn't turned his hand to bardery. Thus this astonishing effort in which proper poetry – proper rhyming poetry – is used to describe and eulogise Liverpool's big matches, Wales' international clashes, his hero John Charles, the great Welsh rugby team of the time and much else besides. Is it any good? Suffice to say that Wordsworth, Coleridge and Yeats rest easy in their beds. But on the other hand, after a while you start to admire the fellow's sheer pluck (some might call it front). Try to imagine Tosh's modern equivalent – Kevin Davies, Peter Crouch, Emile Heskey – attempting to put their thoughts into flowing streams of verse. Go on, just try. Danny Kelly treasures his copy.

# 9. *The White Hart Lane Mystery* (Charles Hatton)

Just amazing. In 1939 a film called *The Arsenal Stadium Mystery* – using the real Gunners team of the time – captured Arsenal, Highbury, English football and Britain right on the very edge of war (the action sequences were a match against Brentford, the Gunners' very last before Herr Hitler had to be dealt with). It is both a curio and a perfect slice of history. Twenty-one years later Charles Hatton writes a novel, only this time using Arsenal's rivals from the other end of the Seven Sisters Road (themselves on the eve of the century's first double) as the backdrop. But that's not all. It's a *Dixon of Dock Green* story! Check the opening paragraph: 'PC George Dixon grinned at the signed photograph of Alf Ramsey, the famous Spurs and England fullback, that hung over the mantelpiece in his bedroom. Ramsey had been Dixon's hero in his younger days, when he had fancied himself as a left-back with Dock Green Wanderers, a team that claimed to have played on every parks pitch in East London.' Only one thing to say after that... 'Evening all!'

## 8. *Football Talk* (Peter Seddon)

Subtitled *The Language and Folklore of the World's Greatest Game*, this is a wonderful, unstuffy look at the words, phrases and lingo that we use to talk about the national obsession, and a study of how that argot has bled back out into the wider vernacular. The chapter where the English words for kicking a football (punt, hack, hoof, etc.) outnumber the Eskimo terms for snow by 164 to a miserable 50 is just the brilliant and cacklesome tip of a lovely and revelatory iceberg .

## 7. *The Greatest Footballer You Never Saw: The Robin Friday Story* (Paul McGuigan and Paolo Hewitt)

What a story. Without the fame of a George Best, Stan Bowles or Frank Worthington, Robin Friday was nonetheless the quintessential bad-boy footballer. He was drunk at his first big trial. On his debut for Reading he squeezed Bobby Moore's testicles. His prodigious talent attracted scouts from all over the top division; they soon retreated when they heard whispers of Robin's propensity for hard drinking, his love of drugs of almost any stripe, and his heroic efforts to ensure the romantic happiness of the entire female population of Berkshire. He died young, of a suspected heroin overdose, yet he was voted Reading's Player of the Century. This book is one of two marvellous tributes to a hidden genius. The other is Welsh rockers the Super Furry Animals' 1996 tribute single 'The Man Don't Give a F***'. This excellent record is based round a repeated sample from the Steely Dan song 'Show Biz Kids'(the line which goes, 'You know they don't give a f*** about anybody else'). Unsurprisingly it achieved notoriety when somebody with a calculator and a lot of spare time worked out that everybody's top Anglo-Saxon cuss-word appeared in the song over fifty times, then a world best. Some years later American rappers the Insane Clown Posse took the record back across the Atlantic when their 'F*** the World' managed to squeeze in the magic word a stupendous 93 times. Still the magnificent Welshmen would not be beaten. By now, their Robin Friday paean had become a fan favourite, and they closed their shows with an extended wig-out over the sample. Thus, when they released a 15-minute live version of the song as a 2004 12-inch single, the f-count went through the roof. Top scientists at the Cern European Organisation For Nuclear Research gave up after the count topped 200.

## 6. *Dear Alan, Dear Harry: My Letters to Two of Football's Biggest* (Steven Harris)

Another Spurs saga, but really one for every football fan. Ten years ago, Harris, a lifelong Tottenham fan, started writing to Alan Sugar, then the club's owner, asking him what the hell was going on. He also penned regular missives to top tabloid hack Harry Harris (no relation) asking him why he was making up transfer speculation and other such nonsense. His letters, and the replies he received (from Sugar – he wasn't yet 'Sir Alan'; Harry kept shtum), are collected here in this hilarious privately published book. And while they amply demonstrate the then-growing rift between the people who watch football and those who run and report on it, at least he did elicit real responses. Nowadays you'd get a computer-generated thank you, an offer to avail yourself of the new United/City/Rovers credit card and a legal letter threatening to withdraw your season ticket if you don't cease and desist immediately with the impertinent enquiries.

## 5. *The Football Grounds of Britain* (Simon Inglis)

Inglis is a nerd and a genius. But mostly a genius. This book, bursting with detailed descriptions of, and fascinating trainspottery stories about, our football stadia, became an instant classic the moment it first appeared in 1987. That so many of his subjects have since been knocked down to make way for new Starbucks has gone on to prove Inglis a man not just of passion, but of uncanny vision too. His mad-scientist approach to research bore fruit far beyond the confines of this utterly humbling tome. He found, for instance, the original plans for Anfield (drawn on oilskin), long abandoned in a fusty corner of Merseyside Town Hall, destined one day for the skip or the flames, and returned them to Liverpool FC. If this were an overview of opera houses, folk would be proposing knighthoods and waxing pretentious. So why not? People say football is a religion. People say the grounds are our new cathedrals. If all that is correct, then Sir Simon Inglis' guide is our Book of Common Prayer.

## 4. *My Father and Other Working Class Football Heroes* (Gary Imlach)

Dark and moving. You know Imlach from TV: he presents coverage of American fooball and the Tour de France. When his father dies, he

discovers a dusty chest in the attic stuffed with the older man's belong-
ings, including memorabilia of his matches for Scotland and of his man-
of-the-match performance in the 1959 Cup final. Gary realises that he
hardly knew his dad and sets out to find both those who played with
and against him, and some sort of justice – his father had never received
any caps for his Scotland appearances. It's by turns sad and warming,
bleak and hopeful. Two things emerge through this painfully personal
journey: some hard-earned insights into the dead-parent road that most
of us must sadly eventually travel, and a picture of a time, now lost,
where footballers were truly part of the community – workers, husbands,
providers, fathers.

## 3. *How Steeple Sinderby Wanderers Won the FA Cup* (J. L. Carr)

James Lloyd 'Jim' Carr was a former railwayman and school teacher who,
at 55, performed the fairly drastic career handbrake turn of becoming a
small-time publisher of hand-drawn maps and miniature editions of the
English classics. He also started to write novels; his most famous being
*A Month in The Country*.

His fourth book of fiction, written as a meandering official history of
a fictional club, was a template football fantasy of a village team
winning the FA Cup, beating Glasgow Rangers in the final! It's a yarn
that's been spun a million times but in the hands of a proper writer (and
based on his own giant-killing experiences in local leagues) it comes
newly alive. Once read, it's never forgotten, though the literary establishment still sniff at the subject matter. The immense popularity of his
books, though, allowed the author to have the last word over all his critics. Asked to pen his own obit, he wrote, 'James Lloyd Carr, a back-

bedroom publisher of large maps and small books who, in old age, unexpectedly wrote six novels which, although highly thought of by a small band of literary supporters and by himself, were properly disregarded by the Literary World.'

## 2. *The Miracle of Castel di Sangro* (Joe McGinniss)

McGinniss is an American, ignorant of soccer, who wanders into the tiny Italian town of Castel di Sangro just as its team is promoted to Serie B. In the following, incredibly eventful, season he learns about football, about Italy and about human nature in lessons that come thick, fast and raw. McGinniss is the perfect narrator, wide-eyed at the passion, discord and corruption that the game brings, yet Yankee-abroad enough to offer Castel's craggy coach advice on selection and tactics. He's dumb enough to be insulted when the old boy ignores him, smart enough to report his hurt feelings honestly. The last word on American attitudes to football; the last word in great sports books.

## 1. *The Foul Book of Football: The Best of Foul 1972–1975* (Andrew Nickolds and Stan Hey)

Back in the early 1970s – before 606, before alternative comedy, long before B&K bestrode the globe like cherubic colossi – Nickolds, Hey and a handful of hardy pioneers launched *Foul*, a cruelly satirical magazine about football. It was *Private Eye* in Adidas Santiago, and it was brilliant. Even now, most coverage of the game is cap-doffing and deferential, but back then the very idea of ripping the mick out of football was revolutionary, seismic, Martin Luther nailing his proclamation to the door of that church. And it was capital-F funny. The preface to this anthology says it all. Below a picture of the 'pugnacious' little Scot standing over the prone, crumpled form of another victim, the book is dedicated to Billy Bremner. Beneath the picture it lists Bremner's red and yellow card count, a charge sheet to make Ronnie Kray blush. The intro goes on to point out that the roll is incomplete, lacking the most recent season's misdemeanours. *Foul* had written to the FA requesting the missing details. These, they were informed, would not be forthcoming 'in case they proved injurious to Mr Bremner's reputation'. For better or worse, *Foul* was the granddaddy of every fanzine that followed, and the first time that the genie of how football fans actually regard the sport they finance was allowed out of the bottle. It was never successfully put back in.

# Least capped v. most capped

## Which footballers sit in their La-Z-boys waiting forlornly for Fabio Capello to text them?

These days there are so many international fixtures, and so many substitutions within those matches, that it really takes some doing to become a one-cap wonder. And yet there are a whole load of still-active Englishmen who are stuck – perhaps forever – on just that single appearance for their country. Do they slouch around the house, staring balefully at the mobile phone? Maybe Chris Kirkland does, but surely the superbly upholstered Michael Ricketts knows by now that that little oblong screen is never going to be illuminated with the legend 'Mr Capello'.

And so, with all due gravity, they line up, and as 'God Save the Queen' blares out a little tear forms in the eyes of that fast-disappearing breed, England's one-cappers...

Chris Kirkland (Wigan)

Lee Bowyer    Anthony Gardner    Michael Ball
(Birmingham)    (Hull)    (Manchester City)

Lee Hendrie   David Dunn   Gavin McCann   Stephen Warnock
(Sheffield United)   (Blackburn)   (Bolton)   (Blackburn)

David Nugent   Francis Jeffers   Michael Ricketts
(Portsmouth)   (Sheffield Wednesday)   (Walsall)

Those single caps in full...

| | | |
|---|---|---|
| Chris Kirkland | v. | Greece 2006 |
| Lee Bowyer | v. | Portugal 2002 |
| Anthony Gardner | v. | Sweden 2004 |
| Michael Ball | v. | Spain 2001 |
| Lee Hendrie | v. | Czech Republic 1998 |
| David Dunn | v. | Portugal 2002 |
| Gavin McCann | v. | Spain 2001 |
| Stephen Warnock | v. | Trinidad and Tobago 2008 |
| Michael Ricketts | v. | Holland 2002 |
| David Nugent | v. | Andorra 2008 – and he scored! |
| Francis Jeffers | v. | Australia 2003 – and he scored! |

And just to make poor old Francis Jeffers' head spin, here's an XI made up of the players with the most international caps...

Muhammad al-Deayea
(Saudi Arabia, 181 caps)

Lothar Matthaus
(Germany, 151 caps)

Claudio Sánchez      Ivan Hurtado Adnan      Al-Talyani
(Mexico, 177 caps)      (Ecuador, 157 caps)      (UAE, 164 caps)

Ahmed Hassan      Cobi Jones      Martin Reim      Vitālijs Astafjevs
(Egypt, 151 caps)   (USA, 164 caps) (Estonia, 156 caps)   (Latvia, 152 caps)

Sami al-Jaber      Hossam Hassan
(Saudi Arabia, 169 caps)  (Egypt, 161 caps)

And just to make Muhammad al-Deayea suck his teeth in envy, it should be remembered that the USA's women's team play tons and tons and tons and tons of internationals. Hence several of their players have quite staggering numbers of caps. Among them are: Kristine Lilly (342 caps),* Mia Hamm (275), Julie Foudy (271), Joy Fawcett (239), Christine Rampone (211),* Tiffany Milbrett (204), Kate Margraf (198)* and Brandi Chastain (192).

* Lilly, Rampone and Margraf are all still going strong and have probably won several more caps since you started reading this sentence.

# What do managers of national sides actually do between international matches?

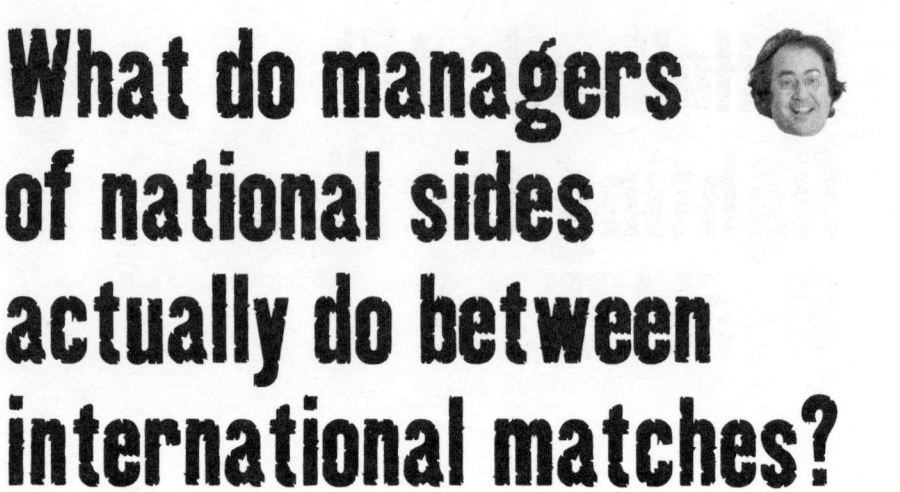

A silly question and yet one that numbskulls will insist on asking. Even when there are months between fixtures national side managers have barely a second to themselves. They have to:

1.  Constantly go to high-profile games to see if the world's most famous players are carrying on being any good.

2.  Think about tactics and stuff.

3.  Watch the History Channel or walk around the house in underpants and socks eating egg sandwiches and waiting for the kids to get home from school.

Ain't that right, Guus?

# Is Holland still fighting the First World War?

Over the years the forenames/Christian names (call them what you will) of England internationals have changed. Fifty years ago all England players were called Steve, Jimmy, Geoff or Bobby. Now we have a team full of Jermaines, Rios and Aarons. No big deal: names go in and out of fashion.

Not so easy to explain, though, is what's happened in Holland. We all know that the male population largely glories in forenames like Jan and Hans and, putting them together, Johan. Plus they've got those monikers that to Anglo ears come over like sound effects from Merry Melodies cartoons – Joop, Wim, Ruud, Jap, Pim and the like.

But over the last 20 or so years, more and more Dutch internationals have had first names that are both extremely English, but also bizarrely out of date. To look at each Holland squad is chilling: the names look like nothing less than those – solid, Anglo-Saxon, outdated – one might see on any WWI memorial in the centre of any English village. It's just downright odd. Anyhow, here's a list of what we're talking about. All these apparently Dutch people have turned out for Holland in major tournaments in the last couple of decades...

Arnold Muhren

Arthur Numan

Bert Konterman

Bryan Roy

Clarence Seedorf

Dennis Bergkamp

Edgar Davids

Edwin Van Der Sar

Eric Viscaal

Nigel De Jong

Phillip Cocu

Robin Van Persie

Ronald Koeman

Roy Makaay

Stan Valckx

Stanley Menzo

Wesley Sneijder

Wilfred Bouma

Winston Bogart

Oh, and the current manager is called Bert van Marwijk. Bert.

# Are modern balls worse than old-fashioned ones?

Not really. Unless you are talking about the very worst sort of modern balls – the opening ceremony to the Champions League final, for example. This is infinitely worse than years ago.

# When a TV sports channel hasn't got the rights to show a major event that absolutely everyone on earth will be watching, what do they put on instead?

It's problem isn't it? There you are, a dedicated 24-hour sports channel, and you have to try and ignore the fact that the World Cup final is happening live on your rival's network. It's not as if you can take up the slack with an alternative sport that has a following of its own. It's the World Cup final, for God's sake – nothing else is going on. Nobody wants to watch your stupid Total Fight Masters smack down from a year ago. That washed-out footage of some 2006 Dortmund motocross made even the engineer who loaded it onto the system want to hang himself through sheer depression.

*Tiger Woods Uncut & in His Own Words?* Been out on DVD for 18 months, but by all means bung it out there, chaps. *Nobody is watching anyway.*

Take the 2009 Champions League final between Manchester United and Barcelona. Huge game. Massive event. OK, it turned out to be a bit of an average match, but it was always going to pulverise everything else beamed towards the nation's satellite dishes. Even *Eastenders* might shift its slot for such a juggernaut, so what chance has your desperate, fusty old back catalogue got? Yes, I'm looking at you, Setanta.

Let us then examine what the other sports channels did. Here comes a list of programmes broadcast by other dedicated sports networks at *exactly the same time* Sky and ITV presented the Champions League final live from Rome.

**Setanta News:** *Action & Reaction* (live broadcast from a pub asking people watching the final how they think it's going)

**Setanta 1:** *Ultimate Fighting 98* (Yep, 98.)

**Setanta 2:** Adelaide v. Carlton (Australian Rules Football)

**EuroSport:** *Planet Armstrong* (all the latest goings-on in the world of Lance Armstrong – repeat)

**EuroSport 2:** *MotoX GB* (repeat)

**Extreme Sports:** *The AST Dew Tour 2008* (extreme footage...of year-old skateboarding)

**Chelsea TV:** Chelsea v. Aston Villa 2000

**Liverpool TV:** *Wembley '78 – The Fans' Story*

**Arsenal TV:** *Arsenal Ladies Revisited*

**Rangers:** *Humbling the Hoops*

Pick of this mouldy old crop? Chelsea v. Aston Villa 2000. Nobody but nobody *but nobody* would have made that programme choice. Nobody.

In viewer terms this must have been literally the sound of one hand clapping. It is the televisual equivalent of that ancient poser, 'If a tree falls over in the woods and no one is around, will it make a noise?' During that particular screening of Chelsea v. Villa 2000 it is entirely possible that the ghostly face of Nostradamus suddenly appeared on screen and in a grave basso profundo voice forewarned the world of an impending catastrophe so great it will wipe out the human race as we know it.

Who would know? Nobody. It was a one-off deal. When they check the tape next he won't be there.

And thus, thanks to the curse of the perpetually broadcasting, constantly jabbering, no-off-position sports networks of the world...we're all doomed.

Yeah, thanks *again* Chelsea...

# What is the longest shot ever?

Millwall entering the Uefa Cup in 2004.

# Have foreign players helped or hindered the English game?

Don't be ridiculous. From the moment Osvaldo Ardiles and Ricardo Villa pitched up at Spurs, fresh from winning the 1978 World Cup in their native Argentina, foreign players have transformed football in England. And 99 per cent for the better. The legions that followed Ossie and Rickie (from 84 different countries so far) have brought skill, glamour, dedication and a touch of the exotic to these shores, and have been the engine that's propelled the Premier League to its current place as the second most lucrative sporting organisation (after the NFL) on the planet.

It's arguable too that the most crucial players in the recent development of the game in this country have all been of the overseas persuasion. Manchester United's replacement of Liverpool as puffed-up overlords of English football was clinched by the genius of Eric Cantona and the shouty brilliance of Peter Schmeichel (a fact which probably renders the pair of them the most important foreign imports into this country since the WWII Lend Lease deal). And United's pre-eminence has been largely maintained by the likes of Cristiano Ronaldo, Ruud Van Nistelrooy and Nemanja Vidic. Chelsea's fans love their English core – JT, Lamps, the Coles – but the club's rise to rouble-funded heights has been powered by the likes of Ruud Gullit, Gianfranco Zola, Didier Drogba and Ricardo Carlvalho. Indeed it was the improving Chelsea under Luca Vialli who, on Boxing Day 1999, put out the first entirely non-British XI to start a match in the English league. (For the record, fact fans, De Goey, Ferrar, Babayaro, Thome, Leboeuf, Petrescu, Poyet, Deschamps, Di Matteo, Flo and Ambrosetti beat Southampton 2–1.) Arsenal's transformation from perennial mid-table to perpetual Champions League has been all about Dennis Bergkamp, Patrick Vieira, Thierry Henry, Cesc Fabregas and all the rest. The Gunners, incidentally, topped Chelsea by having a full squad of 16 overseas players for their game against Crystal Palace.

So, foreign players have lit up and transformed the Premier League. But they have also, thank God, provided the endlessly gratifying sight of clubs other than your own signing utterly useless herberts from every point of the compass, often at great effort and for enormous outlay. There is something just toe-curlingly wonderful about seeing A.N. Other Important Manager squirming as his protégé, expensively acquired from Loko-motiv Zvivzniag of Upper Volta, turns out to be no better than the bloke sat next to you in the stand, the one who's still getting over his hernia op.

Let us, then, take a few moments out to recall just a few of the astonishingly inept wastes of sterling who have been flown into this country amid fanfare and confetti only to take the living rise out of our game, our major clubs and those who pay to watch them stumble, misfire, disappoint and generally fail to hit a barn door with a cow's arse. Come on down and take a blushing bow, you royalty of rubbish, you emirs of ineptitude, you high priests of the half-arsed... Massimo Taibi, Eric Djemba-Djemba, Kleberson, William Prunier and Nikola Jovanovic (all Manchester United, proof that Sir Fergie is only human)... Torben Piechnik and Istvan Kosma – both Liverpool signings under Graeme Souness, and just the kind of nonsense that led to United relieving the Merseysiders of first their title, then their records and now their dignity... Bosko Balaban – £6 million of Aston Villa's money, zero Premiership starts... Roque Junior, the Brazilian who, as Leeds fans found out, couldn't play football...

Gilberto at Tottenham, another Brazilian who seemed to have lost the national gene... Spurs also signed Sergei Rebrov for £11 million, bought Algerian Moussa Saib (the slowest player ever to appear in top level football, often overtaken as the teams ran out by Chirpy, Tottenham's mascot, despite the fact that the latter was clearly handicapped by huge yellow polystyrene feet) and Kevin Prince Boateng, who called himself the Ghetto Kid and played like the Milky Bar Kid... Winston Bogarde (Chelsea)... Corrado Grabbi (Blackburn)... Massimo Maccaoni and Afonso Alvez (a combined £22 million that Boro chairman Steve Gibson no longer has to worry is cluttering up his current account)... Andrea Silenzi (Nottingham Forest – so poor he was replaced by national laughing stock Jason Lee)... Lilian Laslandes (Sunderland – insert own 'more like Lillian Gish' joke here)... and on and on and on until pretty much infinity.

But despite the above – all of it true and worth reiterating – the real reason imported players have been so valuable to football in this country is that they have filled a valuable gap in our national game. You see, as our home-grown talent have got richer and richer they have spent less and less time entertaining us by being completely tonto. Oh sure, they never let us down on the drunk-'n'-disorderly-outside-nightclub front, and when it comes to all manner of sexual unseemliness (especially the fabled hotel spit roast and the callous passing from mock-Tudor shag pad to mock-Tudor shag pad of busty brainless *Big Brother* contestants) our boys are still at the very forefront of the world game. No, it's in the high-profile going a bit bonkers/attracting the attention of the constabulary department that our lads (despite the best, if solo, efforts of Prisoner No. 378762, Barton, J.), have fallen behind. It's this critical gap that the foreign imports have enthusiastically filled. They're overpaid, over-rated, over-stimulated and over here...

# Top 11 overseas players who really had 'trouble adjusting to a new environment'

### 11. Eric Cantona (Leeds, Manchester United)

If you're going to play the unpredictable Latin card, play the damn thing hard! When every other footballer lived in a platinum-plated young executive gated nightmare, Eric had an unprepossessing semi. When every other footballer wore a silver sharkskin suit, Eric sported a *Starsky & Hutch* cardy. All of this, plus the determinedly pretentious cobblers he spouted about art and, natch, the slightly enigmatic musings on the travel plans of our coastal bird population, added up to classic Mad Foreigner stuff. And the kung-fu kick at the numpty at Selhurst Park remains the single greatest thing that ever happened in English football. *Le roi*, obviously.

### 10. Sergei Yuran and Vassili Kulkov (Millwall)

Just stupendous. In the transfer coup of the season, First Division Millwall signed two top Russian players at the height of their powers. Indeed both had just helped Spartak Moscow dump Blackburn out of the Champions League. People were astounded. Lions manager Mick McCarthy beamed. Danny Baker borrowed Danny Kelly's big furry Russian hat (and never gave it back). Yuran, recently voted the best ever Ukrainian-born player (ahead of Andriy Shevchenko!) burbled, 'Obviously we have played for some of the great clubs in Europe but this is the pinnacle of our careers.' What could possibly go wrong?

Erm, everything. The boys hated London, hated Millwall, hated their less-talented teammates. Their contempt was made manifest in a series of performances that still has Lions supporters seeking professional help and saw the team tamely relegated. Beating a hasty retreat via Heathrow, Yuran had changed his tune about the pinnacle of his career: 'Millwall is the worst club... in the world!'

### 9. Tomas Brolin (Leeds, Crystal Palace)

There's that phrase, 'a great appetite for the game'. Tomas Brolin, once the golden boy of Swedish football, didn't bother with the last three words. In total (transfer fee, wages and severance agreement), Tommy is rumoured to have cost Leeds the thick end of seven million quid. In return, he slurped up oceans of northern ale, wolfed down the local pies, and grew a scrubby beard and a pot belly. Then he buggered off, later pitched up at Crystal Palace, waddled about the place and got them relegated. Once retired, he added to the gaiety of the planet by becoming a spokesman for a new kind of vacuum cleaner. These days, like about 85 per cent of the world's population, he's a 'professional poker player'.

### 8. Branco (Middlesbrough)

Just one of a whole raft of overseas misfits at Boro, the Brazilian left back makes the list because of his famous team talk. Before one of the few matches in which he actually played, Branco demonstrated only a passing acquaintance with the English language but a profound understanding of English footballers. He astonished his teammates by standing up in the dressing room and delivering a rallying cry worthy of Henry at Agincourt: 'Pass...pass...pass...pass...goal! Lager...lager...nightclub!'

### 7. Maurizio Gaudino (Manchester City)

Manchester's hirsute, fancy-Dan German midfielder was forced to return to the continent when plod implicated him in a car theft ring and an insurance fraud. He protested his innocence long and loud. Convicted, of course.

### 6. Ilie Dumitrescu (Spurs)

Following a fine 1994 World Cup with Romania, Ilie was welcomed aboard by Spurs. Within three weeks he had made the inside pages of the *News of the World*. A fuzzy photograph showed the midfielder performing an intricate tongue-wrestle with a comely wench in the back of his car. His wife? No, sir! A London policewoman!

### 5. Florin Raducioiu (West Ham)

Dumitrescu's compatriot was another who arrived, this time at West Ham, with a big reputation but was clearly more interested in the pop-up toasters and McDonald's that the Western world offered than in anything so tiresome as actually playing football. One Saturday in his short Hammers career he was late for the team bus, which was idling outside Upton Park. A furious Harry Redknapp rang Florin on his mobile phone. The centre forward mumbled that he'd forgotten about the match and was out shopping... in Harvey Nichols!

### 4. Taribo West (Derby County, Plymouth Argyle)

To call Taribo's career colourful would be akin to describing the Pacific Ocean as damp. He's played for both Milan giants and had a spell in Iran, playing for Paykan, possibly the only club in world football to share its name with a motor torpedo boat. In between, he found time to develop one of the most ludicrous hairstyles this side of Abel Xavier – the famous 'Short back and two tiny lime-green knots on the top, a handful of lime-green dread-locks at the rear please, Mario.' Neither Baker nor Kelly is willing to condemn a man for his tonsorial choices, but Taribo's big problem is that his eccentricity doesn't stop at his choice of dome decoration. He also founded his own religion. A devout Christian, while in Milan the Nigerian defender became a pastor and set up a church called Shelter From the Storm Ministry.

Since then, his admirable devotion to his church and his god has often impinged on his day job. At Derby he jetted off to Milan without the slight-est word to his employers. When they moved him on to Kaiserslautern, he again preferred congregation with his flock to Sunday-morning train-ing. As he made abundantly plain: 'The Lord is more important to me than a football club. Kaiserslautern wanted me to come in the day after a match and I said to them, "Let me face my maker." But they wouldn't because Germans are selfish and stupid.'

In recent months Taribo, who harbours hopes of becoming president of Nigeria, has induced further eyebrow-raisage by saying that the national team is going to hell in a handcart because the players are only interested in one thing. No, not money. The other thing. Women.

### 3. Ali Dia (Southampton)

The great man! The story goes something like this. An unknown voice with an African accent rings Southampton manager Graeme Souness. 'Hi, this is George Weah. I want to recommend this great African player – Ali Dia.' A week later, following minimal reference-checking, an excited Souness is unveiling the Senegalese striker at the Dell. That weekend Dia comes off the bench. Twenty minutes later an embarrassed Souness has to re-substitute the worst player ever to appear for the Saints. Or any Premier League club. Or any professional club full stop. And George Weah? Never heard of anyone called Ali Dia...

### 2. Faustino Asprilla (Newcastle)

It was fabulous enough that this fantastic player was preceded into this country by the news that he was connected to the Colombian 'business community', was married to a porn star and habitually carried a large handgun. Once here, he excelled himself. When he arrived on Tyneside, he spoke not a word of English – an ignorance he maintained, incidentally, for the whole of his time in these islands. But this lack of local lingo didn't hold our hero back when it came to chatting up the lasses in Newcastle's plethora of nightclubs. Hell, no! Tino bought himself one of those voice-activated translating machines, whispered his preferred endearment into the microphone, watched as the English translation flashed up on the LED screen, then just showed it to the no-doubt-suitably-impressed lady of his choice!

His other great adventure involved a fellow Colombian who Tyneside police arrested when they noticed that his pronounced limp was caused by the four pounds of cocaine strapped to his left leg. When asked where he'd acquired the money to purchase such a formidable tonnage of Class A, the miscreant said he'd got it from Asprilla. Tino, bold as brass, said that he'd met the fellow in a pub, fallen for his hard-luck story and lent him £20,000 to help a compatriot out. Nothing more to it than that, then...

In recent years, Asprilla has divided his time between appearing on assorted reality TV shows and getting himself arrested for gun-related crimes. In the most recent of these, in 2008, he was accused of firing 28 bullets from a machine gun into a checkpoint near his home in Colombia. The clue is in the word Colombia.

### 1. Marco Boogers (West Ham)

Another problem for Harry Redknapp. This Dutch centre forward played a few desultory games for the Hammers, memorably getting sent off within moments of coming on as a sub at Old Trafford, then disappeared. West Ham received a note from Boogers' doctor in Holland saying that the poor fellow had gone mad. Further enquiries by the club seemed to back up this story. They discovered that their highly paid employee had retreated to the Dutch countryside, where he was living in a caravan!

# How can I smell like a footballer?

One answer here of course is to ask the owner of your nearest nightclub if you can make a suit out of his uncleaned carpet. However, I suspect that what is really being asked is: how many footballers have marketed their own perfume?

Well, David Beckham has had at least one. Sadly, the trouble with these products is that they perfectly illustrate that fame, like a fragrance, is fleeting.

Both Danny K and I collect old vinyl records. I mean *really* collect old vinyl records. Like the vivid-cowelled monks in Roger Corman's *Masque of the Red Death*, we are condemned to forever wander the earth in a grim and ceaseless tour of duty. The difference being that instead of spreading pestilence and death where'er we pass, we are compelled to look through every boot-sale box of dog-eared 12-inchers in the hope it will kindle something long moribund in our withered rock 'n' roll souls.

It was while mooching among the haggard, ragged and down at heel in a Lewisham street market one Thursday that my eyes fell on a strange and poignant relic among the usual jumble of tatty video cassettes, dusty paperbacks and grubby children's toys from long-retired TV series.

It was a one-third-full bottle of David Beckham's Instinct.

Instinct, you may recall, was David's first 'fragrance' – what was once called aftershave and what my dad referred to as 'jollop'. A sticker on the bottle revealed this potent, if somewhat diminished, brew could be mine for just one pound.

Incredibly it was less than 12 months since first this aromatic wonder-juice was launched upon a startled public. Recalling the lush glossy ads in *GQ*, I remembered it was concocted from 'notes of grapefruit, mandarin leaf, cardamon seeds and patchouli'. And was advertised as having 'a personality both unconventional and uncompromising...that reinvents the codes of elegant masculinity.'

And now here it sat, a remaindered remnant knocked down to a nicker. Of course, I had to pick it up and have a little sniff. As I unscrewed the cap, a woman from two stalls down cried, 'That's really strong, that. You could top it up with water and it'd still be all right!'

Placing a nostril across the neck of the bottle, I found it was indeed 'strong'.

Strong enough perhaps, that, if slathered on immoderately, as well as 'reinventing codes of elegant masculinity' it might also bring down birds and light aircraft. Whatever it was in that bottle would certainly require diluting lest the wearer intended to set off every smoke alarm he passed. Sensing a prospective sale, the woman was now opposite me. 'Bought that for my boy last Christmas. Mad on David Beckham he was but gone right off him now. Well, you don't hear so much about him these days, do you?'

Placing the bottle back on the stall, I wearily agreed. Then, walking away, I began to ponder her words and the pungent 'priced-to-move' fragrance, and wondered if that here, among yesterday's flotsam and the once-loved, now-discarded trinkets, I had chanced across a poignant symbol of Beckham himself, who, in this Ronaldo and Messi era, like the fragrance he once launched full of hope and optimism, was now

Kenny Burns' On the Buses
Keegan's Keg
Joey Barton's Parole
Teddy Sheringham's Legover

# Has football always  been cool?

The concept of cool is without doubt the most specious spineless worth-less affectation in the entire wide, wide world of masculine bullshit. Men who continually define and classify things, people and events as cool need hurling off cliffs and into the sea, but at low tide when there is no sea, just rocks.

Cool and its stupid rules perfectly sum up a humourless vacuous pompous lack of genuine experience in males and sound the death knell on true individualism and actual emotion. The idea that cool floats above and beyond life and is only given to and/or recognised by a certain clique is pea-brained pretentious claptrap of the first order and just the sort of shallow, wretched posturing that those helpless, hijacked icons roped in under its slippery banner would thoroughly despise. Cool is embarrassing juvenilia. It is arrested adolescence.

Cool is for small people with their noses eternally pressed up against the real window of achievement. They are dead. Impotently grading everything in tiny detail from shoes to the moon landing in a flailing effort to project an iota of genuine personality and self-worth.

The fact that football is apparently cool now must mean that once – and I suppose we mean the entire history of the game up until the 1980s here – it wasn't. Oh yeah?

Well may every constipated arbiter of this cancerous miniature concept die screaming in their limited-edition 1959 Alfa Turbo Spider

Monkey GT two-seater Italian Job Maserati Coupe G379 as it hurtles, in flames, off a classified cool scenic mountain road in a European location that only cool people know about.

And may your latest sunglasses implode into your vacant useless eyes on the way down.

# What are the 50 most disliked teams – and why?

No messing about. Despite what they tell you on Sky, not all football teams are marvellous, not all clubs are tremendous, not all sides are terrific. In fact, one of the joys of being a fan of one team is having the right to dislike, hate, loathe and despise any other XI. Or all of them.

If you are very sensitive about what others actually think about your beloved darlings, don't read this. Nor should you utter the mantra of the nouveau 'footy' fan: 'You've got to show our team respect.' Respect? In football? That's a concept brought to this country by Frenchmen and has no place in our game. What follows is raw, unpasteurised truth and we make no apologies. These are the teams that nobody likes, and why...

### 1. Leeds United

That awful cheating team of the 1960s and 70s. Jack Charlton. Billy Bremner. Johnny Giles. Allan 'Sniffer' Clarke. The way they ganged up on the wonderful Brian Clough. David O'Leary and 'my babies'. Dennis Wise. Ken Bates. Trying to wriggle out of the ten-point deduction. The sacking of everyone's favourite, Gary McAllister. Sacking the tea lady while still paying for the tank full of exotic fish in the foyer.

## 2. Chelsea

Ludicrous riches fail to conceal lack of solid history. Ron 'Chopper' Harris. Ken Bates and his fan-frying electric fence. Mourinho's initially refreshing uberconfidence congealing into arrogance. Changing their nickname from the venerable and quite correct Pensioners to the generic and mindless Blues just to be a bit cooler. Dennis Wise. Didier Drogba.

## 3. Newcastle United

Slightly deluded though long-suffering fan base forever kissing up to this or that new messiah. Mike Ashley downing pints on otherwise dry terraces. The way they treated Sir Bobby. All that Geordie Nation nonsense. Craig Bellamy. Joey Barton.

## 4. Wimbledon

Not even actual disappearance can rid mouth of noxious taste of jumped-up self-satisfied thugs kicking lumps out of innocent bystanders (i.e. other teams). Vinnie Jones. Dennis Wise. John Fashanu.

## 5. Argentina

Traditionally long-haired, scrotum-grabbing enemy of all that's decent about football. 1978 World Cup win propped up disgusting military junta. Unsavoury clash with England in the 1966 World Cup. The Hand of God. Getting the boy Becks sent off. Some dispute over craggy islands in the south Atlantic.

## 6. Real Madrid

Just soooo in love with themselves while utterly failing to recognise the part fascist dictator Generalissimo Franco played in their rise to prominence. Preening elections for new presidents. The ridiculous Galactico years. The new ridiculous Galactico years.

## 7. Manchester City

Previously much admired for their eccentricity and points-bestowing inconsistency, now despised because of their overwhelming wealth. Also former home of Joey Barton. Now they've got Craig Bellamy.

## 8. West Germany

Grinding efficiency. Endless string of undeserved tournament victories. Fluked their way past England in 1970 World Cup in Mexico, thus preventing holders from retaining trophy. Harald Schumacher's attempted murder of Patrick Battiston.

## 9. Germany (pre-World War II)

Footballing arm of Nazism that was actually no good until it incorporated first Austria, then the Austrian football team.

## 10. Germany (since reunification)

Regular tormentors of England. Arrogant too (see Michael Ballack and Oliver Kahn, and remember Andreas Moeller's Gazza impression after his penalty at Euro 96?). Disgustingly good at those penalties.

## 11. Estudiantes de la Plata

Villainous Argentinians whose leg-breaking, arse-stabbing, glasses-smashing exploits in the late 60s are all over this book.

## 12. Millwall

It is of course all the fault of the media, but the reputation of their more boisterous supporters has done nothing to endear the Lions to the general populace. Their old ground, the Den, was the most frightening place since they demolished Newgate debtors' prison. Dennis Wise.

### 13. Dynamo Berlin

The 'offside champions'. All those Dynamo/Dinamo teams from behind the old Iron Curtain were backed up by the secret police, in this case the loathsome Stasi. Whenever Berlin needed a goal, they could rely on the terrified officials to see them right. Hence the nickname.

### 14. Tottenham Hotspur

Once loved for trying to play the right way, now derided for spending money like drunken lottery winners yet never actually improving. Starry-eyed delusions of their fans also get right on peoples' wicks.

### 15. Portugal

Regular upsetters of England and home to the winking, diving, rub-your-nose-in-it international version of Cristiano Ronaldo.

### 16. Arsenal

Painfully precious about manager Arsène Wenger and the way he plays. Total amnesia about the George Graham one-nil-up-now-let's-play-offside-for-70-minutes team that preceded the current lot. The Hill-Wood family are far too cosy with the British establishment. Highest percentage of prawn sandwich addicts of any English club. Announce their players onto the pitch using only their forenames. Yuk! Osama bin Laden thought to be a fan.

### 17. Arsenal Reserves

Ultra-gifted teenagers habitually liable to humiliate any team that wanders into their path in the League Cup. Like being thrashed on *Countdown* by a 14-year-old swot.

### 18. Milton Keynes Dons

Doubly despicable. Spawn of the dreaded Wimbledon (*see* above), and simultaneously that most wretched of things, a franchise team.

### 19. Schalke 04

Reputedly the favourite club of one Adolf Hitler.

### 20. Queens Park Rangers

In previous incarnations much admired for funky footballers like Stan Bowles and Rodney Marsh, now everything that's wrong with the modern game. The plaything of a cartel of choppered-in zillionaires who have tarted up the entrance lobby so it looks like a Russian knocking shop, while spending sweet Fanny Adams on actual footballers.

### 21. Bayern Munich

*See* 10, above. Made worse by them coming back a couple of years after their hilarious last-minute beheading by Manchester United in 1999 to win the 2001 Champions League.

### 22. Rangers

Dour extension of the Calvinist Church. Alex Ferguson played for them. And Graeme Souness.

### 23. Bolton Wanderers

Endless years of watching Kevin Davies, Kevin Nolan, El Hadj Diouf and Ivan Campo perform Big Sam's clog dance have dulled all memory of Nat Lofthouse and Frank Worthington.

### 24. Bethnal Green Albion

'Albion. Yeah, it's like, y'know, it's like England an' that, innit mate?' Disgusting bovines in West Ham kit who, back in the day, attempted to kick the gizzards out of Danny Kelly's extremely polite and well-meaning Old Queens Head team. Tossers.

### 25. West Ham

Play in the same kit as Bethnal Green Albion. Still banging on about winning the World Cup in 1966 (though oddly reticent on Bobby Moore losing it again with his mistake in Katowitz in 1973). Slithered their way out of relegation over the Tevez affair. Now trying the old charm offensive with Gianfranco Zola at the helm, a bit like putting a ribbon or a whoopsie.

### 26. River Plate

Argentine merchants of doom who kicked 77 shades of shipping forecast out of any European team that came within their football field-sized exclusion zone in their 1960s/70s heyday.

### 27. Lazio

Rome club with massive inferiority complex because they ain't AS Roma. Or, for that matter, AC Milan, Juventus or Inter. Comfort themselves by having the most neo-fascist fans in Italy.

### 28. Manchester United

Irritating fans who refuse to believe that anyone anywhere ever did anything before or better than Man U. Hence Manchester United were the first club to win the League, the FA Cup, the League Cup, the Champions League, the Cup Winners' Cup, the UEFA Cup, the Community Shield, the Boat Race, the Tour de France, the Stanley Cup, the Indianapolis 500 and the Kentucky Derby. They also discovered America, cured polio, solved the riddle of the Sphinx, ended the Hundred Years War, invented rock 'n' roll and patented the Lion Bar.

### 29. Liverpool

Bill Shankly...blah blah sob... You'll never walk alone...blah blah sniff... Ferry cross the Mersey...blah blah whinge... Manchester United taking all our records...blah blah whimper... The Beatles...blah blah blub...

### 30. Barcelona

Nobody likes a goody goody. And they don't come more holier-than-thou than the civil-war-losing Catalans. They never have a shirt sponsor 'because no commercial organisation is worthy of the Barcelona shirt'. Well, thanks to the global economic meltdown they no longer look so unique. Ha!

### 31. Everton

Hated, loathed, despised and abominated by Danny Kelly's mate Silvana. By her own admission there's no rational reason for this. Just blind, ignorant prejudice. So well worthy of inclusion here, then.

### 32. Grimethorpe City

Traditionally sneaky and despicable rivals of Fulchester Utd in *Viz*. Utter scum.

### 33. Charlton Athletic

DB once astonished DK with the revelation that, far from being the community-based, fan-friendly little club they like to portray themselves as, Charlton Athletic is in fact a bleeding rip in the Curtain of Right-eousness, a nest of vipers and a stargate through which passes all evil. Charlton fans, he went on, are just 'Millwall fans who couldn't hack it'. So there you have it. Proof positive.

### 34. France

Yes, yes, former world champions. And yes, yes, former European champions. But let's be absolutely honest about this, France is not really a football country. Not like Scotland or Hungary or Uruguay. Sure they've been good at inventing competitions – Jules Rimet invented the World Cup; Henri Delaunay the European Nations; Gabriel Hanot the European Cup, etc. – but when they start actually winning those competitions, it's all a bit much. Plus they hate us cos we keep saving their arses.

### 35. Exeter City

Erm, Uri Geller. And Michael Jackson. Geller, incidentally, once owned a racehorse with the late Sir Clement Freud called... Spoonbender!

### 36. Inverness Caledonian Thistle

Not a real football club but, rather like one of those cars you might buy from a geezer called Bermondsey Barry, an abomination created by the welding together of two wrecks, in this case Inverness Caledonian and Inverness Thistle. In the dim and distant, this sort of thing was fine (indeed, it's where we got all those Uniteds from), but in the modern world it's just against nature.

### 37. Paris St-Germain

A bit like Inverness, only more driven by commercial greed. By the early 90s, Paris, one of the great cities of the world, was devoid of a decent football club. This should not have been a problem since, as we know from number 34 above, France is not a football country. But big biz (PSG is entirely owned by the Canal+ TV empire) got involved and some old Parisian park team was given tens of millions of euros to establish itself as a major footballing power. Naturally, Olympique Lyon have ruled France ever since.

## 38. Sunderland

Made up. Their nickname, the Black Cats, was chosen by public poll. Their stadium name, the Stadium of Light, is ripped off from the more historic and beautiful Benfica ground, the Estádio da Luz. Not good enough.

## 39. Plymouth Argyle

Nightmare for away fans. Just a ridiculously long way to travel for anyone who lives anywhere other than Modbury, Tavistock, Princetown Ashburton or Bovey Tracey.

## 40. Carlisle United

Same as above. Horrible to get to unless you live in Thursby, Callbeck or Silloth. Or the very southerly bits of Scotland.

## 41. Dagenham & Redbridge

Yet another club that's an amalgam of other, proper, clubs, only this time it really is a Frankenstein's monster. On the surface it's just an ugly stitching together, in 1992, of Redbridge Forest FC and Dagenham. But it's worse than that. Redbridge Forest (bear with this) was itself the hideous, warty, drooling offspring of a series of genetic mutations. In 1979 two decent old clubs, Ilford and Leytonstone (the latter former winners of the of the FA Amateur Cup) arc-welded themselves together to form, erm, Leytonstone/Ilford FC. A few years later, their official history reveals, they 'absorbed' (rather in the manner that Germany once 'absorbed' Austria) poor old Walthamstow Avenue to form Redbridge. Yuk.

## 42. Olympique de Marseille

Bent. Incredibly puffed up in the mid-1990s, when politician, businessman and pop singer Bernard Tapie poured money into the club. Turned out his club also tried to pour said cash into other clubs as well. In 1994

Marseille were thrown out of the Champions League and forced to give up their 1992/3 French title after Valenciennes players squealed and admitted that they'd been offered bungola to chuck their late-season game against Olympique.

### 43. Melborough
Despised rivals of Melchester Rovers in 'Roy of the Rovers'.

### 44. Monaco
A club whose pitch is on top of a giant car park, for Gawd's sake.

### 45. Steaua Bucharest
Another communist outfit well worth affording a wide berth. Steaua were the preferred team of disgusting Romanian secret police, the Securitate. Their horrible reign as perennial Romanian champions, whether they deserved it or not, only came to an end with the 1989 revolution that eventually saw the noxious dictators Nicolae and Elena Ceaușescu machine-gunned behind a primary school prefab on Christmas Day. You can see that event on YouTube. Still terrific entertainment.

### 46. Denley Moor
Abominable rivals of hapless Barnstoneworth in Michael Palin's *Ripping Yarns*.

### 47. Sheffield United
Relegated from the Premier League in 2007 after a pretty useless season, they've latched on to the admittedly murky goings-on at West Ham and turned their grievance about the Carlos Tevez stuff into a major industry. Over the past two years the directors of Sheffield United have appealed to the Premier League, the FA, the High Court, the House of

Lords, the European Court For Sporting Arbitration, the European Court of Justice, the European Court of Human Rights, the United Nations, USDAW, UKIP, UNESCO, the Upper House of the state of Saskatchewan in Canada, the parliament of Burkina Faso and some blokes they met at Heathrow while on their way to meet the Pope to inform His Holiness of the injustice.

### 48. Crystal Palace

Another hope-nobody-notices change of nickname. Proper nickname, the Glaziers. Concocted nickname, the Eagles. Not buying it.

### 49. Leeds United

No, not a misprint. It just seems churlish in a list this length not to include this shower a second time.

### 50. Darlington

Ideas above their station...flying too close to the sun...delusions of grandeur...hubris... Take your pick. Darlo are one of the most reassuringly hopeless of all English teams, having stayed firmly nailed in the bottom division of English football longer than anyone except the equally loveable Rochdale. The difference between these two perennial losers is that Darlington have actually tried to do something about their terminal stasis. In 1999 local businessman and criminal George Reynolds bought the club (he already owned a yacht, a jet, helicopters and a London address that made him the neighbour of a Spice Girl). Reynolds courted top-class players, first Paul Gascoigne, then Faustino Asprilla, and Tino was actually paraded before the faithful. But on the day he was due to sign his contract, he did a bunk, fled the country and has never set foot on these shores since. Then, to widespread bewilderment, Darlington (average gate five dogs and a man) built a 25,000-seater stadium. Called, naturally enough, the Reynolds Arena. Soon after, Reynolds did not pass Go, did not collect £200 and went directly to jail for tax offences (the authorities became suspicious when they found £500,000 in cash in the boot of Mr R's motor).

Darlington have been in and out of administration ever since. More pathetically, their penniless plight has been cruelly highlighted by the succession of name changes forced on their white elephant of a stadium, each new humiliation the latest attempt to attract a few precious coins in the general direction of their cobwebby coffers. The vainglorious Reynolds Arena became the New Stadium. Then the Williamson Motors Stadium. Then the 96.6 TFM Darlington. Then the Balfour Webnet Darlington Arena. At time of going to press it's called the Northern Echo Arena. Plans are at an advanced stage, when the current sponsorship ends, to call it the Classic Football Debates Sorted Once and For All Volume 1 Arena. George Reynolds, meanwhile, sells perfume in pubs.

# How is my club perceived by the wider public (or word-association football)?

In March 2009 a survey was undertaken for this book in which random passers-by in major city centres were asked to say the first two words that came into their heads when given the name of a British football team. It was first ascertained that these people had no interest in football, and they were asked to answer instantly and without bias. Considered replies, partisan remarks or obvious meanings were disqualified and any of the latter that may be inferred from the final list, while doubtless fun, are entirely a product of your own feverish minds.

When the survey was conducted in shopping malls, the replies sometimes reflected the names and products of nearby stores, and these were allowed to stand. Teams are under no obligation to adopt these slogans, though, once translated into Latin, we think they would make a pretty smart addition to any club badge.

Supporters are urged to try to find some subliminal explanation in the seemingly meaningless associations and then to use the phrases as a private greeting when in a roomful of undeclared allegiances. All original and ingenious connections will be included in future B&K volumes.

The full findings are given here.

Aberdeen: showband hoodies.

Accrington Stanley: conceited spoilers

Airdrie United: above Disney

Albion Rovers: ministers nut

Aldershot Town: fake features

Alloa: shaking mind

Anna Athletic: pop off

Arbroath: eightieth birthday

Arsenal: in Sainsbury's

Aston Villa: button moon

Ayr: popped paper

Barnet: blanket coverage

Barnsley: no nukes

Berwick Rangers: guitar passage

Birmingham City: sock shop

Blackburn Rovers: pizza papers

Blackpool: old teeth

Bolton Wanderers: walking toddlers

Bournemouth: turn coats

Bradford City: advertised late

Brechin City: Good morning!

Brentford: mythical beasts

Brighton and Hove Albion: short shrift

Bristol City: wavy gravy

Bristol Rovers: notorious liars

Burnley: soon come

Bury: half cut

Cardiff City: shampoo makers

Carlisle United: empire made

Celtic: Darwin's mouth

Charlton Athletic: grizzly bear

Chelsea: Herman's Hermits

Cheltenham Town: Bond film

Chester: unlimited texts

Chesterfield: tall order

Clyde: discover Atlantis.

Colchester United: alphabet soup

Coventry City: septic toe

Cowdenbeath: jagged beer

Crewe Alexandra: Grimpen Mire

Crystal Palace: gorilla kings

Dagenham & Redbridge: Dagenham & Redbridge

Darlington: polished brass

Derby County: Philadelphia light

Doncaster Rovers: river creatures

Dumbarton: her fantastic

Dundee: peanuts talking

Dundee United: tri-cornered hat

Dunfermline: wild geese

East Fife: New York

East Stirlingshire: marrow barrow

Elgin City: Derek Jameson

Everton: looted chimpanzee

Exeter City: calm down

Falkirk: messianic foolscap

Forfar Athletic: you understand

Fulham: in bed

Gillingham: mamas & papas

Grimsby: loose sweets

Hamilton Academicals: market prices

Hartlepool United: Angolan capital

Hearts: your sister

Hereford United: hairpin bends

Hibernian: tree trapped

Huddersfield Town: Nan's house

Hull City: Fiona's machine

Inverness CT: pregnant Australians

Ipswich Town: critics' choice

Kilmarnock: all cartoonists

Leeds United: altitude sickness

Leicester City: *Shrek Two*

Leyton Orient: wet dynamite

Lincoln City: stained fingers

Liverpool: Ivor Bloody Novello*

Livingstone: classic track

Luton Town: beyond imagination

Macclesfield Town: ship ahoy

Manchester City: smoking sandwiches

Manchester United: moonlit flit

Middlesbrough: rhythm cooks

Millwall: miniature railway

Montrose: savings everywhere

Morecambe: greedy fatso

Morton: chocolate cigarettes

Motherwell: Lake Placid

Newcastle United: Zulu headdress

*Breaks the two-word rule but we thought it such a great response we left it.*

Northampton Town: archaeological find

Norwich City: Germany awake!

Nottingham Forest: freezing Charlie

Notts County: hand written

Oldham Athletic: Tommy Cooper

Partick Thistle: jewellery stand

Peterborough United: film version

Peterhead: November Nirvana

Plymouth Argyle: broken windows

Portsmouth: skinned milk

Port Vale: snake walkers

Preston North End: face facts

Queen of the South: London taxi

Queen's Park: didn't happen

QPR: gulch apocalypse

Raith Rovers: one glove

Rangers: jump m'lud

Reading: invisible menders

Rochdale: biggest aspidistra

Ross County: nervous Mark

Rotherham United: maxi priest

Scunthorpe United: crackerjack pencils

Sheffield United: Bull Run

Sheffield Wednesday: Clinton's cards

Shrewsbury Town: publicity stunt

Southampton: terrible affair

Southend United: Dutch masters

Stenhousemuir: Cliff's there

Stirling Albion: carrier bags

St Johnstone: Boy George

St Mirren: mum's stocking

Stockport County: sounding wrong

Stoke City: definitely there

Stranraer: indigestion people

Sunderland: Beach Boys

Swansea City: marvellous, terrific.

Swindon Town: sheriff's office

Tottenham Hotspur: fitted curtains

Tranmere Rovers: boiled down

Walsall: King Kong

Watford: Gemini children

West Bromwich Albion: fish guts

West Ham: long ponytail

Wigan Athletic: married astronaut

Wolverhampton Wanderers: deedliography school*

Wycombe Wanderers: long bacon

Yeovil Town: Siegfried Line

* No we haven't a clue either.

# What if they recast  the Star Wars saga using football folk?

'A long time ago, in an LA Galaxy far, far away...'

| Star Wars character (originally played by) | New footballing actor... |
| --- | --- |
| Han Solo (Harrison Ford) | Steven Gerrard |
| Obi Wan Kenobi (Sir Alec Guinness) | Arsène Wenger |
| Luke Skywalker (Mark Hamill) | Fernando Torres |
| Princess Leia (Carrie Fisher) | Kevin Keegan |
| C-3PO (Anthony Daniels) | Peter Crouch |
| R2-D2 (Kenny Baker) | Dennis Wise |
| Chewbacca (Peter Mayhew) | John De Wolf |
| Darth Vader (David Prowse) | Micky Droy (body), Roy Keane (attitude) |
| Uncle Owen (Phil Brown) | Phil Brown |
| Yoda (Frank Oz) | Arjen Robben |
| Lando Calrissian (Billy Dee Williams) | Chris Kamara |
| The emperor (Ian McDiarmid) | Sven Goran Eriksson |
| Chancellor Velorum (Terence Stamp) | Terry Venables |
| Darth Maul (Ray Park) | Joey Barton |
| Mace Windu (Samuel L Jackson) | Ian Wright |

| | |
|---|---|
| Count Dooku (Christopher Lee) | Ken Bates |
| Jar Jar Binks (Ahmed Best) | Rio Ferdinand |
| Jango Fett (Temuera Morrison) | Tim Cahill |
| Jabba the Hutt (Rubber blob) | Mike Ashley |

**Imperial storm troopers (big, slow-moving, blokes):** Nicklas Bendtner, Titus Bramble, Kevin Davies, Sam Allardyce, Sol Campbell, Tony Adams, Martin Jol, Papa Bouba Diop, John Carew.

**Ewoks (small, sometimes hairy, loveable fellows):** Aaron Lennon, Ray Houghton, Paul Peschisolido, José Dominguez. Trevor Hockey, Paul Breitner, Paul Hartley, Shaun Wright-Phillips, Abel Xavier, Derek Hales, Gennaro Gattuso, Gianfranco Zola, Lionel Messi, Carlos Tevez.

# What's going on inside the mind of...?

## Alex Ferguson?

- Obsession with beating all of Liverpool's records
- Horse racing
- Remembering cutting David Beckham's head
- New ways to upset Rafa
- Beaujolais nouveau 1998
- Fury about Rock of Gibraltar
- Birthday present for Gary Neville
- Seething recollections of Pizzagate
- Inexplicable dislike of Red Nose Day
- That day I got off the motoring offence because I had diarrhoea
- Château Mouton Rothschild 1982
- Fury at having to pay the BBC licence fee
- Quietly enjoying Paul Ince's failure
- Simmering resentment of Jaap Stam, Ruud Van Nistelrooy and Gabriele Heinze
- Weird dreams where Berbatov morphs into Verón

## Sepp Blatter?

- Stockings
- Suspenders
- Suspender belts
- Ways to decrease power of European clubs
- Ways to increase number of World Cup teams to 64
- Air miles
- Nostalgia for my great golden goal idea
- Nostalgia for my great silver goal idea
- Fury at inventor of tights
- Five-star hotels
- Stopping England hosting the World Cup
- Hatred of pantyhose
- More ways to punish 'overzealous celebration'
- Ways to award Mexico the World Cup for the 74th time
- Listening to Jack Warner's warbling
- Lingerie catalogues

## Roy Keane?

- Revenge
- Trigger
- I was right in Saipan
- I was definitely right about the prawn sandwich brigade
- Grrrr... Mick McCarthy
- No doubt. I was totally right, on the money, in Saipan
- I wonder if Dwight could play centre back?
- Vengeance

- Grrrr... Patrick Vieira
- Who the hell is President Ahmadinejad?
- Keeping wife Theresa out of the limelight
- Blissful memories of stamping on Gareth Southgate
- Memorising the A roads of Suffolk
- Grrrr... WAGs
- Complete unrepentance re Saipan

## West Ham legend Alvin Martin?*

- My lovely family
- Coy carp
- That boat I bought in Brighton marina
- Big Bert, my ex-copper dad
- Ringing managers about my footballing sons Joe and David
- I spent a lot of money on that boat
- Unhappiness with youth set-up at Tottenham
- My dad the hedge murderer
- Then the blinking boat got keel rot, something like that
- Modern fullbacks don't cut out the crosses
- I should have played against Argentina; I'd have stopped Maradona
- Then the sodding thing sank
- Purple shirts
- Thompson's Sunspots catalogue
- Never even got out to sea... all that dough...

*Danny Kelly works with the excellent Alvin Martin on Talksport. All of this is true.

## Newcastle supporters?

- Sir Bobby will help us win the World Club Championship
- Wor Jackie
- Blaydon Races
- Big Sam will take us to the very pinnacle of European football
- 1969 Fairs Cup victory
- The *Angel of the North*
- King Kev will ensure we win the Premier League
- Big lasses in the Bigg Market
- *Whatever Happened to the Likely Lads*
- Joe Kinnear will see we qualify for the Europa league
- 'Fog on the Tyne'
- Plans to kill Noel Gallagher
- Chrissy Hughton, he's the man to get us a mid-table position
- Cockney b'stads
- Alan Shearer – no way he'll let us get relegated

## Phil Brown?

- Mmmm... Big Sam
- New tanning technologies
- The Next catalogue
- Ooh look... there's a TV camera
- My brilliant half-time-on-the-pitch wheeze
- Special Christmas card for Big Sam
- Harley-Davidsons
- Ooh look... there's a microphone
- Advanced communications technologies

- The Wash
- Touch of Grey For Men
- Ooh look... there's the man from the *Daily Telegraph*
- Bizarre memories of being taught by Brendan Foster
- Nicole Farhi scarves
- Ooh look... there's the girl from the *East Riding Mail*

## Marouane Fellaini?*

- Childhood memories
- The return of Rick Wakeman's *King Arthur on Ice*
- The price of milk in this country
- Vague fear that David Moyes may be concealing a weapon
- Vintage Judge Dredd comics
- The Chi Lites
- Trade in car; get scrappage allowance
- A growing dislike of steak and kidney pudding
- Stephen Fry's book recommendations
- Twiggy versus Mary Quant... hmmm?
- Frizz-Ease by John Frieda
- The disturbing level of pub closures in the Liverpool area
- Capybaras... cute
- Whatever happened to the Aztec bar?
- Being from Belgium, how did I even know about the Aztec bar?

* *Neither of the Dannys has ever met Mr Fellaini, a player they hugely admire. Some of these thoughts, therefore, have had to be invented*

# David Beckham?

- My beautiful lady wife Victoria
- Master Bedroom! No, that's a stupid name for a kid
- Alex Ferguson hurt me. And not with words...
- Sarongs
- Image rights
- Where's my throne?
- Tattoos pregnant with meaning
- Stanley Matthews was still playing for England when he was 87
- Fabio Capello's phone number
- Where am I?
- My 32,876 chums on MySpace
- 327 people pretending to be me on Facebook
- It turns out Americans don't really like football
- Bring a bottle for Tom Cruise's party
- Bobble heads

# Liverpool legend Ray Houghton?*

- My lovely family
- The Royal and Ancient, St Andrews
- Cocking the wrists for the perfect bunker shot
- Sergio Garcia
- Harry Varden and the roots of golf
- The Masters
- Mashie-niblicks

*Danny Kelly works with the excellent Ray Houghton on Talksport. All of this is true.

- New driver technologies
- Seve Ballesteros
- Four days lying on the couch watching the Ryder Cup
- Practising my swing while on air
- Tomorrow's round
- Keeping your head still for the perfect putting stroke
- Tiger Woods
- I really, really should have brought Michael Thomas down that evening at Anfield. I was the nearest Liverpool player. If I'd just caught him and given away the free kick, they wouldn't even have had time to take it. Michael wouldn't have gone through. Arsenal wouldn't have scored. Nick Hornby wouldn't have written *Fever Pitch*. All those other, much worse, football books could have been avoided. Liverpool would have won the 1989 title. And probably gone on to dominate English football for the next 20 years. Why the hell didn't I bring him down?

## Arsène Wenger?

- Carthesian dualism
- Poststructuralism
- Cognitive science
- Scouting trip to Tierra Del Fuego
- Logical positivism
- Coq au vin. Yummo!
- I really do not look like Professor Yaffle
- Scouting trip to Burkino Faso
- Alsatians
- Slight worry about diminishing eyesight

- Wondering if nine-year-olds could win the Carling Cup?
- Nagging fear of a right-hander from Martin Jol
- 33179 Arsenewenger, the asteroid named after him
- Slight disdain for the British and everything about them
- Secret plan to turn on new mate Fergie as soon as we start winning trophies again

## Harry Redknapp?

- Remind people how great I am at managing
- Memories of playing with Booby Moore, Geoff Hurst and Martin Peters
- Organising coaching job for Jamie
- Things that are triffic, inc me!
- Setting the Sky box for *Location! Location! Location!*
- Heathrow arrival times June–September
- Chateau Ste. Michelle and Dr. Loosen 2002
- Sir Bloody Clive Woodward
- Blamelessness for Southampton's 2005 relegation
- Organising coaching jobs for old mates
- Screaming Eagle Cabernet 1992
- Secret glee at West Ham's 2003 relegation
- Reminding people that every club I go to is a basket case
- Pie, mash, jellied eels, nice drop of 1942 Château d'Armailhac
- We only had two points from eight games, y' know

# What is the fewest 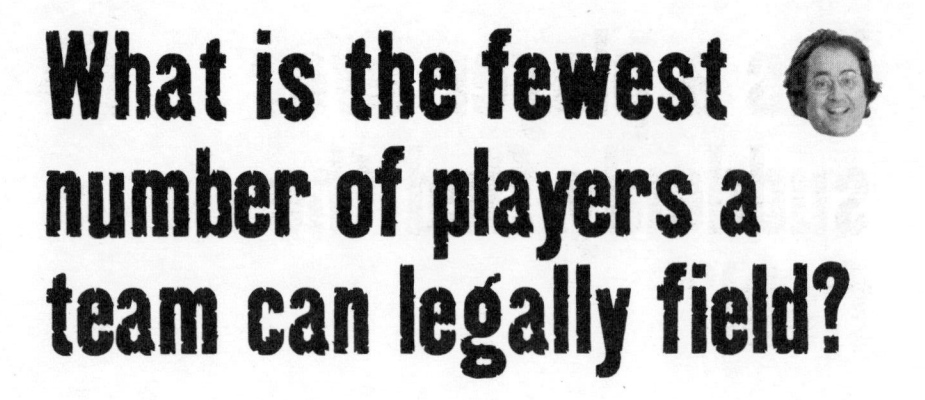 number of players a team can legally field?

Well, rather amazingly, the answer is none. If a side so chooses they can simply refuse to send a side out. This has never actually happened, although in the 1970s the Northhampton Town first XI were found to be hiding, shortly before kick-off, in a Kettering department store after losing their nerve at the prospect of facing Manchester United. The match eventually went ahead with United winning 8–2, George Best famously grabbing six of those.

The actual fewest number of players to ever comprise a team is three. This was York City, who arrived at Gillingham's ground on 5 December 1961 with only their manager and a trio of pros from the first team. The rest of the squad had been left at a motorway service station for taking too long to eat their meal. York manager Bill Langley said of the incident, 'I told them and I told them to hurry up or I was going without them. One of them, and I'll find out who, said, "I'd like to see yer try," and something just snapped. What's done is done. I've told our three lads who are here exactly how I want them to approach this game now but obviously it's backs to the wall.' The match ended 2–2.

# Has a player ever suddenly fled the field?

Dozens. In fact before managers were introduced to the game in 1935 players would often jack it in whenever they felt the game had got away from them or if they had a prior appointment. In must be remembered that in those days even top clubs paid very little by way of wages and most footballers drove trains in the evenings.

No modern British player has suddenly fled the field since Clyde-bank's Paddy Sinclair took to his heels an hour into his club's home tie against Third Lanark in 1981. It transpired that Sinclair, often described a 'jumpy' man, heard a fire engine noisily pass the ground and became convinced that it was his house that was on fire. Despite being caught as he raced through the tunnel and various offers to send members of the youth team to check it out, Paddy became hysterical and even accused several of the backroom staff of 'all being in on it'.

His paranoia was hardly helped when it subsequently turned out that it *was* in fact his home ablaze, although as local fire chief Robert Ferris later said, 'The chance of such an occurrence is absolutely infinitessimal and it should be taken into account that Mr Sinclair has been legging it after our engines in panic for several years now. Every other time he's been wrong, but there you are.'

# Should footballers always play strictly to the whistle?

Well, first off let us say that for our money not enough people take whistles into the ground any more. In the 1970s virtually everyone took a soundalike ref's whistle to matches and, used sparingly, it would amusingly halt play and cause tremendous confusion among the visiting team. Goals scored because of a whistle in the crowd are among the very funniest in the entire annals of the game. What's more you can't be arrested for it. See, it's just a whistle.

Sure it takes a lot of nerve to blow with sufficient volume for all the players to hear, and you will always get one or two stuffed shirts in the crowd who disapprove and point you out to the stewards, but the fact is there is nothing in the programme or in the small print on your ticket that says you can't ref-along-a-match-day with your own whistle.

That splendidly tetchy commentator Barry Davies hated whistles in the crowd. 'And that beautiful sweeping move by Everton had just suddenly come to nothing because of some idiot in the crowd with a whistle. Dear me...'

Of course the whistle itself is a superbly arcane piece of kit in the first place. Think about modern football – Ronaldo, high-tech stadiums, Sky Sport's state-of-the-art graphics, national anthems, billions of pounds at stake – and at the centre of it all a silly tin whistle. *Peep-peep!*

On one of our shows we invited calls about what has been used, at park level, if the referee didn't have a whistle. Children's squeaky toys, black-rubber-bulb bicycle horns and a harmonica all cropped up. The best improvisation though came from a low-level ref himself, who said that despite exhaustive appeals to all around for anything that might make a distinctive sound nothing was forthcoming, and so he was eventually reduced to walking some distance to a pub that had not yet opened for business. The players were astonished to see him emerge from the hostelry after a period of negotiation carrying two match-saving items: a tin tray and a large spoon. With these implements in hand he declared game on.

While we're here we may as well reference the Sunday League referee who had neither red or yellow cards with him. Only realising this at the last second, he held up kick-off and legged it over to a nearby house. When he emerged he had his cards. What were they? The silver-tongued official had sweet-talked the occupants and got them to throw open the doors to their larder. Scissors were then taken to boxes of Weetabix and Maltesers and the day was saved. That said, can you think of anything more ignoble than being ordered off the pitch by a man holding aloft a piece of a Maltesers' box?

But back to the question in hand. Should players always play to the whistle? Well, this very question lay at the heart of one of the most astonishing stories ever put before us.

A Sunday-morning match was being played in a large park in Eltham, south London. The two sides were placed one and two in their league and had a long history of bitter rivalry. With about half an hour to go and the score poised at 1–1 both sides became aware of a vague droning noise seemingly emanating from nearby trees. It was a light aircraft in distress struggling to remain airborne. Players on an adjacent pitch spotted it first and scattered as the plane began to plummet, spinning like a sycamore seed. In the game we are focusing on there was apparently a brief interlude before the teams scrambled for safety wherein, as they say, 'time stood still'. It was in this momentary hiatus that one of the chaps found himself with the ball at his feet, dead centre on the edge of the opposition's area. Everyone else was frozen to the spot staring skyward, transfixed by the descending aircraft. The goalkeeper was some yards to the left of his goal, shielding his eyes and with his back to the pitch.

Now our moral dilemma begins to take shape. I mean these two sides *hated* each other. Yes, the game had stopped and, quite rightly, become insignificant set against the human tragedy unfolding in the bright Sunday-morning sky. But, well, the referee hadn't actually blown...and the goal was just *there*. Wide open. Unguarded. Yawning. The player, quietly and without ceremony, simply side-footed the ball apologetically across the goal line, where it barely even riffled the netting. Then he, like everyone else, raced for cover.

The stricken aircraft thudded into the earth close to the corner flag of the pitch our two rivals had recently vacated. Within moments ambulance crews arrived and police taped off the crash scene. Word soon spread across the park that neither pilot or passenger had survived. During the hour or so that the emergency services performed their grim duties, players all over the park lolled around on the grass, stunned and helpless.

As the last ambulance pulled away, games on other pitches actually began to resume and talk began about the rearranging of our crash-site fixture. Setting a date for the following Wednesday, everything seemed settled...until the following exchange.

'So, we just play the last 30 minutes out or what?

'No, we start from scratch.'

'But we were winning 2–1.'

'It was 1–1. We just start again.'

'It was 2–1. I scored just before you ran away. The ball's still in the net. Look.'

'But you can't count that! That's sick. Blokes were dying.'

'Not when I scored they weren't. The ref hadn't blown.'

'He don't have to blow; it's a plane crash!'

'Not *when I scored* it wasn't.'

'I can't believe you seriously want to count a goal scored when people were dying.'

'I was just playing to the whistle, that's all. It's 2–1.'

And, as you can imagine, this is where things started getting heated. The referee, it turns out, had returned to the changing rooms, ashen-faced and wobbly, long before. This turned out to be no obstacle. After a lengthy face-off, the two sides decided to play out the remaining 30 minutes of the match there and then, skirting around the portion of white tape that encroached onto their pitch and still with the wreckage of the aircraft just a few metres away. Whatever the result at the end of that time, they agreed that would be the result filed with the league.

It finished 2–1. Our correspondent never told us whether this score was allowed to stand but he did send us photocopies of news reports about the incident the following week: GAME CARRIES ON AT DEATH CRASH SITE.

Appalling of course. But, you know, he hadn't blown, had he? And that plane hadn't crashed yet. And the goal was just there. I mean... it's a tricky one, isn't it?

## Danny Baker's thank yous...

For Alex Armitage who can do anything. And for Wendy who regularly sacrifices Grey's Anatomy so I can watch another torpid kick about.

## Danny Kelly's thank yous...

Heartfelt thanks to my clan – mum, Maggie, Mike, Andy, John and Jo – for all your love and support. And to Alex Clark for just being your lovely self. And to Alex Armitage for keeping the faith.

My bits of this book are dedicated to my dad, Andy, without whom the world seems a harder place.